ENCYCLOPAEDIA OF INDIAN GOVERNMENT: PROGRAMMES AND POLICIES

ENCYCLOPAEDIA OF INDIAN GOVERNMENT: PROGRAMMES AND POLICIES

Vol. 8

Defence: Challenges & Strategy

Edited by

Satish Tiwari

ANMOL PUBLICATIONS PVT. LTD.
NEW DELHI - 110 002 (INDIA)

ANMOL PUBLICATIONS PVT. LTD.
4374/4B, Ansari Road, Daryaganj
New Delhi - 110 002

Encyclopaedia of Indian Government: Programmes and Policies

First Edition, 2000

ISBN 81-261-0515-1 (Set)

PRINTED IN INDIA

Published by J.L. Kumar for Anmol Publications Pvt. Ltd., New Delhi - 110 002 and Printed at Mehra Offset Press, Delhi.

Contents

Preface

Encyclopaedia of Indian Government: Programmes and Policies contains authoritative information on about fifty departmental policies and their future developmental programmes.

Organised to be completed in 40 volumes, this gigantic work covers Agriculture; Atomic Energy; Chemicals and Fertilizers; Coal; Commerce; Communication; Culture; Defence; Education; Environment and Forests; External Affairs; Finance; Food & Consumer Affairs; Food Processing Industries; Health and Family Welfare; Home Affairs and Internal Security; Human Resources; Industry; Information and Broadcasting; Labour; Law, Justice and Company Affairs; Non-conventional Energy Sources; Ocean Development; Parliamentary Affairs; Personnel, Public Grievances and Pensions; Petroleum and Natural Gas; Planning and Programme Implementation; Planning and Statistics; Posts and Telegraphs; Power; Rural Development; Science and Technology; Social Justice and Empowerment; Space; States Affairs; Steel; Steel and Mines; Sugar and Edible Oils; Surface Transport; Textiles; Tourism; Urban Development; Water Resources; Women and Child development etc.

Based on the information derived from authoritative sources, this work contains authentic facts and figures. I am deeply beholden to all the scholars whose writings are cited or substantially made use of in the present work. I am also thankful to Anmol Publications Pvt. Ltd. for undertaking publication of this encyclopaedia. I am solely responsible for shortcomings in presentation of matter.

Encyclopaedic in nature, this will prove a dependable reference work for scholars and academics besides those appearing for different competitive examinations.

—Satish Tiwari

1

National Security and Defence

Internal security issues in India

More recently the exploitation of casteist and communal–religious sentiments for plainly electoral purposes in the Indian experience, has added a further dimension to the ethno-political sources of internal conflict. The strenght of the socio-economic causes underlying internal conflict might also be noted, arising largely from the spread of communications through a popular media like television to fan resentments among the under-privileged/deprived. In the totality of its internal security problems during the eighties, India witnessed irridentist militancy in Kashmir and Punjab, ethnicity-related violent movements in its North-eastern states; Naxalite activity in Andhra Pradesh that has now spread to Maharashtra, Madhya Pradesh, Orissa and Bihar; LTTE-associated terrorism in Tamilnadu with similar incidents in other Southern states; regional agitations for Gorkhaland, Bodoland and Jharkand, that could encourage similar demands in Uttarakhand, Poorvanchal, Vidarha, Ladakh and Jammu; casteist violence embodied that is endemic to certain sensitive areas in the country but gained a national spread after demolition of the Babri Masjid. There was an appreciable increase also in domestic law and order problems like riots for non-communal reasons, student and labour unrest, atrocities on women and scheduled categories of the population and so on.

An especial cause for violence has become the call to elections leading to great excitement that finds expression in clashes between the supporters of rival; candidates in the run-up to the elections, and in booth-capturing, prevention of electors reaching polling stations and so on, on election day. An incipient cause of tensions that would become more apparent in the years ahead would arise from rapid urbanisation in India. It is estimated to reach around 30% of the total population by the end of this century, but could reach between 35-40% in the more industrialised states. What is subsumed in these statistics is that around a third of the present urban population lives in slums, and their percentage could increase dramatically as a proportion of the total urban population. Civic servicers in urban areas, including the metropolitan centres, are already under great strain, with basic amenities like water, electricity, sewerage, roads, public transport and communication systems under tremendous strain. The concept of satellite townships has not shown much progress to arrest the ceaseless flow of rural population into the cities, primarily in search of employment. The ghettoisation of this largely itinerant, rootless and psychologically traumatised people living in appaling conditions, could lead to socio-economic tensions and conflicts in future.

The variegated and serious dimensions of the internal security threat to India in the coming years draws attention to the capability of the governance processes to overcome these challenges. The disconcerting situation obtaining is that the instrumentalities of the State, including its law and order apparatus, have suffered a deterioration in quality, but the problems of internal security are becoming more complex and acute. This has affected the basic functions of the State, which remains the maintenance of law and order, administration of justice, provision of communications facilities, and social services for the weaker sections of society. The machinery established for undertaking these various activities has uniformally been adversely affected.

Of interest to the seminal question of national/internal security is the palpable decay in the efficience of the machinery for law and order and criminal justice administration. A large number of reasons like the politicisation of the bureaucracy and the police, the nexus established between organised crime and politics and communalism/casteism, institutional breakdown of the judicial system, and an all-too-eager recourse to deploying the armed forces to handle internal security problems that clearly lie within the competence of the existing police/para-military forces. The problems of governance revealed here draw attention to the growing weakness of the political parties and political institutions of Government that include both its legislative and administrative wings.

Defence

India's defence policy aims at promoting and sustaining durable peace in the sub-continent and equipping the defence forces adequately to safeguard aggression. The Supreme Command of the Armed Forces is vested in the President of India. The responsibility for national defence, however, rests with the Cabinet. The Defence Minister is responsible to Parliament for all matters concerning defence. Administrative and operational control of the armed forces is exercised by the Ministry of Defence and the three services headquarters.

Army

At the Army Headquarters in New Delhi, the Chief of the Army Staff is assisted by the Vice-Chief of the Army Staff and seven other Principal Staff Officers, namely, two Deputy Chiefs of the Army Staff, Adjtant General,

Quarter-Master General, Master General of Ordnance, Military Secretary and Engineer-in-Chief.

The Army is organised into five operational Commands, *viz.*, Southern, Eastern, Western, Central and Northern Command and one Training Command. Each Command is under a General Officer Commanding-in-Chief who holds the rank of Lieutenant General. General Officer Commanding-in-Chief commanding an operative command is the commander of demarcated geographical area and has both field and static formations under the command. The major field formations are Corps, Division and Brigade, commanded by a General Officer Commanding of the rank of Major General and Brigadier, respectively. The major static formations are Areas, independent Sub-Areas and Sub-Areas. An Area is commanded by a General Officer Commanding of the rank of Major General and an independent Sub-Area and Sub-Area by a Brigadier.

The Army consists of a number of arms and services. These are: Armoured Corps, Regiment of Artillery, Corps of Air Defence Artillery, Army Aviation Corps, Corps of Engineers, Corps of Signals, Mechanised Infantry, Infantry, Army Service Corps, Army Ordnance Corps, Corps of Electrical and Mechanical Engineers, Remount and Veterinary Corps, Military Police, Judge Advocate General Department, Army Physical Training Corps, Poineer Corps, Army Postal Service, Territorial Army, Defence Security Corps. In addition, the Army has its own Recruiting Organisation, Record Offices, Depots, Boys Establishments and Selection Centres and Training institutions.

Navy

The Navy responsible for defence and security of India's maritime interests and assests, both in times of war and peace. The Chief of the Naval Staff at the Naval

Headquarters, New Delhi, is assisted by four Principal Staff Officers, namely, the Vice Chief of Naval Staff, the Deputy Chief of Naval Staff, Chief of Personnel and Chief of Material.

The Navy has three commands *i.e.,* Western, Eastern and Southern with their headquarters located at Bombay, Visakhapatnam and Cochin respectively. Each Command is headed by a Flag Officer Commanding-in-Chief in the rank of Vice Admiral. Western Command and Eastern Command have under them operational fleets *i.e.,* Western and Eastern Fleets comprising warships, submarines, aircraft and other support ships. Southern Naval Command is responsible for all training activities of the Indian Navy.

The Indian Navy is a well balanced three dimensional force consisting of sophisticated missile capable warships, two aircraft carriers, minesweepers, advanced submarines and the latest aircraft in its inventory. Many of the warships are of indigenous design and have been constructed in Indian shipyards. These ships compare well with the ships of similar capability constructed by the advanced countries. The Naval forces are maintained and supported by modern dockyard facilities encompassing state-of-the art technology. At present, it has two major Naval bases at Bombay and Visakhapatnam.

Coast guard

The Coast Guard was constituted as an armed force of the Unin in 1978 under the Coast Guard Act, to protect the maritime and other national intersts in the maritime zones of India covering an area of approximately 28 lakh sq km. The force, which in headed by Director General Coast Guard is functioning under the effective control of the Ministry of Defence.

The headquarters of the force is presently located in New Dehli and regional headquaters are at Bombay, Mardras and Port Blair. The three regions, namely, Western, Eastern and Andaman and Nicobar cover 11 districts, one in each of the nine coastal states in the mainland and two in Andaman and Nicobar Islands. At present, the Coast Guard district headquarters are located at Porbandar in Gujarat, Bombay in Maharashtra, Vasco-da-Gama in Goa, New Mangalore in Karnataka and at Cochin in Kerala. Similary on the East coast, these are located at Madras in Tamil Nadu, Vizag in Andhra Pradesh, Paradeep in Orissa and Haldia in West Bengal. In addition independent Coast Guard stations are located at Vadinar, Okha, Tuticorin and Mandapam. Coast Guard air stations are in operation at Daman and Madras and Air Enclaves at Goa, Calcutta and Bombay. Establishment of stations at Kavaratti and Kamorta are being planned.

The force has effectively served national interests in high-risk areas. Foreign trawlers fishing illegally have been apprehended. Coast Guard ships and aircraft have been regularly assisting the customs authorities in anti-smuggling operations. Besides, the force is available for search and rescue operations, anti-pollution and other duties in the maritime zones of the country. The recent oil spill situations off Andaman and Nicobar and Goa were efficiently handled by the Coast Guard.

Air force

The Air Forse is organised both on functional as well as geographical basis. There are five operational commands. These are: Western Air Command, South-Western Air Command, Central Air Command, Eastern Air Command and Southern Air Command. In addition, Maintenance Command and Training Command are two functional commands.

At the Air Headquarters in New Delhi, the Chief of the Air Staff is assisted by the Vice-Chief of Air Staff, Deputy Chief of Air Staff, Air Officer Incharge Personnel, Air Officer Incharge Administration, Air Officer Incharge Maintenance and Inspector General (Flight Safety and Inspection). Each of these six Principal Staff Officers is assisted by an Assistant Chief of the Air Staff.

Today, the Air Force has an array of modern aircraft on its inventory besides other hi-tech electronic and support equipment. The aircraft fleet consists of fighter bombers, air superiority fighters, interceptors, transport and logistic aircraft and helicopters. The fighters force comprises *MiG-21* variants, *MiG-23s, MiG-25s, MiG-27s* and *Jaguars* which represent the modern generation strike aircraft. Older generation aircraft like the *Hunters* and *Canberras* are presently used in training and ancillary roles. *MiG-29s* and *Mirage-2000s* are air defence aircraft of the present generation. The transport fleet consists of *IL-76s, AN-32s,* the indigenously produced *HS-748s, Dornier-228* which are manufactured under licence by HAL and *Boeing 737s* which are used for VIP duties. While the *IL-76s* provides the Air Force with heavylift and strategic capabilities, *AN-32s* and *HS-748s* are also used in training role besides performing air maintenance and communication duties. The helicopter fleet consists of *Chetak, Cheetah, MI-8, MI-17* and the heavy-lift *MI-26* which is the largest helicopter in the world. All these aircraft are used for high altitude operations and provide logistics support to our ground forces. *Chetak/Cheetah* helicopters maufactured by HAL for the Air Force, are also used as Anti-Tank Guided Missile (ATGM) carriers, air borne Forward Air Controller (FAC) and for search and rescue operations. *MI-8* helicopters are specially modified to undertake tasks in Antarctica. In addition, the force has been supplemented with *MI-25* which performed yeoman service for the IPKF in Sri Lanka and

MI-35 attack helicopters. *HPT-32* and *HJT-16 Kiran,* both manufactured by HAL are used as basic and applied stage trainers respectively with the *Kiran* being supplemented by Polish *Iskara* aircraft. A landmark in the IAD was the commissioning of the first batch of women pilots on 17 December 1994. These pilots are now serving in front line transport Squadrons. The next batch women pilots is currently undergoing helicopter training and all have achieved solo flight status on *Chetak* and *Cheetah* helicopters.

The army

As for the Army, the project plans centred around the 155 mm Bofors guns were completely neutralised for reasons well known. In the process the ambitious programme of manufacturing about 1000 field Howitzers aided by technology transfer from Sweden for manufacture of ammunition got stalled. Worse still the Army's urgent requirements of the self-propelled guns of the same calibre got stuck up.

In Spite of the tumult over its acquisition, the 400 odd Swedish Howitzers played a decisive role in both the north-west as well as the north-east borders. Pakistan's repeated attempts togain a foothold in the Siachen Glacier were foiled by the Army's timely deployment and effective use of the Bofors guns.

So too, in the eastern sector, the advent of the 155 mm guns and their potential for long range bombardment in the himalayan heights put the Chinese in check and there were no more intrusions like the one in Arunachal Pradesh in the late 80's.

It would not be out of place to mention that the Indian Army has been involved in the arduous task of neutralising insurgencies in the entire North-East during the last 50 years. Neighbouring countries like China, Burma and the then East Pakistan (Bangaldesh) evinced more than usual interest in provoking various insurgent and ethnic groups in a bid to destabilise the country and bleed our defence forces.

The Indian Army nonetheless tackled the situation with minimum force required and to a large extent has succeeded in winning the sympathy of the people through various aid to civilian population. More than two division of troops had to be deployed and kept on alert to foil underground insurgencies aided and abetted by hostile countries. In fact, this became part of our defence preparedness plans and specialised units and training centres had to be raised.

To relieve the troops from being locked in such insurgency situatons and policing roles, the Rashtriya Rifles has been established. Forty Batallions have now taken up positions in such conflict situations. The Army will concentrate on its primary role to keep fit and trained to face any eventuality from across the borders. In addition, the BSF and Assam Rifles are there to assist the armed forces.

The navy

Although the Navy has been slightly better off with its own naval design Bureau and a home shipping industry, the lack of funds has slowed down the pace of construction of new warships. On this score one cannot fault the Navy for lack of planning. It is more in the sphere of implementation. Yet both government and shipyards have to be congratulated for additions, especially in the field of Corvettes, Missile Boats and Submarine, two of which were built at Mazagon Docks, Bombay. There is an ongoing project for the construction of three destoyers of 6000 tonnes each beginning with the Delhi, Mysore and Mumbai. Three advanced and modified versions of the Godavari class are under construction at the Garden Reach Workshop, Calcutta and the first 'Brahmaputra' has already been launched.

The demand is there for more subs, both of the Kilo and the German Hunter class but government is yet to take a decisison. Fortunately the cash crunch has not affected the progressive addition of Sea Harriers with the Navy but they require an additional platform in time, since Vikrant has already been virtually decommissioned. The life of aircraft carier Viraat is also getting shorter by the Years. Fortunately, both the nodel Ministry and the Navy is in the process of acquiring a sea control ship, possibly from Russia. As a long term option, India of course has the potential to build its own Aircraft Carrier at Cochin shipyard.

The Navy with its spreading blue water capability has no doubt created an impact on neighbouring countries, especially in the East and even caused a sense of alarm in far away Australia which has however with the passage of time been convinced that India has no expansionist intentions except to guard its coastline particularly its Exclusive Economic Zone and Oil Installations on the high seas.

The Indian Navy has also raised the 'Marine Commando Force', a specialised unit which can operate in various under water and off-shore areas. India is the second country after the USA to build up this highly mobile and potent naval commando force. During the operations in Sri Lanka, the Marine Commando Force won laurels and proved its worth as a deterrent to the enemy.

The air force

The maintsay of the Air Force has been the MIG fleet ranging from MIG-21 to MIG-29, supplemented by the Jaguars and the Mirage-2000. It goes the credit of the Air

Force that it showed its capabilities in combined operations first in 1971 and some 20 years later in the Maldives. In 1971, the Air Force was ready to take on the task of dropping a para batallion over Tangail to deliver a deadly psychological blow that hastened the surrender of Pakistani forces in Bangaldesh. Such airborne operations had become imperative due to a threat posed by an American Carrier group heading towards Chittagong. It would not be out of place to mention that the press played the role of a force multiplier. A foreign news agency reported that a para brigade had been dropped on the outskirts of Dacca and that did the trick.

But more outstanding was the reflex action response of the Air Force in fulfilling the requirement of the maldives President Abdul Gayoom in meeting a coup attempt by foreign mercenaries against his democratically elected government. In less than six hours, the Air Force with its giant IL-76 had landed Indian troops in and around Male, the Maldivian Capital and foiled the coup attempt. In this operation, the Air Force displayed its combat and communication capabilities across the Indian ocean and this was indeed an eye opener for Western Powers. Not only this, it was a snub for Pakistan as its offer for help was rejected by the Maldivian President

Fortunately, for the Air Force, it has also a large manufacturing and overhauling base with rich experience in the production and maintenance of almost the entire MIG fleet and Jaguars. It is against this background that these facilities will not only be upgraded but considerably augmented by the project for modernisation of the MIG-21 BIS fleet of 125 fighters. Two prototypes of the upgraded MIG-21 BIS are expected shortly and the HAL will undertake the fabrication of the updated versions. This programme is expected to be completed in less than two years and should amply make up for repeated delays in the LCA project. The air defence of the country would be well secured with the new look MIG-21 BIS fleet, which will be equipped with four times higher fire power against ground targets and would be an even match for F-16 in service with Pak Air Force.

The acquisition of the Sukhoi-30 culminates a long wait by the Air Force, which had spelt out its requirements for this multi-role air superiority fighter far back in 1990. For the first time perhaps India has gone for a new weapon system not merely based on the Pakistan syndrome but with much wider perspective that will cover portions of China, Myanmar and South-East Asia. In addition, the regional security requirements will be amply met by the longer range and sweep of the Sukhois which could neutralise any hostile activity emanating from countries in the neighbourhood like Iran, Afghanistan and even possibly Central Asian States. It will be pertinent to point out in this context that Sukhois will have mid air refuelling capability. India has signed a contract with Russia for 40 Sukhois and significantly this includes the transfer of technology and indigenous manufacture of this multi-role fighter planes. For the first time the Russion agencies have agreed to permit DRDO to participate in R & D and joint development of avoinics of the aircraft.

Commissioned ranks

Following are the commissioned ranks in the three services; each rank is shown opposite to its equivalent in the other service:

Recruitment

The Armed Forces symbolise the unity of the country and the ideals of national integration. Recruitment to the Armed Forces is open to all Indian nationals, irrespective of caste, creed, community, religion and region. The endeavour has been to provide free and equal opportunities to all sections of the population to join the Armed Forces and render service in accordance with the ideals of secularism, democracy and social justice. India's Armed Forces offer challenging openings to our youth. A remarkable feature of recruitment to the Armed Forces is that it is entirely voluntary. The competition for entry into the service is intense, reflective of the increasing numbers of educated youth in the country, coupled with the attractive terms and conditions of service, and the high level of respect commanded by the Armed Forces. Recruitment is made from different states/union territories on the basis of their recruitable male population. Conscious efforts are made to take care of the special needs of the border areas and hilly and other remote areas, by lowering educational and certain other criteria to suit their requirements.

Induction of women into the armed forces

While provision has all along existed for women to join the Armed Forces Medical Services, the Armed Forces Dental Services and the Military Nursing Service, Section 12 of the Army Act provided that women would not normally be eligible for enrolment in the Army. Similar provisions also existed in the cases of the Air Force and the Navy. However, in acknowledgment of the changing times, the Government has approved the induction of women into selected non-combatant branches in the three Forces. The entry of women has however, been restricted to the Officer Cadres, and they are on Short Service Commission basis. Further continuance of schemes would be decided on the basis of the experience gained. In pursance of this decision, several women officers have since joined the Service, in the EME, Signals, Engineers, Army Education Corps, Army Ordnance Corps, Army Service Corps and in the Judge Advocate General Department.

Recruitment of commissioned officers

Entry to the Officer Cadres in the Armed Forces is primarily through the Union Public Service Commission (UPSC). Graduates are eligible to join the Armed Forces through an examination known as the Combined Defence Services Examination (CDSE) conducted by the UPSC twice a year. Candidates who quality in the examination join the Indian Military Academy (IMA), the Air Force Academy and the Naval Academy for pre-commission training. Individuals selected for Short Service Commission are trained at the Officers Training Academy. The candidates seeking a career in the Armed Forces after completion of 10+2 general education join the National Defence Academy (NDA). UPSC holds the entrance examination twice a year for entry in the NDA. They join the respective Service Academies *viz.* the Indian Military Academy (IMA) for the Army, the Air Force Academy for the Air Force and the Naval Academy for the Navy, for their pre-commission training.

There is also direct entry of officers through the Service Selection Boards (SSBs) for the Army and Navy, and through the Air Force Selection Board for the Air Force, without any written examination by the UPSC. Candidates in the age group of 20 to 27 years with Engineering Degree and Post-Graduates in specified subject in the age group of 23 to 27 years are eligible for interview by the respective Selection Boards of the following branches of the Armed Forces: Armed Engineers, Electrical and Mechanical Engineering, Signals, Army Education Corps, Military Farms, Remount and Veterinary Corps: Navy–Electrical and Engineering, Engineering (Naval Architects) Logistics, Law, Education, Air Traffic control: Air Force–Aeronautic Engineers (Electronics), Aeronautic Engineers (Mechanical), Administration, Education, Logistics, Accounts, Meteorology.

In July 1992, the Government approved a University Entry Scheme, initially for a period of three years, for induction of Engineering students in their final year/pre-final into the Army. This scheme is already operating in the Air Force and the Navy. Engineering students of various disciplines studying in the final/pre-final years in recognised universities/institutions are eligible for induction into the technical branches/services of the Army as short service commissioned officers with the rank of Second Lieutenants under this scheme. Their salary, however, is paid in one lump sum on their joining the IMA for training on the successful completion of which they will be granted permanent commission in the Army. An intake of 100 officers per year has been planned under this scheme.

With a view to mitigate the shortage of Technical Officers (Engineering) in the Army, the Government also approved a short service commission (Tech) Entry Scheme. This envisages recruitment of qualified technical graduates through the SSBs and their enrolment in the Officers' Training Academy (OTA), Madras after medical tests for a ten month course. At the end of the course, the successful candidates will receive short service commission. Thereafter, they will be governed by the rules applicable to the other short service commissioned officers.

Recruitment of medical officers in the Armed Forces is done through two sources. All MBBS graduates passing out from the Armed Forces Medical College, Pune are granted Permanent Commission. Apart from this, post graduates/MBBS degree holders passing out from civilian medical colleges are selected through competitive examinations, on an all-India basis, conducted by the Directorate General of Armed Forces, partyly for grant of Regular Commission and partly for grant of Short Service Commission.

Research and development

Defence Research and Development Organisation (DRDO) was established in 1958 by amalgamating Defence Science Organisation and some of the technical development establishments. A separate Department of Defence Research and Development was formed in 1980 which operates through network of 50 laboratories/ establishments. The Department is engaged in the pursuit of self-reliance in critical technologies of relevance to national security. It formulates and executes programmes of scientific research, design and development leading to induction of state-of-the-art weapons, platforms and other equipments required by the Armed Forces. It functions under the control of Scientific Adviser to *Raksha Mantri* who is also Secretary, Defence Research and Development.

Research and development activities of the Department cover important demarcated disciplines like aeronatuics, rockets and missiles, electronics and instrumentation, combat vehicles, engineering systems, naval systems, armament technology including explosives research, system sciences including advanced computing, high altitude agriculture, physiology, food technology, nuclear medicine and allied sciences. In addition, the Department also assists the Services by rendering technical advice regarding formulation of requirements, evaluation of systems to be acquired, fire and explosive safety and mathematical/statistical analysis of operational problems.

The notable development successes of the Department include flight stimulators for aircraft, light field gun, 5.56 mm rifle, charge line mine clearing system for safe passage of vehicles in the battlefield, illuminating ammunition for enhancing night fighting capabilities, cluster weapons system for fighter aircraft, naval mines and new generation bombs for high speed aircraft and low-level bombing. Different radars like low-level tracking radar *Indra-I* and *Indra-II* for Army and Air Force, light weight field artillery radar, battlefield surveillance radar, secondary surveillance radar hae been developed. Bridge Layer Tank-*Kartik,* military bridging system, advanced ship sonar systems, advance sonobuoy, naval decoys, naval simulators, torpedo launchers, advanced materials and composites for military applications are also some of the other achievements of the Department.

The main battle tank *Arjun* having superior fire power, high mobility and excellent protection has been successfully developed. Army has accepted the tank for induction in Service and the tank is now under troop trails in actual field conditions. Simultaneously, planning action has been initiated by Department of Defence Production and Supplies for productionisation of *MBT Arjun.* A Light Combat Aircraft (LCA) is under hardware fabrication and engineering stage and integration of some of the sub-assemblies has already commended. An advanced technology gas turbine engine *GTX-35VS* named *Kaveri* for use in LCA is under development under a separate programme. Integrated Guided Missile Development Programme (IGMDP) comprises four missile system, namely, *Prithvi,* surface-to-surface tactical battlefield missile; *Akash,* medium range surface-to-air missile; *Trishul,* short range surface-to-air missile; and *Nag,* third generation anti-tank missile. The programme also included development of a re-entry technology demonstrator project called *Agni.*

The other major programmes which are in advanced stage of development/productionisation are: Pilotless Target Aircraft (PTA), Composite Sonar and Tactical Weapon Control System-*'Panchendriya'* for Navy, LMG and carbine in 5.56 mm calibre and multi-barrel rocket launching system-*'Pinaka'.* A Marine Acoustic Research

Ship-*'Sagardhwani'* has been designed and built indigenously. The ship is one of the most modern research. A PACE-PLUS parallel processing computer, configured with advanced commercially available micro-processors as computing nodes, has been designed and developed.

The Department has also rendered assistance to para-military and police agencies by way of supply of bullet proof vehicles, bullet proof vests, amenity vehicles, such as kitchen lorry, communication equipment, water pressure jet based anti-riot vehicles and several other types of equipments. The Department also offers specialised training at its two primier training institutions.

Production and supplies

A substantial part of defence stores needed by the Services is now being developed and produced within the country. The responsibility for this has been entrusted to the Department of Defence Production and Supplies in the Ministry of Defence. The Department directs and coordinates production of material and equipment required by the Armed Forces.

Ordnance factories

At present, 39 ordnance factories spread all over India operate a wide-range of technologies and product mix. Some of the important products are field guns, anti-aircraft guns, mortars, various small arms and ammunition for weapons and guns, rockets, projectiles, pyro-technics, bombs, grenades, mines, demolition charges, depth charges, infantry combat vehicles, battle tanks, self-propelled guns, transport trucks and petrol vehicles, high-altitude and combat clothing, optical and fire control instruments, engineering equipment, supply dropping equipmet including parachutes, rubberised items, various knitted and woven items like blankets, web equipment and a wide range of general stores are produced by them. Production of 5.56 mm (indigenously designed) weapon system has started in ordnance factories. These factories are also producing bombs required by Air Force. Besides, liquid fuel required for successful flight trials of *Prithvi* and *Agni* missiles, igniters and copper liners for the warheads were also supplied in the development of *Prithvi* missile. The production of *Ajeya tank (T-72), Sarath (BMP-II),* infantry combat vehicle are carried out at Heavy Vehicle Factory, Avadi and Ordnance Factory, Medak, respectively. A sophisticated opto-electronic production unit has been set up at Dehra Dun to produce the opto-electronic fire control and night vision devices required for *Ajeya Tank (T-72-MI* and *Sarath* infantry combat vehicle is planned from 1994-95. To utilise the sparable capacities, after meeting the services requirements, linear and lateral shift in customer product profiles has been taken up as a major thrust area of operations.

Jonga for civil market

As a part of diversification efforts, Vehicles Factory, Jabalpur (VFJ) has taken up modification and upgradation of Jonga. The vehicle, conforming to military standards, is not only sturdy but also has a very high pick up, high fuel efficiency of 16 km per litre (under test conditions) and a maximum speed of 120 kmph with gradient climbing capability of one in three. It has been decided to launch Jonga in the civil open market. VFJ has a captive capacity to manufacture 20,000 Jonga per annum. Out of this, 10,000 vehicles are to be released in the civil market and remaining 10,000 are reserved for the Army and exports.

Defence undertakings

There are eight public sector undertakings (PSUs) under the Department of Defence Production and Suppliers.

These are: Hindustan Aeronautics Limited (HAL), Bharat Electronics Limited (BEL), Bharat Earth Movers rail coaches, track laying equipments, heavy duty trucks, trailers, diesel engines etc. BEML is a leader in earth-moving industry with over 70 per cent market share. Its equipments and systems are productively deployed in India and over 30 other countries across the globe.

Mazagon Dock Limited (MDL) is the country's leading shipbuilding yard and can build warships up to 6,000 DWT displacement and merchant ships up to 27,000 DWT. It has units at Bombay, Nhava and Mangalore and headquarters at Bombay. At present, its major activities include construction of sub-marines, missile-boats and destroyers etc., for the Indian Navy and off-shore supply vessels and well-head platforms etc., for the Oil and Natural Gas Commission (ONGC). The company also provides diving services as well as services for coating/laying sub-sea pipes.

Garden Reach Shipbuilders and Engineers Limited (GRSE) is a multi-unit shipyard-cum-general engineering company. It has six units in and around Calcutta and a Diesel Engine Plant at Ranchi (Bihar). Its corporate office is at Calcutta. It has three distinct divisions, namely, ship, engineering and engine divisions. It is presently engaged in the construction of war ships and auxiliary vessels of various types for the Navy and the Coast Guard and to undertake repair of vessels of these two organisations. Other products of the company include a variety of high technology ship-borne equipments, portable Bailey type steel bridges, marines sewage treatment plant, dock-machinery items, turbine pumps for the agricultural sector, diesel engines, etc.

The activities of Goa Shipyards Limited (GSL) located at Vasco-da-Gama, primarily comprise construction and repair-reit of ships/vessels. It has undertaken construction/refit of variety of vessels for the Indian Navy and the Coast Guard as well as for the non-defence sector. It is currently building advanced off-shore patrol vessels of in-house design.

Bharat Dynamics Limited (BDL), established in 1970, is primarily engaged in the manufacture of guided missiles and allied equipments. It has units at Hyderabad and Bhanur Medak district. Its corporate office is at Hyderabad. It is also the prime production agency for manufacture of four new missile systems, namely, *Prithvi, Trishul, Akash and Nag,* being developed indigenously. Its activities which had earlier been diversified into a number of Naval projects now proposes to take up manufacture of small arms required for para-military forces of the country.

Mishra Dhatu Nigam Limited (MIDHANI) located at Hyderabad was incorporated in 1973. MIDHANI's product range includes super alloys, maraging steels, heat resistance alloys, controlled expansion alloys, tungsten, molybednum etc., in variety of mill forms.

Resettlement and welfare of ex-servicemen

In order to maintain a youthful profile of the Armed Forces, over 55,000 service personnel are retired/released every year at a comparatively young age. Majority of service personnel at the time of retirement are at an age where they have numerous unfinished responsibilities which necessitate their taking up of a second career. The Government is seized of this problem of rehabilitating them through provision of employment in organised sector or through self-employment. The welfare of ex-servicemen has been accepted as a national responsibility.

The Directorate General of Resettlement (DGR) under the Ministry of Defence (MOD) has been set up to look after all matters connected with resettlement and welfare of ex-servicemen and their dependents. A Kendriya Sainik Board under the Chairmanship of *Raksha Mantri* has been established for laying down general policy for the welfare of ex-servicemen and their dependents, for the administration of welfare funds, and also for coordinating the work of the Sainik Boards in the country. At the state level, the Rajya Sainik Boards, and at the district level the Zila Sainik Boards, have been established. The Government of India bears 50 per cent of the expenditure incurred on the organisations of Rajya and Zila Sainik Boards, the remaining expenditure is borne by the respective state governments.

Resettlement

Resettlement activities for the retired/retiring service personnel consist of the following: (a) training programmes to reorient retiring Defence personnel towards civil emploment; (b) providing re-employment opportunities in government/semi-government/public sector organisations and (c) schemes for self-employment.

In order to equip retiring service personnel for employment, suitable training programmes have been devised. They equip them for employment in civil organisations and for self-employment. For retiring service officers, the following training programmes were introduced during 1994-95: (a) Diploma in Industrial Security and Labour Laws; (b) Coaching for Air Line Transport Pilot Licence/Senior Commercial Pilot Licence/Commercial Helicopter Pilot Licence; (c) Consultant in ISO-9000; (d) Quality Assurance Manager ISO-9000 and (e) Deputy Quality Assurance Manager ISO-9000. Up to March 1995, 882 officers were trained. The vocational training, ITI training and on the job training are presently being conducted for retiring Service personnel other than officers.

Re-employment

Re-employment constitutes a major means of rehabilitation of ex-servicemen. To achieve this goal both the Central and state governments have provided various concessions/facilities. These include reservation of posts, relaxations in age/educational standards, priority in employment etc. The Central Government has reserved 10 per cent of Group 'C' and 20 per cent of Group 'D' posts for ex-servicemen in Central ministries/ departments. The percentage of reservation in public sector undertakings and nationalised banks in these are 14½ and 24½ per cent respectively. Besides, there is 10 per cent reservation for the post of Assistant Commandants in para-military Forces. Reservation under the state governments varies from two per cent to 20 per cent. There is no reservation for ex-servicemen in Bihar, Kerala and Megahalaya.

DGR has been nominating ex-servicemen security agencies to various PSUs and private sector organisations. These security agencies provide employment opportunities for officers and other ranks. There are over 173 ex-servicemen security agencies which are registered with DGR, of which 130 have been sponsored for work. This alone has generated employment opportunities for over 6,419 ex-servicemen and over 250 officers.

There is considerable scope for absorption of ex-servicemen in para-military forces like CRPF, BSF, ITBP, CISF, etc. However, the response of ex-servicemen for joining these forces has been generally poor. With a view to achieve fuller utilisation of reserved vacancies, special recruitment rallies were organised in selected states. During 1993, special recruitment drives were conducted by CISF.

The concept of Ecological Task Force was mooted in

1992 for the purpose of restoring the forest cover in regions where significant deforestation had taken place. These units were initially raised in three states *viz.*, Uttar Prasdesh, Rajasthan and J&K. The task forces are manned by ex-servicemen who are paid salaries as per TA scales. Every individual, irrespective of his rank prior to retirement, is re-employed as a sepoy. Ministry of Defence provides officers to command these units.

Schemes for self-employment

Important schemes for self employment for ex-servicemen are SEMFEX-I, SEMFEX-II and SEMFEX-III. These schemes have been launched in collaboration with the Small Industries Development Bank of India, NABARD and the Khadi and Village Industries Commission for providing extensive self-employment opportunities for ex-servicemen and their dependents.

The SEMFEX-I Scheme was launched in April, 1987. Under this Scheme, financial assistance is provided to ex-servicemen to set up small industrial projects for self-employment. Loans under this Scheme are provided by the respective State Financial Corporation. As on 31 December 1994 there were 6,686 beneficiaries and the amount sanctioned is to the tune of Rs. 179.27 crore since inception.

The SEMFEX-II Scheme was launched in January 1988 by the DGR in collaboration with the National Bank for Agricultural and Rural Development (NABARD) to provide assistance for agricultural and allied activities. Under the Scheme, financial assistance up to Rs. 7.5 lakh for setting up of industrial units/service establishments is given. The ceiling of Rs. 7.5 lakh is, however, not applicable for setting up of units relating to agro-industries. Since inception and up to December 1994 loans amounting to Rs. 12.30 crore have been sanctioned to 2,352 beneficiaries.

The SEMFEX-III Scheme was launched in October 1991 in collaboration with the Khadi and Village Industries Commission (KVIC). It provides self employment opportunities for setting up village industries under the purview of KVIC. Under this Scheme, ex-servicemen and their widows are eligible to take up self-employment ventures. Financial assistance for such ventures is provided under a liberalised pattern of assistance by the KVIC. The loans granted to village industries under this Scheme carry a rate of interest of four per cent and there is no interest on loan for *Khadi* units. The Scheme is picking up. Up to December 1994, a loan of Rs. 1.42 crore was sanctioned in 188 cases.

Schemes have also been launched in collaboration with Bombay Mercantile Cooperative Bank and Oriental Bank of Commerce to provide financial assistance to ex-servicemen and their widows on easy terms. In addition to the above schemes for financial assistance, certain other measures have also been taken to assist ex-servicemen in their self employment ventures. These are: (a) Allotment of sheds/plots; (b) Price subsidy to ex-servicemen units; (c) Allotment of surplus class V-B vehicles; (d) Allotment of repairable typewriters and duplicators; (e) Transportation of bulk LPG; (f) Allotment of Mother Dairy milk booths, fruit and vegetable outlets; (g) Transportation of coal and (h) Allotment of petroleum product agencies.

Welfare

Before April, 1993 there were four separate funds *viz.*, amalgamated Special Fund for War Bereaved, War Disabled and other ex-Servicemen/serving personnel; (i) Flag Day Fund; (ii) ST Dunstan's (India) and KSB Fund and (iv) Indian Gorkha Ex-Servicemen's Welfare Fund. These separate funds have been merged into an 'Armed Forces Flag Day Fund'.

The Kendriya Sainik Board (KSB) administers 'Armed Forces Flag Day Fund' for the welfare and rehabilitation of ex-servicemen, war widows, disabled service personnel and their dependents. The total corpus of the fund, as on 31 March 1995 was Rs. 45.60 crore. The corpus of the fund is invested with Banks/PSUs. The income accruing from interest is utilised for the various welfare activities. In the year 1994-95, Rs. 2.20 crore were spent on the major welfare activities. Financial assistance is also provided to institutions such as Paraplegic Homes at Kirkee and Mohali, Cheshire Homes, Military Hospitals, St. Dunstan After Care Organisations and Homes for taking care or old and physically handicapped ex-servicemen and their dependents. Financial assistance is also provided to individual ex-servicemen suffering from serious diseases for treatment in civil hospitals in case they cannot be treated in Military Hospitals and have not availed similar assistance from any other source. During 1994-95, a sum of Rs. 20,59,719.60 was sanctioned for the treatment of serious diseases.

Census of ex-servicemen/widows

To collect reliable data about ex-servicemen/widows population and update it on a regular basis a census of ex-servicemen is being carried out by DGR through Zila Sainik Boards (ZSBs) with effect from 15 May 1992. The Scheme envisages registration of retired defence service personnel with their ZSBs and issue of I-cards to the eligible ex-servicemen/widows. As per the feedback received, a total of 12.01 lakh ex-servicemen and 2.06 lakh widows have been registered and were reported to be surviving as on 31 December 1994.

Concessions to ex-servicemen

The Government has been granting various concessions to ex-servicemen from time to time. The major concessions granted to different categories of personnel or their dependents cover assistance in the field of education, reservation for wards in professional institutions, reservations in Sainik Schools and Military Schools, medical treatment, assistance for construction/ repair of houses, financial assistance for the marriage of daughters, canteen facilities, rail and air travel concessions. Besides, financial assistance from the Raksha Mantri's Discretionary Fund (RMDF) is given to old and infirm exservicemen and to their widows in indegent circumstances.

The revised rates of financial assistance are: (a) Assistance to old infirm ex-servicemen/widows of ex-servicemen Rs. 250 per month for two years; (b) Marriage of daughters of ex-servicemen/widows in penury Rs. 4000; (c) Repair of house for ex-servicemen/widows in penury Rs. 5,000; (d) Medical treatment-depending upon the nature and gravity of ailment subject to a maximum of Rs. 8,000; (e) Education of children of ex-servicemen/ widows in penury Rs. 35 per month per child for up to three children up to class X and (f) Other cases in respect of ex-servicemen/widows in penury (like natural calamities, accidental death or where RM/RRM feel that the case deserves sysmpathetic consideration–no single transaction to exceed Rs. 8,000.

Inter-ministerial committee

In pursuance of the recommendation of the high level empowered committee headed by the *Raksha Mantri* on improvement in the retirement pensions of Defence Personnel, the Ministry of Defence constituted an Inter-Ministerial Committee to deal with the problems of ex-servicemen other than those relating to pensionary matters. Accordingly, a committe under the chairman-ship of an Additional Secretary in the Ministry of Defence was set up. This committee included representatives from the Ministry of Finance, Ministry of

Law, Department of Pension and Pension and Pensioners' Welfare and other relevant organisations. The Committee considered 53 demands of ex-servcemen. It has recommended/partly recommended 33 demands, noted that five demands were not found justified. The demands which have already been accepted by Government are: (i) Permission for commercial employment after retirement; (ii) Provision of Soft Seed Capital Assistance under SEMFEX-II Scheme; (iii) Non-allotment of oil production agencies to ex-servicemen/widows; (iv) Reservation in purchase from ex-servicemen entrepreneurs; and (v) Issue of Last Pay Certificate along with discharge certificate.

Recruitment of other ranks in army and sailors in navy

There are 12 Zonal Recruiting Officers (ZROs) and 58 Branch Recruiting Officers (BROs) spreasd throughout the country. In addition, there is an Independent Recruiting Office (IRO) at Delhi. In order to inform the potential candidates well in advance of the commencement of recruitment extensive recruitment publicity is undertaken throughout the country, including in remote areas. Recruitment rules provide for relaxation in respect of educational and physical standards to the candidates from certain specified backward, remote and tribal regions to give them due representation in the Army. Relaxation in physical standards is also given to one son and one grandson of serving soldiers, ex-servicemen, widows of battle casualties, etc. The recruitment to the Navy has been clubbed with Army from the beginning. The recruitment demand is projected to Army Headquarters by Naval Headquarters.

Airmen

Recruitment of Airmen to the Indian Air Force is done through the Central Airmen Selection Board located at the Air Force Station, New Delhi. There are 13 selection centres under this Board and they make the necessary arrangements for the conduct of selection tests and final enrolment. After seeking the application through advertisements in national/regional dailies and through the mass media, a written test on an all-India basis is held and the all India merit list is drawn up with help of computers.

A Pilot Project has been undertaken for the direct recruitment of trained manpower from the civil stream in the trades, such as clerks, drives, and Surveyor Automated Cartography. Besides direct recruitment of technically qualified civilian personnel as JCO (Catering) has been introduced.

National cadet corps

The National Cadet Corps (NCC) has emerged as the single largest structured youth movement in India. It was established on 15 July 1948. It has 11.5 lakh boys and girls in the Senior and Junior Divisions in the Army, Navy and Air Force Wings. This strength covers four per cent of the eligible student population in the country. NCC with motto 'Unity and Discipline' has following aims: (a) to develop qualities of character, courage, comradeship, leadership, secular outlook, spirit of adventure and sportsmanship and the ideal of selfless service among the youth to make them useful citizens; and (b) to create a human resource of organised, trained and motivated youth, to provide leadership in all walks of life including the Armed Forces and to be always available for the service of the nation.

Director General NCC located at New Delhi controls and oversees various activities of the NCC through 16 NCC Directorates spread across the country. There is a Central Advisory Committee for the NCC to provide overall policy guidelines. NCC is manned by Service personnel, whole time NCC officers and civilians. One lecturer/teacher in each educational institution is appointed as Associate NCC Officer.

During 1994-95, 21 centrally organised camps were held in which 5,575 cadets participated from Army, Navy, and Air and Girls Wings and 66 National Integration Camps were conducted across the country in which nearly 35,185 cadels have participated. A total of 3,65,151 cadets have attended Annual Training Camps till March 1995. One hundred and sixty girl cadets attached with Air Units attended the ATC at Belgaum and 160 girls attached with Naval Units attended ATC at Visakhapatam. As many as 110 officers and 8,902 cadets participated in attachment training during the year, 853 girl cadets did attachment training with Armed Forces hospitals. Twenty boys and 20 girls did para basic courses at Agra during November-December 1994. Besides, 4,59,992 NCC cadets participated in social service activities such as blood donation, eye donation, Cheshire homes, anti-dowry pledge, adult education etc., and 6,45,369 saplings were planted.

A team of eight officers and 42 cadets (21 boys and 21 girls) visited Canada in July 1994 under Indo-Canada Youth Exchage Programme. A similarly composed Canadian contingent was in India till January 1995. While 57 cadets visited other foreign countries on a reciprocal Youth Exchange Programme and one officer from Singapore and 32 foreign cadets from seven countries attended the Republic Day Camp (NCC) 1995. During 1994-95, 48 NCC personnel were awarded DGNCC's Commendation Cards with badges for outstanding contribution to the organisation.

Great achievments

In talking of operational capability, one must remember with pride, the magnificent contribution by our network of Ordnance Factories which produce almost every weapons system and ammunition used by the three services. What is needed now is a large—scale induction of the latest technology from abroad to meet the specific requirements of the latest acquisitions in the three services. Equally in place is the well deserved tribute to the vast Research and Development activities under the umbrella of DRDO. No doubt, the latest INSAS Rifles systems may have its drawbacks, but as has been rightly pointed out by Ordnance experts there is imperative need for acquiring requisite technology from abroad for improving its design since such guns are already in use in USA and Austria.

India can be proud of its IMDP (Integrated Missile Development Programme) which has now after more than two decades produced four missiles with varied applications-Prithvi, Akash, Trishul and Nag. This family meets the requirements of multifaceted attack and defensive modes. But the crowing glory of defence research has been its development of the Intermediate Range Balistic Missile, the Agni with its range upto 2500, depending on the load.

The entire missile programme barring the Agni, is on the threshold of the production stage and it is here in this context that the defence sector undertakings such as Bharat Dynamics, the nodal agency, the HAL, Bharat Electronics and Bharat Earth Movers Ltd. are putting in integrated efforts to speed up the final fabrication stage. This missile programme has been well designed to meet the needs of all the three services. The Prithvi and the Nag for the Army and Akash and Trishul for the Air force. Both the Prithvi and Trishul can be modified or optimised for use by the Navy for surface to surface firing and surface skimming offensive power respectively.

The thrust of this presentation is also to focus

attention to essential factors if not more on defence preparedness.

We must realise that Policy Planning and Strategy on a macro level are more important than additions to weapons, manpower or support systems.

Need for an open approach

It is in this context one must have Perspective Planning over an extended period of anywhere between five to twenty years. In other words our outlook has to undergo radical change as we have been doing in the field of build up of economic infrastructure in our country. We have taken a very bold step, infact a revolutionary one, in striking a balance between public ownership and control to a liberalised economy throwing open vast avenues of business and industry not only to private sector in India but to direct investment from abroad.

Keeping this in mind we have to evolve a policy of an open door approach and access to the defence sector establishments including Ordnance Factories, both in terms of exports, and induction of technology. The present day policy of outmoded secrecy for the sake of secrecy is a fallacy because whenever imports are made from abroad the seller invariably comes to know what we are doing or plan to do.

The mention of this factor has become imperative because of abnormally slow rate of progress by the defence sector undertaking at Bolangir in Orissa for manufacture of critical ammunition for medium and light guns. This project has been bogged down in controversy. This is a classic case of where defence preparedness has suffered due to lack of coherent policy planning.

This is only a tip of the iceberg. Having dragged our feet on a full production line for the T-72M tanks, it has now been decided as a matter of policy to acquire off the shelf these tanks of advanced versions and also secure technology for their production in India. Infact, as a matter of wrong policy the manufacture of T-72 was stalled with unwarranted claims of imminent productionisation of Indian Arjun MBT.

Another example of faltering and vacilating policy is the induction of AJT and advanced combat aircraft for the Indian Air Force. No doubt it is very wise proposition to perservere with the LCA project to achieve self-sufficiency but to peg India's defence on a system that is yet to make its appearance is too much of a gamble. Fortunately, the present government has been prudent enough to seek at least an additional aquardron of MIG-29 fighter aircraft and given its approval for the induction of Sukhois-30 to give the IAF required strength to take care of national security requirements.

The Indian Armed Forces have many outstanding achievements to their credit. However, as war or any external threat requires total mobilisation in a democracy, maximum transparency alone can ensure cooperation on the part of the people in all respects, says the author.

Independent India was born in the midst of hostilities in Jammu and Kashmir. The holocaust that followed the partition of the country, the migration of people and the sudden attack by pakistan in Kashmir valley in October, 1947 created a feeling of insecurity among the people. The armed forces left behind by the Britishers and the infrastructure then available however proved adequate enough to repulse the Pakistani mischief.

Subsequently, the easy manner in which we secured the integration of Junagarh, Hyderabad and Goa brought in an element of overconfidence. Truely speaking, we were lost in an attitude of complacency believing in the good intentions of our neighbours, particularly China.

The rude shock delivered by China in Oct., 1962 made the leaders at the helm of affiars realise the need for an all weather Army, Navy and Air Force. Fear and insecurity hasd then gripped the people and some had even doubted our capability to protect the territorial integrity of the country. People in the North-East, for a moment, felt they were left to fend for themselves. In the background of these developments, one can say that planning for defence preparedness had its beginning after the humiliating Chinese invasion in the North-East.

Thanks to the assistance extended by the then Soviet Union in the development of our Air Force, Navy and Army, besides the help provided by the United Kingdom and France for expansion and modernisation of sea and air elements, we were able to check a renewed Pakistani onslaught in Jammu and Kashmir and Rann of Kutch in Gujarat in 1665. Pakistan was well and truely beaten and the Tashkent Peace Accord held good till 1971.

Gradual build up

Meanwhile, all the three defence services were gradually building up their strength in terms of armour, aircraft carrier, submarines and air defence fighters. Thus when in 1971, after Sheikh Mujibur Rehman gave a call for a mass freedom struggle on March, 26 in Dacca, the Indian armed forces were definitely in a position of superiority to take on the challenge to protect millions of refugees as well as the borders.

During the last 25 years, defence preparedness, as linked to Policy Planning, has been on an ad-hoc basis, if not in fits and starts. No doubt, there has been the acquisition of the T-72M tanks and the BMP series covering the Infantry Combat Vehicle and the Bofors 155 MM field howitzers. The Navy has gained in the acquisition of the Kilo class submarines, the aircraft carrier Viraat and the West German Hunter Killer class submarines.

The Air force has been steadily strengthened with the induction of the Jaguars, MIG-21, MIG-25, MIG-23, 27 and 29. The Mirage 2000, the AN-32 and the IL-76 long haul transports have also added punch to the Air Force. But this by no means reflects a long—term defence policy planning since all these acquisitions virtually came long after the requirements were made known, resulting in heavy cost escalations.

And some of them were clouded in controversies. As a result of which for nearly a despite urgent needs being repeatedly highlighted by the Armed Forces.

Training institutions

Sainik schools

Sainik schools prepare boys academically and physically for entry into National Defence Academy. There are 18 sainik schools in the country, one in each state, except in Nagaland, Meghalaya, Tripura, Sikkim, Arunachal Pradesh, Mizoram and Goa. These schools are affiliated to the Central Board of Secondary Education and follow the 10+2 pattern, in science stream.

Admission is made to class VI on the basis of an all-India entrance examination held every year in February, in which boys in the age group of 10-11 years are eligible to appear. From 1992-93 academic session lateral admission to class IX has also been started for which the boys have to be 13-14 years of age on 1st July of that year. Since its inception, a total of 4,647 boys from these schools were selected for admission to the National Defence Academy, Naval Academy, Armed Forces Medical College etc.

National defence academy

The National Defence Academy (NDA), Khadakwasla, is a Joint Services Training Institution which imparts academic as well as service training. The NDA has been brought in step with the national education format of 10+2+3. The syllabus of the Academy was reviewed to meet these requirements and has been approved by the Jawaharlal Nehru University for the grant of BA/B.Sc degree, at the time of passing out from Academy. the first course commenced training on revised syllabi in January 1989. After passing out from the NDA, the cadets go to their respective service acadmies for further training before being commissioned as officers in the Armed Forces. The present authorised training strength of the Army, Navy and Air Force cadets at the Academy is 1,800. This includes cadets from Bhutan and other friendly countries on as required basis.

Indian military academy

The Indian Military Academy (IMA), Dehra Dun caters for training of cadets for commission into the Army. Cadets join the Indian Military Academy as per the following modes of entry: (a) on passing out from NDA, (b) on graduation from the Army Cadet College which is a wing of the IMA itself, (c) Direct entry graduate cadets who join on qualifying at the Union Public Service Commission Examination and the Services Selection Board, and (d) Technical graduates and University Entry Scheme. The present authorised strength of trainees at the IMA is 1,200 which includes cadets from Bhutan, Shri Lanka, Maldives, Mauritius and Nepal. The authorised training strength of Army Cadet College is 450.

Officers training academy

The Officers Training Academy (OTA), Madras imparts pre-commission training for the following type of courses, (a) Short Service Commission Course of 44 weeks for university graduates who quality in the Union Public Service Commission; (b) course of six months for lady cadets (Women Special Entry Scheme); (c) Permanent Commission on Special List (PC) (SL) to selected service candidates, who qualify after a training of four weeks and (d) Regimental Commission Course for selected service candidates, who qualify after a training of 13 weeks duration. Authorised training strength of the Academy is 500. So far 50 lady cadets have been granted Short Service Commission.

Rashtriya Indian military college

Education on public school lines is imparted at the Rashtriya Indian Military College (RIMC), Dehradun principally for the boys who subsequently desire to join the NDA with a view to obtaining a commission in the Armed Forces. The College runs classes from eighth to 10+2 class. Selection for the RIMC is through a written examination cum *viva voce* conducted through the state governments. Intake into the RIMC is bi-annual.

National defence college

Inaugurated by Pandit Nehru in 1960, the National Defence College is an Inter-Service Organisation functioning under the Ministry of Defence. The NDC is the highest defence institution in India imparting instructions on all elements of national security and strategy to officers due to become Major Generals and equivalent and attain similar status in the Civil Service. The aim is to equip these policy makers with the necessary background and understanding of the total system of economic, political, military, scientific, international relations, national organisational aspects and the planning necessary for national security, both in its internal dynamics as well as the external comulsions. The head of the College is the Commandant, with five faculty members from the Army, Navy, Air Force, IAS, IFS and an administrative staff.

Army cadet college

Army Cadet College is a Wing of IMA which caters for the training of service cadets selected for commission.

The academic format is similar to the NDA on the lines of 10+2+3, and the syllabus is common. On completion of the course these cadets also qualify for a BA/BSc degree recognised by the Jawaharlal Nehra University.

Other training centres and schools

The College of Combat, Mhow conducts the higher command, senior command and junior command courses for Army officers. It also conducts a Combined Operational Review and Evaluation (CORE) programme for selected senior officers of the rank of Major General and equivalent of the three Services once every year. College of Military Engineering, Kirkee (Pune), imparts training to the officers and other ranks in all aspects of military engineering. Long courses of over two years duration are also conducted to train officers up to degree standards. Military College of Telecommunication Engineering, Mhow imparts basic and advanced technical training in telecommunications and signal tactics. Armoured Corps Centre and School, Ahmednagar, conducts training in tactical handling of armoured fighting vehicles, driving and maintenance. School of Artillery, Deolali, provides training in field branch artillery. The Air Defence Guided Missiles School at Gopalpuron-sea trains personnel of the Air Defence Artillery. The High Altitude Warfare School located at Gulmarg and Sonmarg train personnel in the art of mountain warfare including rock, snow and ice-craft. The Counter Insurgency and General Warfare School, Viairengate, trains officers and men in the art of combating insurgency.

Mechanised Infantry Regimental Centre conducts basic and technical training for recruits of mechanised infantry. In addition, it runs basic and instructor courses on anti-tank guided missiles for officers, JCOs and other ranks of mechanised infantry. It also carries out conversion training of units when they are converted to mechanised infantry or when change in equipment is involved. College of Materials Management, Jabalpur, imparts specialised training in materials management including ammunition and explosives and also in contemporary materials management techniques. Some of the other Army training centres and schools are Army Service Corps School, Bareilly; EME School, Vadodara; Military College of Electronics and Mechanical Engineering, Secunderabad; College of Defence Management, Secunderabad; Remount and Veterinary Corps Centre and School, Meerut; Army Eucation Corps Training College and Centre, Pachmari; Army School Physical Training, Pune; Army/Air Transport School, Agra; Military Intelligence Training School and Depot, Pune; Army School of Mechanical Transport, Bangalore; Corps of Military Police Centre and School, Bangalore; Institute of Military Law, Kamptee; Armed Forces Medical College Pune; Institute of National Integration, Pune and Army Medical Corps Centre and School, Lucknow.

National security and conflict resolution

The international milieu

It is possible to construct a scenario from recent events to conclude that the end of history has been reached by the cessation of the Cold War resulting in the disintegration of the Soviet Union/Warsaw Pact and the triumph of liberal democracy over Communism. A palpable reduction of interational tensions has indoubtably occurred at the uppermost hierarchical levels of the international system, with competition shifting into the economic sphere wherein future contentions might arise between the United States, Germany and Japan. Appreciating the resurgence displayed by its economy China seems destined to play a growing political role in North-east and South-east Asia, although some caution would be necessary herein and political conformism would eventually emerge.

There is some controversy, however, whether 'total war' in the Clausewitzian sense has become obsolete since the end of the Cold War, because the support/assistance of the rival super-powers is no longer available to regional adversaries. Indeed, the efforts of the United States, and the major powers, are more likely to be harnessed for the prevention of conflict, with the United Nations being utilised in more extensive peace keeping roles. Conventional wars, too, have become very destructive with the availability of high technology precision-guided weapons that combine great lethality with high accuracy, as was displayed in Operation "Desert Storms". For these reasons, it could be urged that the possibility of conventional wars, quite apart from nuclear conflict, is steadily becoming remote if not wholly obsolete in future.

But another source of potential contention, if not conflict, arises from North-South issues that are becoming sharply delineated in the spheres of trade and intellectual property rights. These issues, too, would be overshadowed by the technological hegemonism that is being sought by the developed countries over the international system and is embedded in their concerted steps to deny dual-purpose technologies to developing countries on the grounds that they could also be used for military purposes. The control regimes established for purposes of denying/regulating the flow of these technologies–Nuclear Suppliers Groups, Missile Technology Control Regime, Australia Group and COCOM to name the most prominent–have been invigorated and directed to apply their guidelines with greater severity. More disconcertingly, the list of goods, materials, subisidiary items and technologies including within these guidelines for gating are being progressively increased with result that, in a recent case, fertiliser manufacturing technology was denied to India on the tenuous grounds that it could be used for the production of heavy water that could be used in atomic energy reactors which might be used to make fissile materials for nuclear weapons. This situation delineates two possibilities for the evolving technological international order. It could either lead to the establishment of a new colonialism by the developed over the developing world, or it could encourage the developing countries to seek greater cooperation among themselves and work together in the direction of greater self-reliance, if not self-sufficiency. Yet another possibility would be for the technologically more advanced among the countries of the South configuration of nations to enter into mutual arrangements to either generally, or specifically, explore frontier areas of science and technology for cooperative exploitation.

It would be imprudent to suggest that conflict per se, in its numerous manifestations, would become remote and obsolete. The growth of beliefs in the equality of nations in the international system and the spread of the democratic idea and principles of human rights within nations has led to the encouragement of an ethnic consciousness, resulting in movements that seek greater autonomy and even separatism within nation-states. Some weightage no doubt must be given to national/ regional particularities. But the rise of subnationalism in violent forms within the erstwhile Soviet Union and Yogoslavia, for instance, reveals the conflict potential in this new ethnic consciousness, that could affect peace and stability in regional configurations, no less than the nationalism which distinguished the struggles in Vietnam and Afghanistan. It is wholly plausible that external powers might pursue their national interests by intervening such internecine domestic conflicts and exacerbate its dimensions, which presents a generic problem for the international community.

Indeed, the problem of ethno-political consciousness asserting itself highlights the internal roots of conflit coming to the foreground in the international security system during the eighties for causes ranging from the denial of political rights to economic exploitation to identity submergence of ethnic populations within a larger group.

External publicity

Publicity priorities focus largely on image-building and areas of India's unique enduring features such as her luminous history; rich cuvilisation, ethnic, linguistic and cultural variety; diverse and profound religious and philosophical trrraditions; democratic and secular political culture and institutions;pluralistic, tolerant and accommodative social ethos; wide experience in nation-building; and impressive economic and technological achievements. The function of current publicity is to explain and interpret India's foreign policy objectives and actions, and gain acceptance and support for them and intensification of publicity of India's new economic environment and policies. It has been the endeavour of the Ministry of External Affairs to counter unfair and biased reportage by transparency, and to project a balanced perspective through the mainstream media and other opinion-making channels.

To meet the challenge of the world-wide information revolution, the Ministry of External Affairs is gearing up its communications technology by moving to an integrated use of communication by fax and computers as a first step. New publicity and public relations strategies are also being adopted in an effort to keep pace with the changing scenario.

Indian missions abroad arranged telecasts of new documentary fijlms and brought out special supplements in local newspapers on the occasion of Independence Day 1994 and/or arranged telecasts of films to mark the 125th birth anniversary of Mahatma Gandhi.

India's response to negative reports and perceptions on Jammu and Kashmir has been to remind the world about the correct historical background leading to the unambiguous legal accession of Jammu and Kashmir to India, the circumstances leading tot he UN Resolutions on Jammu and Kashmir, the reaffirmation and endorsement of this option by the people and political parties of Jammu and Kashmir through successive elections held under the Indian Constitution and by the Constitutent Assembly, the non-fulfilment by Pakistan of crucial requirements under the Un Resolutions resulting in its non-implementation and absolescence, and the supression of the UN Resolutions with the signing of the Shimpla Agreement enshrining a solemn commitment by India and Pakistan to sort out all problems bilaterally.

Overseas Indians

There are nearly 14 million overseas Indians all over the world who include Indian citizens settled abroad as also persons of Indian origin who have taken foreign citizenship. Government is sensitive to the emotional urges and cultural bonds that overseas Indians have with India as also to their deeply felt desire to nurture their roots in the mother country. Government makes every effort to remain informed about their well-being. Consular work with regard to Indian nationals abroad continued to get constant attention. Indians in Rwanda and Yemen were evacuated to Indian due to internal problems in those countries. Indian Missions in Kampala, Sana'a, Aden and Djibouti rendered assitance to these persons by issuing them duplicate travel documents and arranging for their transportion back to India. Missions abroad provide assistance to Indians insettling differences with local employers, repatriation of destitute Indians, maintaining contacts with Indians in foreign jails, assisting with formalilties for Indians who have died abroad, either in the performance of last rites or return of the dead body to India.

Propagation of Hindi abroad

The Ministry of External Affairs in its endeavour to propagate Hindi abroad extends all possible help to foreign universities, educational institutions and individuals engaged in promotion of Hindi through Indian Missions. During 1994-95, Hindi typewriters/ computers softwards were provided to foreign institutions/individuals. Indian Mission in Buenos Aires, Budapest, Ulaan Baateor, Seoul, Paramaribo, Port of Spain, London and Port Louis contimued to play a major and significant role propagation of Hindi. The High Commission of India, London organised *Kavi Sammelans* in Manchester and London which were attended by poets from India while the Indian Embassy in Kathmandu organised a Hindi-Nepal *Kavi Sammelan*. The Indian Missions in Paramaribo, Budapest and Kathmandu successfully organised *Hindi Diwas* wherein natives of the respective countries participated actively and enthusiastically.The Ministry liaised with Department of Education, *Kendriya Hindi Sansthan,* Agra and Indian Missions abroad for nomination of suitable foreign candidates for scholarship to study Hindi at Kendriya Hindi Sansthan, Agra.

2

Security Environment

Developments over the past ten months, particularly the nuclear tests conducted by India on May 11 and 13,1998, have helped forge a relatively stable national security environment for India. There is already a greater international acceptance of the compelling logic for India to develop a credible minimum deterrent against the use or the threat of use of weapons of mass destruction.

India's approach, is aimed at greater regional and international stability and is entirely in consonance with its consistent efforts towards the ultimate elimination of all weapons of mass destruction. This global disarmament process has to be based on universal and nondiscriminatory treaties and on the principles of equal security for all.

The emergence of ideology-linked terrorism, abetment of and support to separatist insurgencies in other countries, economic crises and the spread of small arms are some of the factors that link India's security directly with its extended neighbourhood. This security overlap particularly includes India's neighbouring countries and the regions of Central Asia, South-East Asia, the Gulf and the Indian Ocean. India has a direct stake in the security of this entire region but is not hemmed in by it.

India's national security objectives are served by:

(a) Defending the country's borders as defined by law and enshrined in the Constitution and protecting the lives and property of its citizens against terrorism and insurgencies.

(b) Having a secure, effective and credible minimum deterrent against the use or the threat of use of weapons of mass destruction against India. The profile of this deterrent, including accurate and refined delivery systems, will not be circumscribed in range and payload by any outside pressure or influence but will be determined by the country's threat perception at any point of time.

(c) Insulating the country from the effect of individual or group restrictions on the transfer of material, equipment and technologies that have a bearing on India's security, particularly its defence preparedness. This involves a greater emphasis on in-house research, development and production of the nation's requirements and recourse to feasible alternative sources.

(d) Promoting further co-operation and understanding with neighbouring countries and implementing mutually-agreed confidence-building measures.

(e) Working with countries of the Non Aligned Movement to address key challenges before the international community and engaging in co-operative security initiatives such as the ASEAN Regional Forum (ARF).

(f) Pursuing security and strategic dialogues with major powers and key partners.

(g) Following a consistent and principled policy on disarmament and international security issues based on the principles of supreme national interest, universality, nondiscrimination and equal security for all.

India's neighbours

China is India's largest neighbour. India's relations with Chine have improved in recent years. India has expressed its interest time and again in resolving the boundary dispute with China peacefully and through bilateral negotiations as quickly as possible. China's assistance to Pakistan's nuclear weapons programme and the transfer of missiles and missile technology to Pakistan affect the security situation in South Asia. India does not regard China as an adversary but as a great neighbour with which it would like to develop mutually beneficial and friendly relations.

Exchanges at the governmental, parliamentary, non-governmental, people-to-people and other levels have continued during the year. The first ever visit by a Chief of General Staff of the Chinese People Liberation Army to India took place from April 26- May 1, 1998. India's Deputy Chairman, Planning Commission met the Chinese Foreign Minister during the ASEAN Regional Forum (ARF)- Post Ministerial Conference (PMC) Meeting in Manila on July 27, 1998. Such high-level political and military contacts serve the objective of flirthering mutual understanding between the two countries and reassuring each other about their peaceful intentions. The Agreement on the Maintenance of Peace and Tranquillity Along the Line of Actual Control in the India-China Border Areas signed on September 7, 1993 and the Agreement between the Government of the Republic of India and the Government of the People's Republic of China on Confidence-Building Measures in the Military Field Along the Line of Actual Control in the India-China Border Areas signed on November 29,1996 provide a reliable framework for the maintenance of peace and tranquillity in the border areas.

Prime Minister, Shri Atal Behari Vajpayee's landmark visit to Lahore on February 20-21, 1999 on the inaugural run of the Delhi-Lahore bus service, once again demonstrated India's deep desire for peaceful, friendly and cooperative relations with Pakistan. It is significant that in the Lahore Declaration the two countries condemned terrorism in all its forms and manifestations and affirmed their resolve to combat the menance. The two countries also undertook, in the Lahore Declaration, to refrain from intervention and interference in each other's internal affairs.

A Memorandum of Understanding was signed by the Foreign Secretaries in the presence of the Prime Ministers in Lahore on February 21, 1999. The MOU identifies measures aimed at promoting an environment of peace and stability between the two countries. These measures include bilateral consulations, advance notification of ballistic missile flight tests, reducing the risks of accidental or unauthorised use of nuclear weapons and improvement of communication links between the defence establishments of the two sides. These steps would contribute in a tangible way to the objective of fostering a climate of stability and security in the region.

During the Defence Secretary-led talks on the Siachen Glacier issue in New Delhi in November, 1998 (as part of the composite dialogue process) the Indian side made concrete suggestions that aimed at establishing a regime of peace and tranquility in a limited area Of the state of Jammu & Kashmir, which is an intergral part of India in its entirety, through a ceasefire, freezing the present ground positions and working out a bilateral mechanism to monitor the ceasfire. Along with political initiatives taken by the Government, the alterness of India's security forces has managed to contain the level of militancy. The effective and coordinated action by the security forces has led to the elimination of over 3000 militants since 1996 and the arrest of over 6500 in the same period in the Jammu & Kashmir sector.

India's relations with its other neighbours have a strong security dimension since mutual understanding and coordinated action of these countries with India can lead to the eventual establishment of peace and stability in the region for the benefit of all the South Asian countries. India has traditionally enjoyed close and stable ties of friendship and cooperation with both Nepal and Bhutan. High-level interactions have provided direction and impetus to the wide-ranging and multi-faceted cooperation between India and these countries. The state visit of the President of India to Nepal in April 1998 and that of His Majesty, the King of Nepal to India as the Chief Guest at Republic Day Celebrations in January 1999 were an important landmarks in our relations with that country. Cooperation on security related issues is monitored through regular meetings of the Joint Working Group on Border Management and Home Secretary level talks which has helped coordinate the efforts of both countries in managing the long open border between them and to prevent its misuse by elements acting against the interests of either country. Priority has also been attached to the consolidation of the close cooperation between the armed forces of the two countries.

The official visit of His Majesty the King Of Bhutan to India in October 1998 was another milestone in the tradition of frequent high-level contacts between India and Bhutan, and provided an opportunity for a comprehensive and wide-ranging review of the bilateral relationship. Regular dialogue with Bhutan has also resulted in close coordination and cooperation on security related issues of interest to both countries.

With Bangladesh the dialogue on security and border management was sustained during the year. Talks between the two countries at the level of Home Secretary and the border security forces complemented the exchanges between the Chiefs of Staff of India and Bangladesh.

Issues covered during these talks related to security, insurgency, illegal immigration and border management. India has maintained a regular dialogue with Myanmar on areas of mutual interest in security such as border management and drugs trafficking.

India continued to pursue a policy of the development of close bilateral relations based on friendship, mutual understanding and trust with Sri Lanka and Maldives. India remains supportive of a peaceful, political solution to the internal conflicts in Sri Lanka consistent with a long-term commitment to the sovereignty, unity and integrity of the country. The warmth and co-operative spirit of India's relations with Maldives translate into common endeavours in defence-related areas such as training, supply of equipment and the maintenance of a high level dialogue between the political leadership and defence officials of the two countries.

East and South East Asia

India's relations with South East Asia have made considerable progress. As a full dialogue partner of the ASEAN and as a member of the ASEAN Regional Forum (ARF), India has been engaged more closely than in the past with efforts to promote regional and international security. The essential mutuality of interests between India and ASEAN countries has been reflected in the deliberations of the several conferences and workshops under the ARF process. This was evident at the 5th ARF meeting held in July 1998 after the Indian nuclear tests in May 1998. India expects to continue to make a constructive contribution to this process and to benefit from this interaction in keeping with close bilateral relations with each of the ASEAN countries. India is also keen on developing mutually beneficial defence-related linkages with countries of the ASEAN and the Pacific regions, such as visit of naval ships, training of service personnel, repair facilities for military equipment, spare parts supplies and joint development of equipment and technologies required by the armed forces. India and Malaysia have a mechanism for a structured bilateral defence dialogue on an annual basis. The launching of Bangladesh-India-Myanmar-Sri Lanka Thailand-Economic Cooperation (BIMSTEC) grouping in June 1997 has created additional linkages and scope for co-operation between some member countries of the ASEAN with some from the SAARC.

Central Asia

The insoluble and violent conditions in Afghanistan continued the sufferings of the Afghan people; they also complicated the regional security environment. Taliban success in Northern Afghanistan including their occupation of Mazar-e-Sharif (August 10) and Bamyian (mid-September) increased the area under Taliban advance but was also able to recapture some territories gained by the Taliban especially in the Takhar province. The events of 1998 also made it abundantly clear that the military resolution to the Afghan situation was not possible. The situation in Afghanistan further contributed adversely to the regional security situation through the existence of terrorist camps and the export of narcotics. India which has major security interest in Afghanistan continued to monitor the Afghan situation very closely. As a neighbouring country with a land border with Afghanistan, India remains committed to its unity, sovereignty, territorial integrity and independence. It believes that a solution to the Afghan situation can only be found through negotiations which would lead to the establishment of a broad-based government with the participation of all ethnic groups.

Central Asian countries and India have a common stake in countering negative phenomena such as religious extremism, terrorism, ethnic conflicts, etc. Bilateral contacts with the countries of Central Asia at the political level and sustaining a dialogue through governmental and non-governmental channels on security issues is a regular feature of bilateral relations. In 1997 India, iron and Turkmenistan signed a trilateral transit agreement to facilitate trade with Central Asia. India has also participated with a positive and constructive approach in regional security initiatives such as the Conference on Interaction and Confidence-Building in Asia (CICA). In addition to enhancing co-operation in the military-technical field, India has made all efforts to promote linkages in the areas of military training for the benefit of defence personnel of Central Asian countries.

West Asia, North Africa and The Gulf

The Persian Gulf region is an integral part of India's extended neighbourhood. Developments in the region directly impinge on India's security interests. It is a primary source of India's energy needs, including crude oil, petroleum, petroleum-products and gas and will remain so in the foreseeable future. India also has very substantial other economic interests in the region, with annual bilateral trade exceeding US$ 10 billion and yearly foreign exchange remittances in excess of US $ 4 billion. A strong Indian community resides in the region reinforcing its civilisation links with India and contributing to the economic life of the countries where they live. Bilateral visits at the Chiefs of Staff have been exchanged with the Persian Gulf and West Asian countries. During the year Indian Navy ships have visited Oman, Saudi Arabia, UAE, Iran and Bahrain. The aircraft carrier *Virat*, accompanied by other ships is scheduled to visit the Gulf region in March 1999. These goodwill visits underscore India's abiding interest in and friendship for the countries of the region.

India is vitally interested in peace and development in the West Asian region. India believes that a just, comprehensive and lasting peace in the region can only be established on the basis of UN security Council Resolutions and the principle of 'Land for Peace.' India welcomed the Wye River Memorandum of Understanding signed between Israel and the PLO on October 23,1998 in Washington DC to facilitate implementation of the Interim Agreements. With some countries in, west Asia & North Africa, India has concluded bilateral agreements to combat terrorism and organised crime and to give a global focus to this problem. The West Asia & North Africa region is economically important also as bulk of phosphate and phospheric acid is imported from here.

Indian ocean region

India's maritime interests in the Indian Ocean region stem from a geopolitical and economic reality. A coastline of 7,683 kms., and EEZ of 2.01 million sq. kms., the movement by sea of a substantial part of India's external trade and the need to protect the island territories of India, are some of the factors which determine the strategic importance of the Indian Ocean region to India's security. India's active participation in the Indian Ocean Rim Association for Regional cooperation is part of an effort to develop mutually beneficial relations with key countries of the region. India continues to attach high importance to co-operation with the navies of Southeast Asian and other Indian Ocean states. India also has co-operative programmes such as bilateral exercises with important maritime powers of the world. India would be taking part in *Blue Crane* exercises in co-operation with South Africa and other SADC countries. This participation would be of a tri-Service nature. The Indo-South African joint Committee on Defence held its first meeting in August 1998 in Pretoria. There has also been a frequent exchange of visits at the level of Chiefs of Staff of the Services. India believes that multifaceted bilateral defence co-operation with South Africa based on an understanding and appreciation of each other's security concerns has a considerable potential.

P-5 countries

India and Russia have taken determined steps to raise bilateral defence co-operation to a level of strategic partnership between the two countries. There is a considerable overlap in the security perspectives of the two countries on key regional and international issues. On a bilateral plane defence co-operation between the two encom-passes a strategic dialogue, defence supplies and interaction between defence production and R&D facilities. This co-operation is an chored on a deep understanding and appreciation of each other's security concerns and priorities. In December 1998, India and Russia signed a bilateral agreement on co-opera tion in the military-technical sphere until the year 2010. The programmes of co-operation under this agreement are designed to meet the futuristic requirements of both parties. Other dimensions of ongoing co-operation with Russia include service-to-service ex changes, ship visits and military training.

The development of India's relations with France is reflective of the increasing ties with individual countries of Western Europe and the European Union. Raksha Mantri, Shri George Fernandes, visited France from January 11-14, 1999. The discussions reinforced the determination of the two countries to strengthen and diversify defence co-operation between India and France and underscored the common philosophical underpinning of the approach of India and France to contemporary challenges confronting the international community. The Indo-French High Committee on Defence met in May 1998 commencing a broad strategic dialogue between the two sides. India expects to develop relations with other countries of Western Europe also on the principles of mutual benefit, mutual respect and a mutual understanding of each other's security concerns and priorities.

Regular substantive high-level political dialogue and close economic interaction between India and the countries of Western Europe individually and the European Union (EU) as a whole, continued during this period. There have been moves towards opening a discussion on NATO's nuclear doctrine and its scope of activities, even as it prepares to accept three new members from next year. The continuing exchange of high level visits between India and the countries of Western Europe, the political dialogue with the EU Troika and the strengthening of economic linkages, represents the interest on both sides in intensifying bilateral co-operation for mutual benefit.

India has a continuing interest in improving bilateral defence co-operation with USA based on mutual respect, mutual benefit equality and understanding. Although then have been sporadic contacts between high level military officials since May 1998, the institutional framework for co-operation that had evolved over the years including the, Defence Policy Group, the joint Technical Group and Steering Groups at service-to-service level remains suspended by the USA. India hopes for an early revival of normal defence ties. India and USA are engaged in a high-level dialogue to bring about greater convergence on security issues. During these talks, India has reiterated its balanced and constructive approach on security matters within the framework of its vital security interests. However, like the United States, India will be guided by its supreme national interests in defining its essential security requirements without unacceptable constraints and limitations.

India's Nuclear Policy, Disarmament and International security

— After India conducted its nuclear explosive tests in May 1998, its nuclear weapons policy can be encapsulated as follows:

— India's security interests require the maintenance of an effective and credible minimum deterrent. This flows from the principle of minimum sufficiency which precludes an arms race with anyone.

— India has made a formal commitment to no first use of nuclear weapons.

— India maintains a unilateral moratorium on explosive nuclear tests. It is now engaged in discussions with key interlocutors on a range of issues, including the CTBT.

— India is engaged in negotiations in the Conference on Disarmament on a treaty banning the production of fissile material for nuclear weapons or other nuclear explosive devices.

— India has an effective export control mechanism in place to prevent the unauthorised transfer of sensitive equipment, material and technologies. This mechanism is continuously refined and updated.

— India's nuclear deterrent is based on the principle of strict political and civilian control. Such control would be exercised through appropriate scientific, technological and military management of the nuclear assets of the country to prevent unauthorised or accidental use.

India's policy on disarmament and international security issues is predicated on certain fundamental principles that are based on a broad national consensus. These are:

— The primary factor in India's security calculus is the supreme national interest of safeguarding the sovereignty, independence and territorial integrity of the country.

— Global nuclear disarmament and elimination of nuclear weapons is an indispensable requirement for regional and global security and for genuine and durable non-proliferation.

— Disarmament and non-proliferation cannot be addressed in a piecemeal manner in artificially defined regional compartments. The all-pervading threat arising from the possession of weapons of mass destruction can only be removed with a holistic and global approach to the problem.

— International disarmament and non-proliferation treaties should be universal and non-discriminatory and must provide equal security for all.

— The clandestine and illegal transfer or receipt of sensitive materials, equipment and technology by some countries should not be overlooked or condoned for the sake of political expediency.

— There is a need for the international community to develop effective safeguards against the danger of sensitive materials and weapons of mass destruction falling in the hands of extremist and terrorist organisations by accident or by the acts of governments that support such organisations.

By ratifying the Chemical Weapons Convention (CWC), India has demonstrated its commitment to international disarmament treaties, which are non-discriminatory in character. The implementation of all obligations assumed by India as an original state party to the Convention and related activities has proceeded satisfactorily.

India is a party to the 1972 Biological and Toxic Weapons Convention (BTWC). India actively participated in the work of Ad Hoc Group of State Parties to the Convention in Geneva during 1998 to negotiate a Protocol to the Convention on the basis of the agreed mandate. India envisions the Fissile Material Cut-off Treaty within the overall context of its security imperatives and the broader goal of universal nuclear disarmament. A limited moratorium covering individual countries is completely unacceptable,

The proliferation of small arms to non-state actors, the qualitative improvement in the lethality of small arms in terms of the impact of high technology and their easy availability had drawn the attention of the international community to the problem of small arms proliferation. Apart from a deliberate transfer of small arms to parties involved in low intensity conflicts there is also a widespread clandestine movement of such arms in the international market. The weapons recovered by Indian forces from terrorists and insurgents in Jammu and Kashmir alone, which are enough to equip regular army divisions, are indicative of the magnitude of the problem and the need to prevent the deliberate proliferation of such arms. The problem of curbing the indiscriminate use of antipersonnel landmines became an emotive issue with numerous countries and NGOs calling for their total ban. India believes that while the concerns expressed are justified on humanitarian grounds, a phased approach is desirable till such time as alternative technologies are developed. Countries plagued by landmines do not have the necessary manufacturing capability and are usually importers of such devices. The focus should thus be on restricting access coupled with increased demining activity. The use of mines should be permitted for the long-term defence of borders, perimeters and peripheries of states.

Non-military challenges to India's security

Militancy in regions of India by groups actively supported from across the border has vitiated the security environment in the country. Governments that support such militancy must be careful of the long-term repercussions of fostering terrorism as a potentially destabilising factor for social peace and stability within their own countries. The international community also has to guard against the spectre of the diversion of weapons of mass destruction, sensitive materials and technology to non-state actors. India is alive to the danger of the use of instruments such as currency counterfeiting and drugs trafficking as non-military challenges to security.

The over-all level of militancy in Jammu and Kashmir continues to show a downward trend. The key characteristics of present day militancy are the increased dependence on alien mercenaries, targeted attacks on those who have eschewed militancy and other soft targets as well as determined efforts to ignite and fuel communal tensions. During Foreign Secretary level talks in Islamabad in October 1998 Pakistan was unambiguously told that India was aware of Pakistan's active involvement in promoting terrorism in India and that India would use all means necessary to stamp out the scourge of terrorism and insurgency. Meanwhile the revival of political activity in Jammu and Kashmir state, increasing disillusionment of the people with militancy and effective operations of the security forces has been largely responsible for the improved situation.

In the North Eastern region, militant activities of the various insurgent and extremist groups and ethnic tensions have kept the security conditions disturbed in several areas. The networking amongst the various militant groups in the region, reliance on trans-border bases, continuous efforts to arouse separatist tendencies, projection of alleged human rights violations and the so-called neglect of the region are some of the important aspects of the militancy in the region- The ceasefire in the state of Nagaland, which was initially declared from August 1, 1997 for a period of 3 months, has been extended from time to time and was last extended for a period of one year with effect from August 1, 1998. Pakistani agencies operating from Nepal continued to launch operations against India. Pakistan provides support to organisations such as Tehrikul-Mujahideen, Al-Umar and Jammu & Kashmir Islamic Front. Another dimension to the security climate in the North-East is the number of ULFA and Bodo camps that have been set up on the borders of certain countries neighbouring India. Countries bordering this area have a common stake in uprooting terrorism and violence from e region to enable the overall development and prosperity of the people.

Non-military challenges to India's security also include the linked problems of drugs trafficking, terrorism and organised crime. India is located in the middle of two of the world's leading narcotics producing and exporting regions. North West Pakistan and Afghanistan on one side and Myanmar on the other. The involvement of insurgent an criminal groups in the drug trade is especially worrisome.

Energy security

Energy security is particularly crucial to India for two main reasons: the country's dependence on the imports of fossil fuels and the physical proximity of the two energy rich areas of the Gulf and Central Asia where competitive access rivalries contain inhere tendencies towards conflict involving outside powers. Inspite of improvements in indigenous production, dependence of energy sources like crude, petroleum products or imports continued. India's energy security would need to take into account some or all of the following factors:

— Mutually beneficial arrangements with India's eastern neighbours as well as Nepal for long term energy exploitation and sharing.

— Protection of the energy infrastructure within the country from disruption by terrorists and militants.

— Energy co-operation and sharing arrangements only with countries whose actions do not undermine India's security and which have demonstrated a willingness to co-operate meaningfully with India.

— International transit of energy destined for India only through stable, secure and friendly countries where there is no danger of disruption of supplies by state and non-state actors for political ends.

— Taking carefully calibrated actions to insulate India from disruption of supplies from 9 outside by greater domestic production and recourse to nuclear and non-conventional energy sources.

— Co-operating with other interested parties in protecting the sea-lanes of communication.

— Diversification of supply routes within India.

— Focussed investments in maritime and naval assets to ensure adequate reach and endurance.

— Greater involvement in exploration projects overseas pertaining to oil and gas resources.

3

Foreign Affairs

The kingpin of India's foreign policy has broadly been dictated by a principle of equidistance form the Superpower rivalry until the dissolution of the Soviet Union. In any assessment of India's role to ensure global peace, non-aligned movement played an important part. Although the movement never functioned on any bloc concept, it became the voice of vast multitudes of people spanning four continents belonging to the developing world.

The non-aligned movement was launched in Belgrade in 1961. Eminent statesmen who pioneered the movement were Prime Minister Jawaharlal Nehru, President Tito of Yugoslavia and President Gamel Nasser of Egypt. The movement which had only a handful of members initially later grew into a formidable number. The current chairmanship of Colombia, once believed to be an Americanally in Latin America, is a clear proof that the movement's appeal was spreading to South America, usually considered as "backyard" of US sphere of influence.

The disappearance of the Soviet Union brought an end to Superpower rivalry. It had its effect on the non-aligned movement. Except the coordinating bureau of non-aligned countries at the United Nations, the movement never though it appropriate to have a headquarters. This never gave rise to absence of cohesion in the movement's functioning. In contrast, the Organisation of Africa Unity (OAU) has its headquarters in Addis Ababa, while the Arab League is located in Caero.

Non-aligned movement could have been more powerful as a political force at international level had China preferred to join it. Mao Zedong divided the world into "three worlds" according to the level of economic development. Surely, China fitted in with the concept of "third world", embracing the developing countries. But at no point of time since 1961China a expressed the desire to be part of non-aligned movement, although China rightly belongs to the developing world.

India's third conribution to world peace came from its unremitting support to the anti-apartheid movement in South Africa and its support to decolonisation. New Delhi never gave up the cause of the black South Africans and the Black Africans in the rest of the continent, despite repression on their movement and denial of basic human rights by the colonising powers. One after the other, the French, Portuguese and Dutch colonisers left territories ruled by them. But South Africans were yet to see the light at the end of the tunnel.

The paths to peace and freedom and equal rights were strewn with thorns and hurdles were placed at all steps. the White rule became a blot on the world conscience. Denial to right to live brought an upsurge among the Black South Africans. In their struggle, they found India and the Indians settled there as a great source of inspiration. It was not because Mahatma Gandhi's association with South Africa in the initial years of his political life that made India so receptive to the aspirations of the Black South Africans.

Perhaps in the South African freedom movement and

struggle for equality was seen the same psyche of the Indian people who suffered humiliation, imprisonment and torture in India during the long independence struggle. Indians felt genuinely for the Black South Africans. So did the goverment.

In less than a decade's existence as an independent nation, India brought before the world a new concept of governance based on the principle of "Panchsheel". It was but natural for a country that has a long tradition of tolerance. India with numerous languages and multiplicity of religion itself symbolises co-existence. Mutual respect for each other, irrespective of differences, demonstrates Indian ethos.

It is in this context, the Bandung conference in April 1955 that adopted "Panchsheel" created a new concept for the world already handed over to violence and turmoil. The Bandung conference had five proponents: India, Indonesia, Burma, Sri Lanka and Pakistan. The Bandung conference was preceded by the bombing of the Air India plane carrying delegates and journalists over South China sea. Evidently, forces that wanted the settlement of disputes through terrorism asserted their right to show their way of solving issue and problems.

India's main foreign policy objectives are based on peaceful co-existence, self-reliance and co-operation, non-alignment, support for de-colonisation, disarmament, restructuring of the inequitous International Economic Order and the global fight against racialism. India's first Prime Minister, Jawaharlal Nehru, laid down the basic parameters of India's foreign policy and his unique contribution was the concept of non-alignment. The fundamental aim was to preserve India's freedom of option and decision-making in an autonomous way, in a world bristling with animosities and block antagonism. Consistent with our traditional values, Nehru ceaselessly promoted the universal cause of disarmament, racial equality, international cooperation for economc develpment and the peaceful resolution of disputes and gave India a conceptual framework which was based on cooperative and peaceful co-existence and non-violence which we continue to adopt in evolving our foreign policy. Basic considerations which governed the structuring of our foreign policy and its implementation are: preservation of India's national identity as a plural democratic and secular society, India's territorial integrity, and well-being of our people. Indian peace-keeping operations formed an element in India's foreign policy, being reflective of India's desire to play a positive role to promote normality at a time of need on the part of certain frientl developing countries in difficulties.

India's Neighbours

Nepal

Indo-Nepal relations which have been a long tradition of friendship and shared history and culture continued to develop smoothly during 1994-95. Several high-level visits took place between India and Nepal which include the crown prince of Nepal's first official visist abroad to India in August 1994. India-Nepal economic relations also gained from the liberalisation of both economies and from the stable and positive framework provided by the Treaties of Trade and Transit. Nepalese exports to India during 1993-94 were worth Rs. 1,176.3 million and imports from India were worth Rs. 7,874.63 million. The new Sirsiya bridge at the Raxaul border linking the two countries at the point where the traffic in goods and people is the heviest, was completed. The Rajbiraj industrial estate was formally handed over to Nepal.

Bhutan

Economic cooperation between India and Bhutan has provided a solid basis for a close and warm relationship marked by mutual understanding. the King of Bhutan, Jigme Singye Wangchuk visited India privately in December 1994 when he met the President and the Prime Minister. india is actively invoived in implementing portions of Bhutan's Seventh Five Year Plan (1992-97). Major projects such as the airport terminal building at Paro, Kurichu Hydel Project in Eastern Bhutan, hospitals, schools, roads and bridges, transmission lines, rural electrification, survey project, etc., are underway. India also continued to cooperate with Bhutan in the field of higher education, survey and training, and for renovation of culturally important places.

Bangladesh

The level of interaction between India and Bangladesh remained high during 1994-95 by exchange of several high level visits. The first meeting of Indo-Bangladesh Joint Working Group took place in New Delh to discuss, *inter alia,* security-related issues, cross-border movements, the existing visa regime, and the situation along Indo-Bangladesh border. The Border Security Force and the Bangladesh Rifles also held talks in New Delhi and Dhaka to discuss illegal immigration of Bangladesh is into India, trans-border crimes and repatriation of Chakma refugees from Tripura to Bangladesh. During February to August 1994, 5,198 Chakma refugees from Tripura were repatriated to Bangladesh strictly on voluntary basis.

Inspite of India's efforts for arriving at a long-term comprehensive and equitable arrangement on water-sharing, Bangladesh continued to raise the issue in international fora. On 20 December 1994, the Bangladesh Festival of Arts was inaugurated jointly by the Bangladesh Ministry for Cultural Affairs and India's Deputy Ministry of Education and Culture in New Delhi. The second meeting of the Indo-Bangladesh Joint

Business Council was held in Dhaka in August 1994. On 4 January 1995, Bangladesh Railway signed a US dollar 10 million agreement with RITES to purchase 10 diesel metre gauge locomotives. India's exports to Bangladesh in 19930-94 were valued at Rs. 1,349.69 crore while imports from Bangladesh were Rs. 56.09 crore.

Myanmar

India's working relationship with Myanmar continued to improve during 1994-95. There were several exchanges of visits between India and Myanmar. During the visit of a Survey delegation from Myanmar to India, operational matters relating to boundary demarcation were discussed. Official level talks with Myanmar for operationalisation of the Border Trade Agreement were held in January 1995. Twenty-eight trainees from Myanmar came to India in 1994-95 for course on farm machinery, computers, news agency operations, journalism, survey, diplomacy, banking, railways and telecommunications. India continued to support the restoration of democratic government in Myanmar.

Sri Lanka

Relations with Sri Lanka continued to be based on friendship, understanding and good neighbourliness. India conveyed her interest in further boosting bilateral ties to Chandrika Bandarnaike Kumaratunga who assumed office as Prime Minister in August 1994. India also expressed her shock at the tragic assasination of UNP Presidential candidate and offered the forensic and ballistic assistance in the investigation of the assasination. The Sri Lankan Foreign Minister visited India in October 1994 and briefed the Indian leadership about the Sri Lanka Government's agenda including the peace process, constitutional reforms and economic policies and stressed Sri Lanka's keenness for sound and cordial relations with

India and the Government of India fully reciprocated these sentiments.

The second session of the Indo-Sri Lanka Joint Commission held in New Delhi in April 1994 decided on several measures such as the restoration of preferential tariff margins on Sri Lankan cloves, reduction in tariffs on select items of export interest to Sri Lanka such as ceramic tiles, glycerine, graphite and rubber; extension of a new line of dollar-denominated credit; permission to Bank of Ceylon to open a branch in Madras; and enhanced seat capacity for airlines following civil aviation talks in July 1994. Indo-Sri Lanka trade stood at Rs. 877.3 crore from January to August 1994 with exports valued at Rs. 830.8 crore and imports from Sri Lanka valued at Rs. 46.5 crore. About 8,000 Sri Lankan Tamil refugees returned to their home country in 1994 on a voluntary basis.

Maldives

The traditionally close and friendly relations with Maldives were further strengthned and consolidated during 1994-95. President Maumoon Abdul Gayoom pad a State visit to India in March 1994 and held wide ranging talks with Indian leaders. There were also visits by a parliamentary delegation led by the Speaker of the Citizens' *Majlis,* Maldives Minister of State for National Defence and Security for discussions regarding the operations of Air Maldives to India, which began shortly thereafter, and by Minister of Health and Welfare of Maldives. Ships of the Indian Coast Guard visited Maldives in April 1994 and conducted joint exercises with the ships of Maldivian National Security Service. The Indira Gandhi Memorial Hospital at Male commenced out-patient work on 15 October 1994 where 56 Indian deputationists are stationed to help start work in the hospital. Fifty-nine Maldivian nominees received training in India during 1994-95 in various fields such as medicine, nursing, etc.

Pakistan

India-Pakistan bilateral relations continued to show a downward trend. Pakistan's sustained efforts to internationalise the Kashmir issue, its unabated support to subversion and terrorism directed against India, its intransigence on the issue of resumption of a bilateral dialogue with India, and its persistent negative approach have vitiated the atmosphere and prevented and meaningful progress in bilateral relations. In addition to training, equipping, funding and guiding militants, Pakistan has stepped up its transborder terrorism by inducting mercenaries from third countries into Jammu and Kashmir. India has strongly urged Pakistan to conduct inter-state relations as a responsible member of the international community and to eschew the threat of terrorism held against India. Consistent with her policy to resolve defferences with Pakistan bilaterally and peacefully in accordance with the Shimla Agreenment, India has conveyed to Pakistan on several occasions her readiness for the resumption of bilateral dialogue without any pre-conditions. In March 1994, Foreign Secretary renewed the offer for the resumption of Foreign Secretary-level talks. The Minister of State for External Affairs, Shri R.L. Bhatia reiterated India's offer of dialogue when he met Pak Foreign Minister in July 1994 at Dhaka. Foreign Secretary followed this up with a letter to his Pakistan counterpart inviting him for talks. On 3 November 1994, India once again formally conveyed to Pakistan her offer for dialogue. During his visit to Islamabad in November 1994 to attend the Commonwealth Senior Officials Meeting (COSM), Foreign Secretary conveyed to his Pak counterpart India's readiness to discuss all bilateral issues. The Human Resource Development Minister during his visit to

Pakistan to attend the Commonwealth Education Ministers Meeting (November 1994) reiterated India's desire for normalisation of relations. Unfortunately, Pakistan's response has been conditional and negative.

India propose on 7 April and 12 July 1994 to hold consultation for a review of the implementation of the Code of Conduct for treatment of diplomatic/consular personnel in India and Pakistan, in the light of numerous incidents of intimidatory surveillance and harassment meted out to the Indian diplomatic officials and their family members posted in Indian Missions in Pakistan. This proposal, however, did not find favour with Pakistan. Pakistan has persisted with her restrictive visa policy and other negative measures which further impeded people-to-people contacts between the two countries. On 17 March 1994, Pakistan unilaterally and without justification announced the closure of its Consulate in Bombay. Subsequently, on 26 December 1994, Pakistan asked India to close down the Indian Consulate General in Karachi. These actions of Pakistan are regret-table and are patently designed to create perception of tension between the two countries. Pakistan also assumed an exaggerated air of panic towards the isolated reports of incidents of plague in India.

Pakistan's campaign to internationalise and communalise the Kashmir issue continued. At the 50th session of the UNHRC (March 1994), Pakistan had decided to move a resolution on the Human Rights situation in Jammu and Kashmir and aggressively campaigned for support but, subsequently, withdrew its resolution at the behest of a number of friendly countries. At the 49th session of the UNGA, Pakistan made yet another attempt to table a resolution. However, this attempt also failed. In the face of

Pakistan's campaign of Jammu and Kashmir issue, India apprised the international community of the politically motivated act by Pakistan and emphasised that all outstanding issues between the two countries need to be resolved peacefully and bilaterally within the framework of the Shimla Agreement.

Afghanistan

There have been some high level exchanges with Afghanistan in 1994 in spite of the unstable conditions in that country. Afghan Minister for Civil Aviation visited New Delhi twice in Macrh and July 1994 as a Special Envoy of Afghan President. Afghan Ministers for Martyrs and Disabled Affairs and for Agriculture paid visits to India in 1994. India has been able to resume some technical cooperation (training facilities, scholarships, medical facilities, etc.) during 1994. India has an abiding concern for welfare and prosperity of the Afghan people. During 1994, India supplied tea, medicines, etc., worth Rs. one crore as relief assistance to Afghanistan. India stands for a united, stable, non-aligned and independent Afghanistan, and supports a peaceful political settlement which is acceptable to all sections of the people of Afghanistan and the ongoing peace initiative of the UN, and stands ready to make a contribution to peace efforts.

INDIA AND THE WORLD

In 1972 Prime Minister Indira Gandhi emphasized at the UN Conference on Human Environment at Stockholm that the removal of poverty is an integral part of the goal of an environmental strategy for the world. The concepts of interrelatedness, of a shared planet, of global citizenship, and of 'spaceship earth' cannot be restricted to environmental issues alone. They apply equally to the shared and interlinked responsibilities of environment and development. The global community must address the issue of global development in order to move towards and environmentally sound planet. But the problem of poverty remains as serious today as it was then. Speaking recently at the opening meeting of UNCTAD at Colombia, UN Secretary-General Boutros Boutros Ghali emphasized poverty as one of the most urgent issues facing the international community. It is the goal of removing poverty, of development at the global level, which must be addressed if environmental problems are to be tackled.

The South has a difficult task ahead of it. It has to achieve economic development with minimum damage to its environment, for this alone can sustain development. Unlike colonial powers that could exploit the vast resources of their colonies and industrialize rapidly, and pollute the global ecosystem, the developing countries today are searching for more sustainable and environment friendly solutions. But these solutions have a cost. The developing countries would require access to the latest technologies that would enable them to avoid the dirty-industry route to development.

History has led to vast inequalities, leaving almost three—fourths of the world's people living in less developed countries and one-fifth below the poverty line. The long—term impact of past industrialization, exploitation and environmental damage cannot be wished away. It is only right that development in the remaining part of this century and in the next be more conscious of its long—term impact. Our common future can only be achieved with a better understanding of our shared responsibility. Shared responsibility for the present and the past.

At a global level, the common future depends on sustaibable use of natural resources. The current pattern of development based on high resource consumption, high waste and low recycling, as practised in the North, is not sustainable and yet it is in this direction that much of the South is heading.

The alternative paradigm of improving standards of living without infliciting heavy environmental damage poses its own problems. Many of the technologies required are new, some are as yet being developed. the major costs of pollution control, and the limiting options from an environmental point of view, are factors that the early developing countries in the North did not have to consider. However, it is the cost of these more stringent norms that is the price of development today. These costs need to be shared if the developing countries of the South are to follow an alternative path. A path that bypas the route of severe environmental damage.

Sharing responsibility means sharing costs, rather than charity or aid. Funding mechanisms that are essentially donor driven need to be replaced by moe open participatory mechanisms which involve developed and developing nations. It si inherent in the concept of shared responsibility that funding becomes obligatory, rather than an optional charity. It is only on this basis that we can approah the building of a common future.

Developing countries are equal partners in any process that discusses global issues like environment and development. Their inputs are essential in decision—making to bring in local perspectives and to prevent generalized solutions. Evolving alternatives can only be done through a proper understanding of the local situation. This is best done where decision-making is not centralized.

Environmental standards and mechanisms to deal with environmental issues also need to be worked out on a country by country basis, if not in a more decentralized way. An international funding mechanism or a trade policy should not become the insturment to impose environmental conditionalities.

The countries of the south are among the richest in terms of biodiversity. This biodiversity is the source of a number of products that today benefit all humankind. Advances in biotechnology have increased the range of products in pharmaceuticals, agriculture etc. by modifying and combining the genetic resources collected largely from the South. With the much greater financial and research capability in the North, these new products are being made available through companies of the developed world. When the original genetic resources was collected there was no payment made to the country from which it came. Today these living resources are being patented and sold aback, often to the very countries from which the original genes may have been taken.

Issues of biodiversity must be discussed along with the sharing of biotechnology, sharing of the results of R & D and the commercial benefits derived from the bio-materials. The traditional knowledge base of the rural and indigenous communitites is usually the starting point for identifying particular species for particular applications. This must be kept in mind in any discussion of intellectual property rights (IPR) related to biotechnology. Indigenous communities have over centuries worked towards developing and improving crop varieties. For instance the more than 50,000 varieties of rice found in India have provided a tremendous base for research on rice. One recognizes that biotechnology research must be adequately compensated. But mechanisms other than the presently prevalent system of intellectual property rights are required. The researcher has to be compensated without restricting use as implied in IPR.

Access to environment friendly technologies also needs to be easier and much more widespread. In many cases, existing technologies would need to be replaced. The cost of the new technologies and of pollution control mechanisms is likely to be higher than that of the older processes. However it is important that the wrong decision is not taken owing to short—term financial constraints faced by developing countries. Mechanisms would therefore have to be found to subsidize this change over.

India shares the concern about ozone depletion and understands the need for coordinated action in this area. But it also recognizes that the problem has essentially been created by the developed countries who must also accept the principal responsibility for it. A situation cannot be accepted which while reducing emission levels of CFCs in the North, prohibits even the small levels of CFC-use that arise from refrigeration and other requirements which are, if anything, more necessary in the much hotter tropical countries of the South. The solution is in terms of a quicker and less costly method of transferring the newly developing alternative technologies to the South with international funding mechanisms bearing part of the costs.

India has expressed these concerns in relation to the Montreal Protocol, and now amendments have been made to enable countries such as India to sing it. Of course it must be realized that even today India's CFC consumption is far below levels presecribed by the Protocol. But India has constituted a task froce to draft its own strategy for containing CFC consumption within the country.

Global warming is another concern that India shares

with the international community. The scientific basis for calculating some of the figures related to this issue are being debated at the international level and India is bringing its perspective into this discussion. But apart from the details, India is of the view that developed countries, whose total emissions are far larger than those of the South, must shoulder the principal burden of bringing down emissions so that there is a uniform, sustainable per capita emission level. It is inevitable that in this process, countries which are developing will invariably have an increase in emission levels of greenhouse gases arising out of the development process.

In the final analysis, as Mr. Kamal Nath, India's Minister for Environment and Forests, said at the special session of the UNEP Governing Council at Nairobi in February 1992, "It is not a question of assistance or aid, but of global partnership in working towards making our planet healthier, safer and more productive."

International Cooperation

India realizes the vital need for international cooperation, bilateral and multilateral programmes and regional initiatives in dealing with issues of environment and development. At the governmental level, the Ministry of Environment and Forests acts as a nodal agency for relations with international agencies like UNEP, SACEP, IUCN, World Bank, FAO, UNDP, SAARC and EEC, Independently, NGOs in India have taken several initiatives towards global cooperation and exchanges of ideas. They have, through dealing with international NGOs and participation in international forums, created awareness of a South perspective. They have played an important part in highlighting some inherent shortcomings in international thinking and in international conventions.

Ozone Layer

India acceded to the Vienna Convention for the Protection of the Ozone Layer (March 1985). Under this framework Convention, the Montreal Protocol on Substances that Deplete the Ozone Layer was adopted in September 1987. This Protocol lays down a timetable for the phasing out of the more widely used CFCs. The Protocol came into force on 1 January 1989. India refused to sign it because of the regional treatment given to developing countries and the large economic burden which would have to be borne by them even though they have contributed almost nothing to the problem. In June 1990 the parties tot he Protocl agreed to comprehensive amendments so that developing countries such as India could participate in the global action without deterimental effects to their economies. India would be able to accede to the Protocol once the London amendments came into force. In any case, India is at present far below the targets specified by the Montreal Protocol.

Migratory Species

India signed the Convention on the Conservation of Migratory Species of Wild Animals (the Bonn Convention) in 1979. The convention came into force on 1 November 1983. The Convention on Protection of Migratory Birds between India and the former USSR was retified by both countries and came into force in 1986.

International Support

India has received financial and technical support for environment related projects from multilateral institutions like the World Bank, FAO, UNDP, UNIDO and EEC. On a bilateral basis, USA, UK, Japan, Canada, Sweden, Germany, the Netherlands, France, Norway, Australia, and some other countries have been collaborating extensively with India.

Pollution

India is signatory to the International Convention for the Prevention of Pollution of the sea by Oil, 1954 (LOndon); the international convention on Civil Liability for Oil Pollution Damage (as amended), 1969 (Brussels); the International Covention on the Establishment of an International Fund for Compensation for Oil Pollution Damage (as amended), 1971 (Brussels); the Protocol of 1978 relating to the International Convention for the Prevention of Pollution from Ships; the United Nations Convention on the Law of the Sea, 1982 (Montege Bay); and the Basel Convention on the Control of Transboundary Movements of Hazardous Wastes and their Disposal.

Antarctica

India holds consultative status to the Anatractic Treaty (1959) and is a signatory to the Convention of the Antarctic. India is also considering ratification of a Protocol on Environmental Protection to Antartica under the Antarctica Treaty.

South Perspective for UNCED

To further India's efforts toward South cooperation and to evolve a common strategy among the developing countries to deal with global environmental issues, and international conference of 21 developing countries was hosted by India in New Delhi in April 1990. As a follow-up to this, a ministerial level Conference of Developing Countries was organized by the People's Republic of China in Beijing in June 1991, which was the first such conference of developing countries. At this conference, the 41 participating countires adopted a declaration which articulates the concerns of these countries. India participated actively in putting forward the concerns of the Group of 77 countries. G-77's initiatives at the Preparatory Committee Meeting held in Geneva in 1991 have emphasized the centrality of certain developmental considerations in the agenda of UNCED.

India and World Peace

Right from the beginning as a free nation India has chosen the path of non-alignment to ensure global peace. India gave the world a new concept of governance based on the principle of "Panchasheel" and also played a major role as a peacekeeper under the aegis of the United Nations.

In the formulation of foreign policy of any nation, the determining principle is its long-term goal. A large degree of flexibility and predictability is its final reliance and resource.

India's foreign policy, in this broad perspective, has been guided by its commitment to world peace. It is little wonder that India should choose the path of non-alignment right from the beginning as a free nation since 1947.

While assessing India's contribution to world peace over the past half a century, I have chosen to concentrate on the principal pillars on which rest the edifice of foreign policy that has stood the scrutiny of the Indian people. Indian domestic policy has been subject of intense debate by diverse political entities but the foreign policy has almost enjoyed a monopoly of public opinion based on the principle of consensus.

In the order of importance, Indian policy on nuclear-free world and elimination of nuclear weapons aimed at achieving a comprehensive disarmament within a time-frame has been widely acclaimed all the world over.

It is an unequal world in which we live, and also a world in which political expendiency is placed above morality. The 15th century born Italian statesman and political philosopher Machiavelli may have died his physical death in 1527. But his spirit lives on and his doctrine of statecraft indealing with foreign relations still is a guidding star for many nations.

The latest battle that India fought was on the issue of Comprehensive Test Ban Treaty (CTBT) at Geneva and New York. Almost single-handed India put up a lone fight against virtually the rest of the world with the exception of a few likeminded countries. It looked like an instance of being stonewalled by representatives of countries led by nuclear-haves both at the United Nations and at the Conference on Disarmament in Geneva.

Even when it was known that India under no circumstances would agree to the CTBT draft, rest of the delegates representing their respective countries listened to India's point of view with bated breath. Till the last moment India stubbornly stuck to its policy decision that there was no in-between position on total nuclear disarmament.

Critics of India accused it of being inflexible, and the main charge against New Delhi was that it lacked realism in asking for disarmament under a time bound programme. Instead, experts argued that a time-frame of 10 years was realistic. Between now and the end of cold war with the collapse of the Soviet Union in 1991, the global nuclear arsenal has come down to half. Interestingly, the former Soviet President Mikhail Gorbachev's last call for total elimination of nuclear weapons had also set a time limit for 10 to 12 years. In the early nineties nuclear warheads were put at 57,000. This means that more than 28,000 nuclear weapons are still in the possession of nuclear weapon states.

While advocating a step-by-step approach to eliminate nuclear weapons, none of the states possessing them has ever wished to take the first step and make any firm commitment for their elimination.

Among the five permanent Security Council members, China is the only Asian nuclear weapon state. In his analysis of India and the CTBT, Director of Institute for Defence Studies Analyses Jasjit Singh said in the Institute's September 1996 issue, "there are major uncertainties about the future strategic scenario (in Sino-Indian relations)."

Jasjit Singh says: "it needs to be recalled that China carried out a nuclear test within hours of giving a commitment (during the NPT extension conference in 1995) that required the utmost restraint in carrying out nuclear explosions. It has continued to test since then at sites less than 1,000 kilometres from India. According to reports, the US Defence Secretary stated that China has been providing nuclear weapon technlogy to Pakistan in the recent past."

The world knows that India's concern about nuclear proliferation relates to China possessing a nuclear arsenal. That China's sole objective was to become a nuclear weapon state is evident from the fact that China neglected the peaceful use of neclear energy until late eighties. Ten years after China had experimented with its first successful nuclear test in 1964, India entered the nuclear scene for the first time in 1974 and there it has ended,. Besides, Pakistan has a clandestine nuclear programme fully assisted by Chinese technology. For the first time, China publicly asserted that India must ratify the CTBT. A conclusion is inescapable that those who wanted India to ratify the CTBT would have liked to see that India's security interests are mortgaged to other countries.

Indian and South Asian Region

As the set of Asian economies achieving impressive economic performance has expanded from the Gang of Four (Korea, Taiwan, Singapore and Hong Kong) to many more (e.g., Thailand, Malaysia, Indonasia and that largest of them all, China), the South Asian region is more of an exception in not participating in this economic transformation in the continent. As the economies to India, Pakistan, Bangladesh, Nepal and Sri Lanka adjust to the requirements of the newly emerging global economic scenario and restructure their economies of face the new challenges, is there any scope for co-operation and co-ordination? The answer is unambiguously yes. The South Asian Association for Regional Cooperation (SAARC) was born of such perception in December, 1985.

Whatever the achievements and weaknesses of SAARC there is not denying that this regional organisation has created an overall atmoshphere in which it is possible to communicate on regional perspective as viewed from each nation's vantage point. Placed below are a few important economic issues which should be on the agenda for co-operation among the nations present at this conference.

Areas for Cooperation

Promoting trade and investment between the countries of the South Asian region is a venture which will benefit them all in course of time. Intra-regional trade is not only less than 3 per cent of the total foreign trade of these countries at present but the share has declined in the eighties. India has large trade surpluses with individual countries in the region. There are pressures from neighbouring countries on India to throw its markets open. While India is passing through a phase of lowering its foreign trade barriers as part of the ongoing process of globalisation, promotion of trade with the SAARC countries is better pursued within the framework Sapta agreement such as (South Asian Preferential Trade Agreement). A framework agreement of SAPTA was signed by SAARC countries and adopted in April, 1993, and concessions by individual countries are to be worked out by December, 1993. Progress on this front, however, has been slow, and Pakistan in particuar has been very slow in the follow up.

An active exploration of trade possibilities and choices within the region does not preclude the option of globalising the individual economies to gain access to investment, technology and markets. Working within a regional framework creates an atmosphere in which some bilateral irritants (e.g., Pakistan's refusal to grant Most Favoured Nation Treatment to India) are easier resolved. Growing economic inter-dependence among countries of the region is also in the long run interest of peace in the region.

The importance of regional infrastructure utilising the enormous potential provided by the resources of the region cannot be emphasised enough. The possibilities and potential in the area of water resources has been extensively analysed in numerous studies at the Centre for Poicy Research. The most recent study concludes that the differences that divide the nations which share the Ganga-Brahamputra-Meghna basin and the quantitative values involved in their water disputes are relatively small compared to the far greater benefit that each of them could realise through co-operation. It recommends that numerous trade-offs can be considered in order to even out specific gains and losses so that South Asia will emerge a stronger region.

In the critical area of food security, steps have already been taken to build a SAARC Food Security Reserve which came into force on August 12, 1988. The

Reserve consists of 241,580 tonnes of foodgrains of which India's contribution has been 63 per cent. While the Reserve has not been utilised so far, it holds out the promise of crucial assistance in critical times of need.

As for the common goal of poverty alleviation from the region, there is need for exchanging information and experience in direct programmes for poverty alleviation. The Report of the Independent South Asian Commission on Poverty Alleviation (1992) which was discussed at the 7th SAARC summit in April, 1993, is a good beginning. It was agreed at the summit that a national level pro-poor plan would be drawn up by each member state and the experience and progress will be compared at the next SAARC summit. Co-operation and concerted effort to fight poverty in the region must remain the top priority for the countries of the region.

Guidelines for building a new order in South Asia

Objective conditions are emanating from international change for building a conflict-free cooperative South Asia. Subjective inputs are still lacking, but those who have the destinies of one-sixth of humankind in their hand are coming under increasing pressure from the objective realities that are pathways to a new world order.

The world's growth area has shifted from Europe to the Asia-Pacific. The EEC has shown the way how nations, despite their resistance to parting with national sovereignty, are laying the foundations of economic and technological supranationalism, leading, sooner rather than later, to the foundation of willingly diminished political sovereignty. The Asia-Pacific region is much more diverse and larger than Western Europe. It is a region mostly of newly independent states who carry on their bodies the scars from their struggles for national revolution. In this region, too, several cooperative groupings are either in the process of forming or are conceptually in the air. President Clinton talks of a new Pacific Community and has plans to convene an informal summit next year of the members of the Asia-Pacific Economic Community, which is still to be formally launched. Japan's diplomacy is now vigorously seeking an area of "PARTNERSHIP" with ASEAN and other Asia-Forum with which several non-ASEAN countries like the Indo-China states, China, Japan, the US and even Russia are linked. It is committed to the creation of an ASEAN common market. Gorbachev's cry for an Asia-Pacific Helsinki is now echoed faintly by Bill Clinton and loudly by President Nazarbayev of Kazhakstan. The US, Japan and Korea, together with Taiwan and Hong Kong, are thinking in terms of setting up an East Asian caucus. In the Western hemisphere the U.S. Canada and Mexico have signed an agreement to establish a North American Common Market. Nations of Latin America are in the process of engineering two or perhaps three regional grouping. To be sure, none of these groupings, whether formed or in the process of forming, are from those who have had the old order in their grip for several decades.

South Asia, home of one fifth of human kind, is still lagging behind other regions in coming together for faster economic development and common security. However, SAARC is now committed to create the region as a preferential trade bloc by 1997. Not al SAARC members are equally ethusiastic about the idea, but the fact that none has rejected it is evidence enough to forecast that this conflicted region too cannot live in conflict and in isolation from one another for a long time. The convergences that we see around South Asia cannot skip over our region. In the medium run, Indians and Pakistanis will become good, if not friendly neighbours. Regional cooperation in peace, development and security is now on the agenda of each nation of South Asia and of the region as a whole. As and when the South Asians build their own regional system of economic and security cooperation, they will have to learn from the history of conflicts and from their own indigenous civilsations and heritages. They will need to renounce the use or even the threat of use of force to settle disputes and differences. They will have to resolve their territorial disputes through negotiations. They will not interfere in one another's internal affairs nor allow their respective territories to be used against the inerest of other members of the regional community. Bilateral and regional treaties of cooperative security will guarantee their individual and collective territorial unity, integrity and soveregnty. This will make it possible for them to do with the minimum essential defence expenditures and harvest a peace dividend that will be used to improve people's, conditions of living.

Mass poverty is a cause for insecurity of regimes and states, and South Asia has the dubious distinction of being the home of the world's largest mass of poor and deprived humanity. The countries of South Asia must rebuild their own domestic orders with creation of wealth. From a preferential trade area in theory as well as practice, they have to graduate to a South Asian common market. They will have to create a South Asian pool of technologies and share the benefits of imported high technology. They must learn that improvement in living conditions in any one of the countries countributes to the advancement of the region as a whole. Freindly competition must be the other side of the coin of friendly cooperation.

In a new South Asian order, no nation must aspire after hegemony or sphere of influence. Each one will be the equal of the others. In building relationships with extra-regional powers, each member of the South Asian community will ensure that the interests of no other members are hurt. The weak in the community must receive the constant attention of the strong in the filed of economy and technology. To the extent possible, the community must coordinate and harmonise their increasing international trade. To the maximum degree possible, they must trade directly with one another. Customs barriers will be gradually lifted. South Asians must be able to travel freely with dignity and honour throughout the region, and build regional tourist facilities so that the region a whole becomes a major international tourist attraction. Differences will always arise between and among nations. Cooperation, practised for long years, will minimise differences, as it has happened in ASEAN.

Finally, South Asia will have to fall in line with regional and global trends. One of the most important trends is that institutions, practices and outlooks are becoming more alike across national frontiers. Economic and technological convergences are pressing for national political and defence convergences. Governments are being judged not by their claims to ideological enthusiasm or rectitude, but by their performance. Performance is now determined by answers to a set of questions. Are governments practising or inhibiting development? Are they ensuring a fair distribution of the benefits of development to the weak and are they protecting those who need social protection? Are they improving the quality of life of ordinary people and protecting the environment for their children? Are they conducting foreign policies in ways that reinforce the security and national pride of their regional collectivities. Are the governments being run for the benefit of the governed?

Draft Declaration

South Asia must leave behind its legacy of confrontations and conflicts and import from the world and retrieve from its own ancient heritage and culture qualities of cooperative peace, development and security, its leaders and peoples must take up in earnest the long-delayed task of resolving bilateral differences and disputes, and impart to SAARC the synergy of creative regionalism. All countries of South Asia are now democracies. It is imperative therefore of each nation and of the region as a whole to improve the quality of life of its teeming poor and deprived humanity. More than one-half of the billion-plus population in the region lives in abject conditions. South Asia has lived for almost fifty years obsessed with its historical cleavages. Now, as the planet moved towards the third millennium, South Asia must look to the future and build itself as a peer of other regions, which have joined the efforts of likeminded nation-states in collective endeavours to improve the quality of life of the governed.

South Asia is unaware of the rich natural and human resources of the seven nations that constitute the regional community. Now, in the post cold war world, the region is baffled and bewildered by the complexities of its humanscape. Its governments are strained by confrontations and conflicts at the bilateral level, weakened by the failure of the member states to build bridges of cooperation, and afflicted by domestic ethnic and religious cleavages that take a heavy toll of human life. While several other regions of the world have made impressive progress in regional cooperation for development and security, South Asia, home of ancient civilisations and great religions, lags behind them in making the best use of economic and technological convergences that are the hallmark of the era initiated by the end of the cold war.

Insurgencies, ethnic conflicts, caste clashes, sectarian violence, drug traffic, custodial deaths, violation of human rights, and religious fanaticism conspire together to keep South Asia in the backwoods of the modern world. Behind these effusions and fusillades of blood and hatred, however, lies an uprecedented awakening of the long-inert poor and deprived in a region whose societies are mutli-lingual, multi-ethnic, multi-cultural and multi-religious. A South Asia governed on the high principles of social justice and human resource development, will also be a South Asia of good neighbourliness and regional cooperation.

Leadership failures over a long period of time has created a broad divide between People and Power. Entrenched power structures resist participatory democracy with the principle of self-government extended to the frontier village. These interests, sometime linked with external forces, have places a high premium on conflicts and cleavages between South Asian countries. Power structures are often uninterested in horizontal development and unwilling to part with the enormous power and privilege they have enjoyed since independence.

It is the imperative of the presenet and future generations of South Asian peoples to work for a region that will match ASEAN and other regional communities in cooperative development and security. South Asian leaders must without further loos of time address themselves earnestly to conflict management, control and resolution, peaceful solution of divisive issues, the formation, stage by stage, of a common market and a free trade area, giving protection at the same time to weaker industries, and establishing a regional pool of technologies. South Asians must be able to resolve their differences without the intervention of outside powers. Peace is always an offspring of give-and-take, live-and-let-live, of compromises with dignity. Absolutist positions do not make peace.

Above all, South Asians must develop an elevating vision of the future. Their visions must be hewn from the constructive, integrative and cooperative trends and processes released by the collapse of the Berlin Walls of the cold war, not from the rhetoric of threats, and conflicts that still proliferate in the planet. Only united and together can South Asia, in cooperation with other regional organisations in the developing world, sucessfully frustrate efforts by the developed to keep the developing majority of the international community at a level of technological and economic inferiority.

All national constitutions have something akin to a bill of rights, howsoever named. Derogations are permitted but the frequency and facility with which these have been resorted to calls for introspection and review. South Asian nations should be urged to subscribe to various international covenants and instruments and, having done so, must ratify them expenditously. National laws should be reviewed and, where necessary, upgraded to measure up to these international commitments.

The right to development and poverty alleviation is imperative. South Asia must cooperate to improve the quality of life of its people. But all rights are indivisible and there is no hierarchy of rights.

It would be useful to establish links between official and NGO human rights organisations in the region. SAARC could consider an initiative in this regard by establishing a small human rights cell. Strengthening and closer monitoring of the criminal justice system in countries of the region would go far towards underpinning human rights. Special courts could be one remedy. These could promote specialisation and avoid undue delay. Cross-border violations, drug traffiking and migration pose common problems and common danger. Mutual discussion and special mechanisms might be considered to concert action and defuse tensions.

Awareness and legal aid are prime factors in promoting human rights and environmental protection.

Primary education and health and population control are of fundamental importance for the region. They merit the highest priority in national planning, investments and implementation.

South Asia should develop a common approach to the protection and advancement of its tribal populations who should be encouraged to develop in accordance with their own genius without being treated as separate groups divorced from the mainstream of national life and aspirations of which they are an integral and equal part.

South Asia is made up of plural societies embracing a rich diversity. This plurality, including all minorities, must enjoy equal rights and opportunities.

South Asian societies are deeply religious. There must be respect for all faiths, cultures and traditions. Fundamentalism of whatever brand, poses a threat to harmony and stability in each country and must be constructively countered through education and dialogue.

The environment is a trust. The countries of the

region must work to pursue and accelerate policies that will stem degradation and start a restorative process. All new programmes, equipment and infra-structure should be based on upgraded environmental norms. All must strive to conserve nature, promote sustainability, avoid waste and ostentatious consumerism, and ensure greater equity.

While South Asia's environmental concerns are linked to subsistence and survival, it must be willing to cooperate to ameliorate global environmental problems. SAARC should endeavour to evolve a common aproach towards dealing with these global issues and environmental protocols under discussion.

The foregoing discussion would re-emphasise our contention at the beginning of this paper that the choices available to South Asia are plainly evident. It could either proceed to deepen its ties in various spheres of their bilateral relations, especially lower key areas like cultural, economic, social and academic activities to erode the edges of suspicion and mistrust that afflict political relations between the South Asian countries. It would be tragic if, on the other hand, mutual differences continue to exist, and bedevil the relationships between the sub-continental neighbours, and they persist in wasting their resources on activities that have no useful result.

Above all, it requires greater understanding that the locus of tensions and instabilities has shifted from the external to internal polity, and the roots of the problems of internal security, whether they arise from ethnic, communal or socio-economic causes, lie in the absence of a just order. The various forms of deprivation, that include the denial of political, economic or social rights, need to be more seriously addressed by the countries of South Asia in the interests of managing their internal polities in the years to come. For this purpose also, it is very necessary that the tensions and instabilities that confront their external polities from within the region are sought to be resolved by patient and earnest endeavours.

The South Asian Association for Regional Cooperation

The 14th session of the SAARC Council of Ministers held in Dhaka in July 1994 reviewed the progress in the implementation of the Agreement on SAARC Preferential Trading Arrangement (SAPTA). A report adopted by the SAARC Workshop held in New Delhi in March-April representing a collective position was presented at the World Conference on Natural Disaster Reduction held in Yakohama, Japan in May 1994. The Meeting of Finance/ Planning Ministers of SAARC countries held in Dhaka in July 1994 decided that a mechanism should be set up for exchange of information on experiences of the SAARC countries in the implementation of poverty alleviation programmes. The SAARC Ministerial Conference on Youth held in Male in May 1994 adopted a resolution known as "Male Resolution on Youth". SAARC Documentation Centre (SDC) has been established and located at the Indian Scientific and Documentation Centre, New Delhi. India organised a SAARC Meeting of Experts on Rehabilitation Techniques for Disabled Persons from November-December 1994 at the National Institute for Mentally Handicapped, Secunderabad.

South-East Asia and the Pacific

In keeping with India's desire for greater integration with the Asia Pacific, South-East Asia continued to be an area of prime focus during 1994-95. Numerous high-level contacts helped to rekindle interest in India in those countries. Efforts to synergise the complementarity in the economies of India and the region succeeded in numerous productive ventures in both sides. There are 96 joint ventures in countries in South-East Asia. Currently, India's exports to the region are in the range of Rs. 5,500 crore, a little less than 10 per cent of her global exports.

India's bilateral relations with Singapore continued on a dynamic course. Prime Minister's visit to Singapore in September 1994 was instrumental in turning a new chapter in India's relations with Singapore. Public housing, power generation, telocommunications, tourism and civil aviation were identified as sectors for possible cooperation with Singapore in India. The Prime Minister suggested Singapore's involvement in commercialising new technologies developed by CSIR and also flagged India's interest in further strenthening defence cooperation in areas such as training and equipment. a Memorandum of Understanding on Foreign Office Consultations and a dozen corporate agreements were signed during the visit. Prime Minister Goh Chok Tong's visit to India again in January 1995 after his earlier visit in January 1994 signified the growing informality and closeness in the relationship of mutual benefit.

Prime Minister's visit to Vietnam in September 1994 reaffirmed India's traditionally warm and close relationship in the changing environment. While acknowledging the strength and continuity of bilateral relations between India and Vietnam, both sides agreed that there was need to upgrade economic linkages. Several new areas including sugarcane cultivation and processing, dairy farming, rubber plantation and manufacture, vegetable oil production, leather processing, etc., were identified. Four agreements were signed during the visit on Avoidance of Double Taxation, Facilitation of Visas, Defence Cooperation and Foreign Office Consultations. The visiting Indian business delegation also signed six corporate agreements relating to investments and joint ventures in Vietnam.

With Thialand, there is an excellent understanding at the political level reinforced by periodic exchange of high level visits which include the visit of the Thai Parliamentary Committee of Religion, Art and Culture in September 1994, Thai Deputy Foreign Minister's visit in October 1994 and Deputy Prime Minister of Thailand's visit to Calcutta in January 1995 in connection with Confederation of Indian Industries (CII) Centenary celebrations. Secretary-level talks between India and Thailand were also held in January 1995 in New Delhi. The first meeting of the India-Thailand Joint Business Council aslo took place. India's bilateral trade with Thailand showed a welcome sign of growth with the overall value reaching US dollar 601.60 million (approximately Rs. 1,800 crore) during 1993-94. From Thialand, investment proposals worth US dollar 120 million (approximately Rs. 360 crore) were approved in 1993. The Aditya Birla group is the largest Indian investor with three joint ventures.

India's close relations with Indonesia continued to be strengthened during 1994-95. The visit, of President Soeharto to New Delhi for the reconvened G-15 Summit in March 1994 offered a fresh opportunity for bilateral exchanges and interaction in diverse fields. The volume of trade in 1993-94 was US dollar 354.36 million against the previous year's figure of US dollar 197.19 million. India has 15 joint ventures in Indonesia with investments worth US dollar 189 million.

Prime Minister Mahathir's special gesture of visiting India in March 1994 for the reconvened G-15 Summit after his visit in the same connection three months earlier, contributed to the strengthening of India's bilateral relations with Malaysia. Several major projects involving Indian companies have been cleared over the last year. There are 18 Indian joint ventures in Malaysia and another 14 under various stages of implementation. Malaysian investment in India continued to look up with approved investment reaching Rs. 830 million in 10 projects in various areas. Over 100 Malaysian Air Force personnel are currently undergoing training in India as per the defence cooperation between both the countries.

With the Philippines, India's relations have remained cordial and friendly. The Foreign Office Consultations in Manila in November 1994 underlined the need to step up bilateral economic cooperation and a Joint Business Council was set up. Meat exports from India to the Philippines resumed after a gap of almost thirty years. Senator Leticia Shahani, President Pro-tempore of the Phillippines Senate visited India twice during 1994-95.

India's relations with Brunei Darussalam are also gathering momentum. Brunei's Minister of Communications visited India in January 1995 when a Memorandum of Understanding was signed to discuss matters relatingto the conclusion of an Air Services Agreement and introduction of scheduled air services between the two countres.

With Camboida, India continues to enjoy close and cordial relations. Former Deputy Prime Minister and Foreign Minister visited India in June 1994. A Memorandum of Understanding on Foreign Office Consultations was signed. It was also decided to establish a centre for artificial limbs in Cambodia.

The Lao Foreign Minister visited India in August 1994 and a Memorandum of Understanding on Technical Cooperation and a Cultural Agreement were signed. The visit imparted a much-needed impetus to the bilateral relations.

Relations between India and Australia continued to be cordial. Vice President Shri K.R. Narayanan visited Australia in April 1994 where he inaugurated the Festival "India Today 1994" a two-month long diversified programme of events featuring arts, music, culture-organised by the Austrialia-India Council. Former Deputy Premier of Victoria visited India in February 1994 to identify specific areas for expanding trade an investment and the Australian Chief of Defence Forces visited in April 1994 besides several business/ trade delegations also visited India. The third meeting of the India-Australia Joint Ministerial Commission was held in February 1994 in Sydney. A business cum investment seminar was organised in Sydney and the India-Australian Joint Business Council's meeting held in Perth in April 1994. The bilateral trade during 1993-94 was worth Rs. 2,855.08 crore with adverse balance of trade against India. Australian investment in India has been rising steadily and during January-September 1994 it was Rs. 385 crore, the fourth largest after USA, Germany and NRIs. An Honorary Consul General of India was appointed in Melbourne in November 1994.

The traditional friendly relations between India and New Zealand were maintained. Bilateral consultations at Secretary-level were held in April 1994 in Wellington. Bilateral trade registered an increase of 20 per cent in 1993-94 to Rs. 342 crore. About 12 joint ventures in various fields have been launched. The fourth meeting of the Indo-New Zealand Joint Business Council was held in Auckland in April 1994 while the fourth meeting of the India-New Zealand Joint Trade Committee was held in Wellington in June 1994.

India has declared that the Fijian Government

should accelerate the review process of the racialy-biased 1990 constitution with a view to achieving an early solution acceptable to all the sections of the Fijian population and India has decided to establish diplomatic and consular relations with Federated States of Micronesia, a UN member.

Other Sources of Inter-State Conflict

If some prominence has been given here to Indo-Pak tensions it is because they constitute the overarching reason for SAARC not developing faster to knit together a pattern of regional cooperation in the region.

Apart from the Indo-Pak contention, in its various dimensions, the other sources of tensions in South Asia that could escalate to inter-State conflict might be recognised to arise from:

(i) Territorial disputes arising from divergent claims over areas in the region;

(ii) Ethnic tensions within nations that spill over inter-State boundaries; and

(iii) Population flows within the region reflecting inter-State tensions and leading to refugee exodus, or voluntary emigration in search of socio-economic betterment.

Territorial disputes are, prominently, a potent source of tensions and conflict in South Asia and, in a manner of speaking, Kashmir quintessentially represents a territorial dispute of massive dimensions, which remains unresolved and could be the cause of conflict between India and Pakistan. So does Siachen, and the absence of any agreement about delineation of the border in this area has led to a confrontation between the armed forces of the two countries that has occasioned a great deal of expense in terms of finance and lives lost to the extreme climatic conditions on the glacier. Lesser territorial disputes have obtained between South Asian countries focussing upon the Kachativu and Moore island controversies, or relating to the demarcation of naval boundaries in the Sir Creek between India and Pakistan, or in the Bay of Bengal between India and Bangladesh, but have a limited potential to ignite inter-State conflict.

The growth in ethnic-consciousness and resultant tensions in South Asia are of greater consequence, and could be placed within a theoretical construct, as being occasioned by the zeitgeist, which favours the assertion of sub-national particularities withn domestic polities. The spread of democratic forms of governance gives strength to ethnicity. Similarly, the rise of religious fundamentalism as part of a global phenomenon, would heighten this sense of ethnic particularity. These aspects of current international developments are apparent withn South Asia, in ethno-political movements ranging from Sindh to Kashmir/Punjab/Assam to the Chittagong Hill Tracts to the Tamil majority areas in Sri Lanka. In the historical perspective these entho-political movements represent the disintegrative processes that have traditionally affected the integrity of political structures in South Asia. It provides a powerful rationale for the SAARC modelity to enable an integrative process take shape in the region that would preserve the structure of the various nation-States by submerging their sub-national ethnicity in a larger supra-national identity.

The danger to South Asian peace from this resurgence of ethno-nationalism and inter-State conflicts ensuing therefrom springs from these which impinges on the latter's political economy. This occurred most recently with the ethnic Tamil crisis in Sri Lanka, and its spillover into Tamilnadu, which created its own political dynamics for the Indian federal system. More generally, ethno-political movements in one South Asian country can spill over its borders and adversely influence the politics, apart from the economy of the neighbouring country. This calls for greater inter-State cooperation in the resolution of such problems. Else the possibility obtains that both countries involved would be embarked on a collision course as occurred in the crisis of 1971. It might be added that the instrumentality of militarily assisting a particular ethnic group to reach a favourable solution of its demands vis-a-vis the national government is fraught with unpredictable consequence, as India discovered following its deployment of the IPKF in Sri Lanka to bring peace and stability into the Tamil majority in Tamil province of Sri Lanka.

Inter-State population flows of migrants in search of a better way of life in a neighbouring country or as refugees also has the potential to endanger inter-State tensions and conflicts in South Asia. It is worth remarking that all such population flows have taken place into India over the decades following partition, that would include emigration from Nepal, Bangladesh, and most recently, Sri Lanka. Clearly, the population outflows from Nepal and Bangladesh have a nexus with the aspirations of the migrants to improve their socio-economic condition in India. It is unfortunate that such migrants do become socio-economic problems for the receiving country and can become the pawns of domestic politics by their mobilisation into vote-banks, as occurred with the East Bengal/Bangladesh migrants in the Indian states of West Bengal and Assam. After a process of time the indetification of migrants presents growing problems as India is discovering in its efforts to pushback Bangladesh entrants. This issue has polarised the national political arena with the BJP making the forced return of these migrants a major plank in its foreign policy agenda. Any attempt to evict large populations by force clearly has the potential to engender inter-State tensions and conflict.

A different situation arose with regard to the Tamil refugees fleeing Sri Lanka in the wake of the SLAF campaign against militant groups in the Tamil-majority areas of Sri Lanka. Fortunately, the 1,000,000-1,50,000 Tamil refugees that still remain in India are being re-patriated in terms of an agreement reached between the two countries. Earlier, the conflict potential of the fleeing Tamil refugees lay in the ethnic Tamil problem in Sri Lanka political issue in Tamilnadu leading to competitive jingoism by regional parties demanding the use of force to settle the issue. Further, this question became an issue in Centre-State relations. A similar problem of population outflows, and related to ethno-political tensions, is occurring with the ouster of the Nepali-origin population from Bhutan, and Chakmas from the Chittagong Hill Tracts. Any possible solution to stem these outflows, whether they are natural or forced, would require bilateral negotiations between the countries affected to contain the influx. The question does arise as to what should be done if these efforts fail.

The empirical evidence would suggest, however, that external intervention into Intra-State ethno-political and/or migratory issues could produce wholly unitended effects for the intervening power. India's utilisation of the Tamil militants has lever to resolve the ethinic crisis in Sri Lanka has resulted in a marked deterioration in the law and order situation in Tamilnadu and, to an extent, in other South Indian

States. They are believed to have been used by political parties in Tamilnadu to further their electoral prospects. A similar entree of the Afghan mujahideen into the body politic of Pakistan ensued following their utilisation to serve Pakistan's foreign policy interests by assisting the American strategy of arming the mujahideen to wage war against the occupying Soviet forces in Afghanistan. Pakistan is now left with an exce bation of its law order problem and the establishment of a Klashnikov culture in the country. The empirical evidence strengthens the need therefore for South Asian countries to seriously discuss this new set of issues because they have the inherent potential to destabilise border areas in the region.

Any process of bilateral or multilateral dialogues within the South Asian region needs to appreciate the reality that serious political differences exist between them, that hinders the possibilities of greater cooperation in the sub-continent. These differences cannot be wished away and need to be firmly brought on the agenda for discussion and the search for solutions. The other reality which cannot be wished away is the looming (hegemonic) image of India. No doubt, India must understand the right of the South Asian countries to be apprehensive about it; but is equally the obligation of the other regional countries to appreciate the assurances given by India. There remains the question of underlying doubts and suspicions, which points again to the relevance of the SAARC forms to articulate apprehensions, and declare reassurances.

More specific measures can be suggested to further these objectives:

(1) Regular intervention in the public debate through all media forms to engender a greater awareness of how the existing and newer

sources of tensions and conflicts are bedeviling the region, affecting the developmental process and, at one remove, subverting the processes of democratic governance.

(2) Highlight in public forums the value of multiatcral/bilateral dialogue between South Asian countries and the SAARC process, to erode tensions in the region. Apart from suggesting newer cooperative instrumentalities for this purpose, the existing agreements reached by SARRC, but lie dormant, like the Terrorism Convention and Agreement on Narcotic Drugs/Psychotropic Substances need being recognised as steps requiring vigorous implementation to clear the regional atmosphere of lurking doubts and suspicions

(3) The appreciation could also be underscored that certain natural channels of commerce have traditionally obtained in South Asia, and artificial barriers in their way have only succeeded in directing them into informal and illegal routes. This is occurring with regard to trade via third countries, that is within the knowledge of the countries concerned; hence the need to make overt what is the obtaining reallity. Besides trade these natural channels of commerce would include both capital and labour flows that need to be freed. The logic of commerce points to South Asia developing into a common market. The politics of the region will not permit this dispensation at present, but the strategic direction required might be recognised more clearly.

(4) Academic needs to be more greatly sensitised to the need for undertaking conflict resolution

studies relating to the South Asia, pertaining especially to ethno-political and migration issues in the region, which seems destined to become significant in future. It would serve this purpose admirably if joint studies were undertaken by scholars belonging to the countries affected by these problems, as is being attempted by the newly established Regional Centre for Strategic Studies. Furthermore, the possibility of establishing positions for visiting scholars in the prestigious institutions represented in the South Asian Dialogue to undertake such studies could be another modus to achieving this end.

The Second South Asian Dialogue of 1992 had emphasised the need for stabilisation and structural adjustment in the countries of the South Asian region, particularly in the context of the changing global scenario. Emphasising that the agenda for economic reforms should be defined domestically, the Indian experience was extensively discussed and analysed for possible lessons in economic policy making for other countries of the region. An active domestic debate on the various policy options and an emerging consensus were seen as key ingredients for the success of the economic policy reforms within a democratic polity.

Against the background of this discussion, the developments in policy making and economic performance in India during the last year are sketched out here with a view to updating the record. This is followed by a broader discussion of the nature of regional co-operation and economic integration required to bring about the overall development of the countries of the South Asian region.

The Nuclear Dimension

The obtaining nuclear overhang in South Asia can now be discussed. The Report on Regional Non-Proliferation in South Asia submitted by the White House to the U.S. Congress in May holds that India and Pakistan have established the capability to manufacture nuclear weapons at short notice and also prossess credible means of delivery to attack value targets. This conclusion is in line with independent Russian assessments. Estimates of the nuclear capabilities available to the two countries have also been made by several organisations based on the quantities of fissile material believed to be in their possession. India and Pakistan are, uniquely, the only adversary but cryptonuclear powers in the world. There are other unique aspects of the nuclear situation in South Asia. India's present policy of keeping its option open which, incidentally, seems to have informed Pakistan, without either expressing or foreclosing that option is singular in the so-called non-proliferation regime.This policy enjoys wide domestic support in the two countries, but it also needs greater appreciation that they could only possess crude fission devices with their means of delivery premised on aircraft. It would require a series of tests to miniaturise nuclear warheads and gain assurance about the reliability/accuracy of their missiles, apart from the political/military leadership acquiring confidence that such last-resort weapons will function when they need to be utilised.

Despite these technological constraints there is a considerable body of opinion which holds that the present ambiguous nuclear situation in south Asia has led to a stabilisation of the mutual relationship. Witness the caution displayed by the armed forces of the two countries and their political leaderships during the various crises in relations during the last few years, e.g., Brasstacks Exercise (1987), Kashmir-related escalation of border tensions (1990), and the recent (1992-93) attempts by JKDA activists to violate the Line of Control. There are contrary arguments to suggest that availability of nuclear weapons at short notice constitutes a dangerous situation, with the likelihood of a nuclear exchange being triggered by inadvertence, if not design, and being occasioned by an escalation of conflict from the conventional level. It could, however, be argued that this entire question is somewhat irrelevant, since the primary threat to India arises from ethno-political and other domestic tensions in the polity, which can be inflamed by external powers intervention, and the nuclear weapons provide no defence against this range of problems. It might be further added that the economic costs involved would constrain any overt deployment of nuclear forces. These economic costs would not merely involve the expenses, incidentally, on establishing a nuclear force which, in the case of India, most address the presence of a nuclear China on its security horizons, but also the likelihood of bilateral/multilateral financial assistance getting prejudiced by such proliferation actions.

A word about the present state of the non-proliferation regime. There is optimism about its growing acceptability by events like the accession of France, China and South Africa to the UNP, Argentina and Brazil agreeing to a system of mutual inspection of their sensitive nuclear facilities, signing of major arms control agreements like START-I and START-II, withdrawal of tactical nuclear missles by the U.S., Russia and U.K., and moratoria placed by these nuclear weapons powers on nuclear testing and so an. At the same time, developments in the former Republics of the Soviet Union must cause the most profound concern. All tactical nuclear weapons have reportedly been shifted into Russia. There is no assurance, however, that fissile material, nuclear cores, if not entire nuclear weapons, are fully accounted for. Indeed, materials accounting procedures in the erstwhile Soviet Union were neither detailed nor strict because the nature of its political system permitted confidence that theft or misappropriation of such materials were not possible and could be easily detected. No such confidence is presently available with the break-up of the Soviet Union and the autonomy of its former Republics. The possibility of fissile materials, nuclear cores, if not entire nuclear weapons, remaining unaccounted for is real, and points to the extraordinary-danger of their falling into the hands of nuclear aspirants. There is besides newer problem accosting the non-proliferation regime after South Africa's self-confessedly admitting to making and, thereafter, dismantling six nuclear weapons. There can be no assurance that all its nuclear weapons have been uncovered and/or the fissile materials to produce a further number have been satisfactorily accounted for North Korea has highlighted the escape route available to NTP-signatories to withdraw from the Treaty whenever they chose; Iraq has revealed the clandestine path to the nuclear capabilities. These developments must be construed as adverse to the non-proliferation regime's containment.

The foregoing discussion provides the backdrop against which proposals for controlling, limiting and eventually eliminating nuclear weapons from the region must be considered. This parallels the American objective to "cap, then over the time, reduce, and finally eliminate the possession of weapons of mass destruction and their means of delivery" in South Asia. The technical implications of this measure would require ceasing production of fissile materials and work relating to missiles. It would also require that imports of materials, equipment or tecnnology that could further the military nuclear or missile programme should be stopped. Equity demands that all such proposals should be universal and non-discriminatory. Restricting these proposals to particular regions does not address the true nature or dimensions of the non-proliferation problem, especially in a milieu wherein the dilemma of fissile materials, nuclear cores/weapons/technology, apart from unemployed nuclear scientists and engineers, seeping out of the erstwhile Soviet Union and becoming available to nuclear aspirants has not been credibly resolved. There is, besides, the related dilemma of defining regions. In India's security perceptions the region must include China for the purpose of evolving any methodologies to control, reduce and eliminate nuclear weapons from South Asia.

There remains, however, the question of managing the nuclear situation in South Asia and, in particular, the crypto-nuclear adversarial relationship between India and Pakistan. The various confidence-building and tension-reducing proposals that could build upon existing arms control/confidence-building agreements in the nuclear and conventional areas, could comprise the following:

(1) Extending the agreement not to attack each other's identified nuclear facilities and installations to designated population and high value economic assets;

(2) The "hot-line" communications between the military leaderships could be extended to the political leaderships at the highest levels and upgraded with multiple-redundancy linkages to permit fail-safe communications at all times. This becomes of extreme importance in the ambiguous state of the nuclear relationships;

(3) Periodic meetings of military officials could be formalised into regular meetings at fixed intervals to sort out subsisting border problems, apart from ad-hoc flag meetings to settle local dispute between field commanders;

(4) The agreement for providing advance information on troop movements/military exercises could be widened to include deployments of offensive weapons systems like tanks, combat aircraft, and surface-to-surface missiles within specified border zones to reduce the likelihood of surprise attacks, apart from allowing military observers to be associated with field exercises;

(5) Similarly, the agreement to prevent violations of air space could be broadened to an "open skies" arrangement that would permit aerial reconnaissance of the specified border zones to be mutually undertaken for gaining confidence that no unwarranted military movements and force re-deployments were taking place.

There are further confidence-building measures at the declaratory level that could be considered for unilateral action like no-first-use pledges, no-nuclear-test declarations, promises to adhere to the guidelines of the Nuclear Suppliers Group and the Missile Technology Control Regime, besides innovative measures like sharing information on the location of strike corps elements, and so on.

It would, indeed, be advancing a counsel of perfection to suggest that all these measures are subsumed within the need to normalise bilateral relations between India and Pakistan. One pathway for proceeding purposively here would be to widen people-to-people contacts by meetings at various levels between academicians, journalists, professional and business groups, and increasing the two-way flow of information through various media channels, apart from bilateral trade via formal ageements. In short, the measures enuisaged in Article III of the Shimla Agreement need to be seriously implemented.

At the official level, however, the need for dialogue between the two countries cannot be over-emphasised and this must be extended to the nuclear dimension. Indeed the gaps in understanding and the dangerous consequences of misunderstandings stand accentuated by frequent statements made by Pakistan's leadership about their nuclear prowess and India's reticence in this regard. Why such inflamatory rhetoric is deemed necessary could be considered in this dialogue. There is besides the impermissible actions that could lead to an overt expression of nuclear capabilities, the peronage(s) designated to exercise release authority and so on. The nuclear game has it own rules and nuclear weapons possess their own intrinsic logic. Consequently, these measures, that were found necessary by the existing nuclear weapons powers, cannot be inapplicable to crypto-nuclear powers. Hence the need to address these basic issues relating to the military atom within the structure of an Indo-Pak dialogue.

There are different strands in Indo-Pak relations that give rise to cautious optimism in the possibilities of their betterment, which includes the signficant confidence-building measures that have been reached between them, and have been detailed above. some cause for greater optimism is possible from the manner in which the JKDA attempts to cross the Line of Control had been prevented with firmness by the Pakistan army but, more importantly, in close collaboration with the Indian army. This reinforces the belief that major crises in Indo-Pak relations like the Brasstacks affair and build-up of tensions in 1990 were handled by both countries with considerable adroitness and maturity. These sensibilities lie dormant presently, but are available to address the larger issues of adversarial Indo-Pak relations, if the political will could be generated on both sides.

Dimensions of Inter-State Conflict: the Indo-Pak case

Moving to the sources of inter-State tensions and conflicts in South Asia, and ways to mitigate them, it requires early recognition that the spirit of detente has not struck roots yet in the region. Neither has the example of neighbouring ASEAN, which shares many geo-political similarities with South Asia, like the preponderance of Indonesia in the region, established a standard for emulation by SAARC. We might question here ingrained beliefs that the dominance of India over the South Asian polity is the chief reason for concern, and the major impediment to its greater integration. Admittedly, India is the focus of the foreign policies of the smaller nations in the sub-continent some further reflection, however, on the causes for tensions and conflicts in the region would isolate the Indo-Pak contention, which possesses historical, political, religious and geo-strategic dimensions, and has now acquired a worrisome nuclear dimension. This needs to be discussed at greater length.

Kashmir

This would not be the place to detail the entire gamut of Indo-Pak disputes that have emerged since their independence, but we may identify the Kashmir issue as the principal contention between them that could escalate to armed conflict. The relative merits of the case pesented over the years by India and Pakistan to press their claims are too well-known to bear reiteration. The danger from the continuance of the Kashmir issue arises from its latent possibility of triggering violence, and it bears recognition that Kashmir has been either the cause or the chief theater of conflict between the two countries in the past Indo-Pak wars. A low intensity conflict proceeds at present in Kashmir, which has its roots in the partition of the country and certain errors made by India in the past. It cannot be the case, nevertheless, that external intervention by the provision of moral and material assistance and sanctuaries to Kashmiri militants would help in evolving a solution. Beliefs, morever, that the low intensity conflict in Kashmir would become India's Spanish ulcer do not acknowledge that India cannot abandon Kashmir to be either integrated within Pakistan or become an independent state. Any such action would raise several contentious questions, and, more significantly, the reliquishment of a Muslim-majority area would have serious repercussions for India's secular polity and might lead to extensive communal violence engineered by nationalistfundamentalist forces in the country.

It must be conceded that Pakistan also has a national position on Kashmir. A serious dialogue would seem to be the only way out, and, perhaps, by recognition of the Line of Control as the de jure division of the historical State of Kashmir. Of course, dialogues with the indigenous populations of the historical state of Jammu and Kashmir, and of the different regions comprising it, are essential as well, and matters like the sequencing of all these dialogues will also have to be considered at the proper time. But an over-riding necessity is that the leaders and peoples of India and Pakistan should realise that non-resolution of the Kashmir issue is bleeding both the countries by their common need to station large forces in this area, and their requirement for large armed forces to be maintained, equipped, modernised and expanded due to the prevailing atmosphere of tensions in the bilateral relationship.

Even if it was argued that India's other security concerns warrant periodical upgradations of its armed forces, it might be appreciated that a major portion of its military expenditure is designed against the threat assessed from Pakistan, whilst the security threat from China is reducing, and might largely recede as the recently-signed peace and tranquility agreement. Expenditures being incurred by India and Pakistan deriving, from their adversarial relationship, bear significant opportunity costs in terms of development outlays otherwise possible. A compromise on the Kashmir issue, preceded by a disengagement in Siachen, would permit the relationship to develop within more normal channels of international behaviour, and erode the most prescient cause for inter-State conflict in the sub-continent.

The International Context

This focus on the Kashmir issue might be enlarged now to consider it within the larger international context, and the peace dividend promised by the end of the Cold War. The spirit of detente apparent in the international system has permitted various stubborn regional conflict situations being addressed towards evolving a solution eg., Cambodia, Namibia and Cyprus, the long-outstanding problem of apartheid in South Africa and enfranchisement of its black population is on the way to resolution. Of particular relevance to the Indo-Pak adversarial situation is the agreement signed between the PLO and Israel to usher peace into the most disputed area in the world. The conflict between them involved disputed territory and contention between opposed ideologies viz., nationalism and Zionism.

The rhetoric on both sides had traditionally argued for maximalist solutions to the problem e.g., refusing to accept ground realities like the entity of Israel (PLO), and the recognition of the Palestinians as a people (Israel). Assuredly, there will be many difficulties in translating the different steps envisaged in the peace agreement into political action, and there are powerful domestic constituencies that firmly oppose the agreement and would make strenuous efforts to obstruct its fruition. But, the significance of this momentous first step to bring peace into the Middle-East cannot be minimised, nor its promise disregarded, to resolve a most obstinate regional security problem. Without straining the simile too greatly there are important lessons in this event for India and Pakistan. First, that compromise in long-held maximalist positions in regional disputes is essential to break from sterile unproductive controversies. Second, there is wisdom in not seeking outside intervention, but not rejecting it either to promote the principle of bilateralism in Indo-Pak relations. Third, there would be value in quiet, low-profile discussions, perhaps in another country between duly accredited representatives of India and Pakistan to find solutions. Fourth, and this is central to the exercise, the realisation must dawn, as it did with the PLO/Isreal, that it was not possible for them to destroy each other and, therefore, necessity requires seeking the path of reconciliation.

National budgets, including defence allocations, are under considerable strain in India and Pakistan. The two defence establishments are, besides, finding it progressively more difficult to maintain the operational status of their weapon systems due to problems in arranging for their maintenance, spares and ancillaries from their principal suppliers viz., Russia and the United States. These constraints might assist this process of realisation in the wisdom of reconciliation. It is also conceivable that an additional factor in promoting this realisation might be renewed pressures from the international community to compose the Kashmir issue specifically and Indo-Pak disputes generally. The recently negotiated agreement in the Middle-East highlights the value of quite diplomacy and a step-wise methodology to reach the ultimate objective, besides the possibility of transcending U.N. resolutions.

Western Europe

The process of continuing change in post-cold war Europe and in India's own external environment has provided an impetus for internsification of relations between India and countries of this region based on complementarity of interests and mutual benefit. India's historical and cultural interaction with Europe also provides a unique dimension that further serves to strengthen mutual understanding and affinities. Over a million persons of Indian origin live in Western Europe, a tenth of them Indian citizens. Both the European Commssion and individual members of the European Union evolved new strategies to strengthen political dialogue and economic relations with Asian countries, including India. This trend was compelmented by India's economic reforms and efforts to globalise the Indian economy.

India's trade with the EU countries increased by 20 per cent over the previous year to reach dollar 14.89 billion in 1993; this upward trend continued during 1994. Collectively the largest trading partners of India, the EU countries accounted for 30 per cent of India's exports and imports. Similar progress was registered on the investment front. The share of West European countries in FDI approvals went up from 20 per cent in 1993 to 30 per cent in 1994. Actual investment inflows from Western Europe since the launching of India's economic reforms in July 1991 comprised 31 per cent of total inflows. West European countries also continued to be a leading source of development assistance, technology and collaborations and joint ventures.

The new Cooperation Agreement between the Republic of India and the European Community on Partnership and Development came into effect on 1 August 1994. The 8th Session of the India-EC Joint Commission was held in Brussels in October 1994. The broad principles of a strategy for economic and development cooperation with the EU up to the year 2000 was agreed on, focussing on continued assistance from the EU to India's development efforts.

India's relations with Germary, India's leading economic partner in Europe, was given further impetus through the exchanges of high level visits during 1994-95. German Minister for Development Cooperation visited India in February 1994. The German Minister for Economics attended the 11th Session of the Indo-German Joint Commission held in New Delhi in April 1994. An Indian Parliamentary delegation led by the speaker of the Lok Sabha, visited Germany in June-July 1994 and interacted with a wide cross-section of German Parliamentarians and leaders of various political parties.

The Vice-Chancellor and Foreign Minister of Germany visited India in July 1994 accompanied by a high-level business delegation. He underlined the central position occupied by India in terms of Germany's "Asia Concept Policy" and stressed the importance attached by Germany to developing closer relations with India on the basis of partnership in political, economic and cultural fields. He also reaffirmed Germany's support for the resumption of Indo-Pak bilateral dialogue and welcomed India's policy of transparency on human rights. He expressed support for a permanent seat for India in the UN Security Council. The German business delegation accompanying him evinced keen interest in increasing their presence in the Indian market through investments, particularly in the fields of power, chemicals and transportation infrastructure.

The Indo-German-Consultative Groups, which has emerged as a strong catalytic force in Indo-German reactions, held its Third Session in Bonn in August and submitted recommendations covering bilateral cooperation in political, economic, scientific, cultural and media fields.

Prime Minister paid a visit to the UK in March 1994. The visit marked a new era of relations between the UK and India, reinforcing trends towards a long term partnership based on mutual confidence and trust, shared values and mutual benefit. A Bilateral Investment Protection Agreement was concluded with the UK during the visit.The Indo-British Partnership Initiative (IBPI), launched in January 1993, extended for another year, achieved major success in promoting awareness of opportunities for trade and investment opened up by India's economic reforms. Indo-British trade continued to register a high rate of growth during 1994. There were several exchanges of visits between India and UK during 1994-95. Instruments of ratification of the Indo-UK Bilateral Investment Protection Agreement were exchanged during British Foreign Secretary's visit to India in January 1995. During the year, a Commercial Office of the British High Commission was opened in Bangalore and a decision taken to establish a Consulate General of India in Glasgow.

A delegation of the French Senate led by President of the Senate Committee for Foreign Affairs and Defence visited India in February 1994. In a letter to the Prime Minister, the French Prime Minister Edouard Balladur affirmed the desire of the French Government to impart new momentum to Indo-French relations in the political, economic and cultural fields. French Foreign Minister visited India in April 1994. He expressed French resolve to intensify relations with India particularly in the economic field. From the Indin side Ministers for Agriculture, External Affairs and Health and Family Welfare visited France.

President of the Italian Senate visited India in Februray 1994. Trade and economic relations with Italy, the fourth largest market for Indian exports to Europe, continued to expand. Commerce Minister visited Italy for the 11th meeting of the Indo-Italian joint Economic Committee. The Italian President paid a State visit to India in February 1995 coinciding with the participation of Italy as partner country in the Indian Engineering Trade Fair. A Memorandum of Understanding concerning cooperation in the field of defence equipment was concluded between India and Italy on 4 November 1994.

Minister of State for External Affairs paid official visit to Ireland and Spain in October 1994. The visits focussed on strengthening bilateral trade and economic relations with these countries. A partimentary delegation led by the Speaker of the Lok Sabha visited Ireland in July 1994. A Consulate General of Portugal was opened in Goa in April 1994 to promote Indo-Portugese relations in the areas of trade, tourism and culture. The 11th Session of the Indo-Swedish Joint

Commission for Economic, Industrial, Technical and Scientific Cooperation was held in Stockholm in May 1994. The Indian delegation was led by Minister of State for Industry. The meeting provided impetus to trade and economic relations between India and Sweden.

Minister of State for Communications visited Denmark in May 1994. Ministers of State for Surface Transport and for Petroleum visited Norway. The Norwegian Minister for Development Cooperation visited India in May 1994. Official level consultations between India and Norway on economic, industrial and technicasl cooperation were held in New Delhi. Minister of State for Defence paid a visit to Grecce in October 1994. The visit coincided with the first ever participation by India at the Defence Production Fair "Defendory" which was held in Athens in October 1994. Shri Mallikarjun's visit and India's participation in "Defendory" strengthened prospects for Indo-Greek cooperation in the field of defence production. In November 1994, protocols were concluded with the principality of Andorra establishing diplomatic and consular relations between India and Andorra. During 1994-95, double taxation avoidance agreements were conceded with Malta, Cyprus and Switzerland.

Eastern Europe

There was considerable interaction between India and the countries of the Commonwealth of Independent States (CIS) as well Central and Eastern Europe during 1994-95. With practically all these countries, India has had longstanding relations of friendship and cooperation based on trust and confidence. The evolution of these countries in direction of democratic pluralism and market-oriented economic structures has brought them closer to India in terms of basic orientation. India has established a mutually beneficial economic and commercial interation with all the countries in East Europe. Direct contacts between the Indian Parliament and the parliamentary systems in many of these countries are emerging as an important new dimension in the bilateral relationships.

India's relations with the Russian Federation are friendly and multifaceted, encompassing political consultation on matters of mutual interest, significant economic and commercial interation and cooperation in science and technology, defence, atomic energy, space, culture and education.

Prime Minister, Shri P.V. Narasimha Rao visited Russia from 29 June to 2 July 1994. He was accompanied by the Ministers for Commerce, Civil Aviation and Tourism, the Ministers of State in the Prime Minister's Office, and for External Affairs Shri R.L. Bhatia and senior officers. The Prime Minister had separate delegation level talks with President Yeltsin and Prime Minister Chernomyrdin. Deputy Prime Minister and Culture Minister called on the Prime Minister. The Prime Minister addressed a representative group of Parliamentarians from both Houses of Russian Parliament.

The visit ushered in a qualitatively new stage of Indo-Russian relations. The Moscow Declaration on the Protection of the interests of Pluralist States sets out the post-cold war challenges posed to the viability of large, multi-ethnic, multi-lingual, multi-cultural and multi-religious states by the forces of aggressive nationalism, religious and political extremism, terrorism and separatism and the need to combat these challenges thorugh democracy, tolerance, secularism and the rule of law. It is recognised as a unique document in international relations and has subsequently been circulated as a UN Document at the joint initiative of India and Russia. The Declaration on Further Development and Intensification of Bilateral Cooperation underlines the broad identity of views of the two countries on important regional and international issues, and identified priority areas and directions of cooperation between the two countries. In addition, Agreements and Protocols were signed on cooperation in tourism, environment, space, science and technology, standarsation and metallurgy. The 1992 Agreement on defence credit was extended for a further period of two years and an agreement on setting up of a joint venture in military aviation was signed. The first meeting of the co-chairmen of the Inter-Governmental Joint Commission, Indian Minister for Commerce and Russian Deputy Prime Minister was held in Delhi in June 1994. Priority areas of cooperation were identified and the Joint Commission held its first meeting in Moscow in September 1994. Nine Working Groups-on Trade and Economic Cooperation; Power and Non-Conventional Sources of Energy; Petroleum; Ferrous and Non-Ferrous Metallurgy; Science and Technology; Culture; Coal; Information Technology; and Environment-held meetings and identified their respective areas of cooperation.

The Home Minister visited Russia during August-September 1994. The visit gave a fresh impetus to bilateral cooperation, particularly in areas such as combating terrorism, organised crime and narcotics trafficking. Leader of Opporsition in Lok Sabha and Chairman of the Standing Committee on External Affairs headed a Parliamentary delegation to Russia in January 1995 and had a number of high level meetings.

A nine-member Parliamentary Delegation led by the Chairman visited India in November 1994 while the Russian Prime Minister VS Chernomyrdin visited India on 23 and 24 December 1994 along with a high level delegation. He had discussions with Prime Minister followed by delegation level talks and also called on President and Vice President. Eigth documents, including agreements in promotion of mutual protection of investment, shipping, exploration and peaceful uses of outer space, implementation of the programme of defence cooperation upto the year 2000 and purchases of commodities in India for the period 1995-97 were signed. During the year several rounds of Foreign Office Consultations were also held between the two countries.

Indo-Ukrainian relations were given direction and impetus by the visit of Foreign Minister Zlenko in April 1994. During the visit, three agreements were signed: Protocol of Consultations between the Minister of External Affairs of India and the Minister of Foreign Affairs of Ukraine; Agreement on the Inter-Government Joint Commission on Trade, Economic, Scientific, Technological, Industrial and Cultural Cooperation; and Agreement on Economic and Technical Cooperation. The first meeting of the Indo-Ukrainian Joint Commission and the Foreign Office Consultations were held in Kiev in December 1994.

The State visit by President Dr. Shanker Dayal Sharma from 26 to 29 May 1994 emphasied the importance India attached to relations with Bulgaria. The President had discussions with President Zhelev, addressed the Bulgarian National Assembly and was awarded an Honorary Doctorate by the University of Sofia. During the visit six Agreements on Quarantine and Plant Protection; Veterinary and Sanitary Agreement; Avoidance of Double Taxation; Combating Organised Crime, International Terrorism, Illegal

Trafficking in Narcotics and Psychotropic Substances; Protocol on Foreign Office Consultation and Cooperation; Cooperation in Tourism–were signed and a Joint Statement was issued. Bulgarian Culture Minister paid an official visit to India during February-March 1994 and the Cultural Exchange Programme for 1994-96 was signed.

President Dr. Shankar Dayal Sharma paid a State visit to Romanian from 30 May to 2 June 1994. The President held discussions with President Iliescu; addressed the Joint Session of the Romanian Senate and the Chamber of Deputies; and received an Honorary Doctorate from the University of Bucharest. During the visit, an Agreement on Combating Organised Crime, International Terrorism, Illicit Trafficking in Narcotics and Psychotropic Substances and other Illegal Activities; an Agreement on Cooperation in Tourism; a Declaration of Principles and Directions of Cooperation and the Cultural Exhchange Programme for 1994-96 were concluded.

President of the Republic of Poland Lech Walesa paid a State visit to India in March 1994. Delegation-level talks led by the Prime Minister on the Indian side and by President Walesa on the Polish side were held and were followed by a tele-a-tele between the two leaders. Minister of State for Defence visited Poland in June 1994 to discuss further prospects for cooperation in defence.

Hungarian Political State Secretary for Defence visited India in March 1994 and State Secretary for Foreign Affairs paid and official visit to New Delhi in September 1994. A Protocol on Foreign Office Consulations was signed during the visit. A Hungarian Parliamentary delegation led by the Speaker of the National Assembly visited India in November 1994.

Minister of State for Defence visited the Czech Republic in June 1994 and Foreign Secretary visited Prague on 9 August 1994. The Czech Republic upgraded its diplomatic representation in India to that of Ambassador Extraordinary and Plenipotentiary. The Joint Trade Committee on Economics, Trade and Technical Cooperation held its first meeting at Prague in January 1995.

Minister of State for Defence visited the Slovak Republic in June 1994. He called on Slovak President and Prime Minister and Foreign Minister. Prime Minister of the Slovak Republic, Jozeh Moravcik paid an official visit to India in June 1994. He called on the President, Vice President, and had talks with the Prime Minister and he also met Indian businessmen and industrialists. A Protocol on Foreign Office Consultations; a Memorandum of Understanding on Cooperation in Science and Technology; and a Memorandum of Understanding concerning Indo-Slovak Joint Committee on Trade were also signed. It was also agreed to open a resident Indian Mission in Bratislava. The Union of Slovak Industry and CII also concluded a Memorandum of Understanding. The Slovak Republic upgraded its diplomatic representation in India to that of Ambassador Extraordinary and Plenipotentiary and also established an Honorary Consulate in Calcutta.

An Armenian delegation led by Minister of Science and Higher Education visited India in March 1994 and held discussions with Minister of State (Prime Minister's Office and Science and Technology). An Agreement on Cooperation in Science and Technology, a Memorandum of Understanding on concluding an Agreement on Economic and Technical Cooperation were signed. Armenia established its diplomatic representation in India by appointing an Honorary Consul. India has offered humanitarian assistance of medicine valued at Rs. five lakh to Armenia.

Deputy Prime Minister of Moldova paid an unofficial visit to New Delhi in May, 1994 and held discussions with Minister of State for External Affairs, Shri Salman Khurshid. A Lithuanian delegation led by the Minister of Energy visited India in March 1994. He held discussions with Minister of State for External Affairs, Shri R.L. Bhatia and senior officers in the Ministry of Power. Lithuania established its Honorary Consulate in New Delhi in October 1994. India kept a close watch on the developments in the Former Yugoslavia, particularly the continuing criss in Bosnia-Herzegovina. India supports the efforts of the Interanational Conference on Former Yugoslavia, basically because to-date it is the only attempt at finding a settlement that is based on regard for legitimate aspirations and interests of all parties to the conflict. India recognised Bosnia-Herzegovina on 11 May 1992 along with the Republic of Croatia and Slovenia but not as a Muslim State.

India's Ambassador to Croatia, presented his credentials in June 1994. Commerce Minister visited Croatia on 17 September 1994. An Agreement on Trade and Economic Cooperation was signed during the visit and the Croation Assistant Minister of Economic Affairs led a delegation to India in November 1994 during the India International Trade Fair.

The Americas

The year 1994-95 witnessed rapid and diversified growth in the Indo-US relations following Prime Minister's visit to the USA from 14 to 20 May 1994. Prime Minister Shri P.V. Narasimha Rao and President Clinton promised to cooperate in the search for solutions to global challenges posed by weapons of mass destruction, AIDS, environmental degradation, population growth, poverty, international terrorism and narcotics trafficking. Agreement was also reached to expand the pace and scope of high level exchanges on the full range of political, economic, commercial, scientific, technological and social issues. The two leaders agreed to seek ways to expand their cooperation at the United Nations. Two Memoranda of Understanding-on Cooperation Measures to Increase Awareness and Support for Efforts to Combat Production, Distribution and Use of Illegal Drugs and on Planning, Conservation and Management of Natural and Cultural Heritage Sites-were also signed.

Commercial and economic interaction remained the most vital sector of Indo-US cooperation through 1994-95. Bilateral trade in 1993 equalled US dollar 7.3 billion with a trade surplus of US dollar 1.8 billion in India's favour. The USA remained the single largest investor-country in terms of direct foreign investment in India, with approved investments from the US between January to September 1994 amounting to Rs. 14,302 million. Actual FDI inflows from the USA from 1991 to September 1994 amounted to Rs. 2,039 million. US Energy Secretary visited India in July 1994 leading a large Presidential Mission when four joint statements were signed and 11 cooperative projects between private companies of the two countries were announced. US Commerce Secretary led a Presidential Business Development Mission to India in January 1995 and during the visit the two countries signed a Memorandum of Understanding setting up the Indo-US Commercial Alliance.

Minister of Power visited USA in November 1994. Several agreements were signed during the visit. Minister of State for Non-Conventional Energy Sources visited the USA in December and a number of Memoranda of Understanding for cooperation between Indian and the US institutions/firms were signed during the visit. Air Chief Marshal visited US in August 1994 while Chief of Army Staff visited in September 1994. The second round of talks on a new Indo-US Extradition Treaty was held in Washington in October 1994.

Democrat Congressmen Gary L Ackerman, Jim MC Dermott accompanied by Congresswoman Barbara-Rose Collins visited India in November 1994 while Commander-in-Chief of the US Pacific Command visited India in December 1994. In September 1994, the Indian and US Navies conducted a joint Special Operations exercise at Ratnagiri (Mirya Bay). Defence Secretary visited India in January 1995 and an Agreed Minute on Defence Relations between India and the USA was signed. It was agreed that growth of bilateral defence relations would be evolutionary and related to convergence on global and regional issues.

India and the US held a further round of discussions on non-proliferation regional security and disarmament in London in April 1994. The two countries also agreed to intensity cooperative efforts to achieve a Comprehensive Test Ban Treaty (CTBT) and a verifiable global ban on the production of fissible material for nuclear weapons purposes. US pronouncements on the human rights situations in India gave rise to considerable misunderstanding. Differences in perception continued over Pakistan's support to terrorism. However, the situation improved later in the year as a result of greater restraint and objectivity exercised by US authorities.

Indo-Canadian relations witnessed greater interation, especially in the economic and commercial spheres. From January to September 1994, foreign direct investment approvals for Canada amounted to Rs. 417 million as against the total Canadian investment approvals for 1993 of Rs. 300 million. Canadian imports from India during January to May 1994 totalled Canadian dollar 178 million, registering an increase of 30.5 per cent as compared to the imports during the same period last year. Canadian exports to India during January to May 1994 registered a marginal increase of 5.1 per cent as compared to the same period last year. The Canadian Minister for International Trade accompanied by a large Canadian business delegation visited India in October 1994. Home Minister visited Canada in October 1994 and Mutual Legal Assistance Treaty on combating terrorism, drug trafficking and organised crime was signed during the visit.

India maintains very good relations with all the Latin American and Caribbean countries. During 1994-95, India's relations with these countries were consolidated by several exchanges of high level visits, joint commission meetings and contacts at various levels. The Foreign Minister and Minister of Environment of Brazil also visited India. Minister of Civil Aviation and Tourism visited Brazil and discussed various means of close cooperation in tourism. Minister of Textiles, Deputy Minister for Education also visited Brazil in 1994, the latter to participate in the Conference on 'Education for All.'

A three-member delegation led by Minister of Parliamentary Affairs attended the inauguration ceremonies of the new President of Mexico. President Dr. Carlos Saul Menem of Argentina visited India in March 1994 to take over Chairmanship of G-15 and extended his stay to pay a bilateral visit. The leaders of India and Argentina discussed important international issues and matters of bilateral importance. Several agreements on bilateral cooperation were signed during the visit. Minister of Civil Aviation and Tourism visited Argentina in June 1994 to promote tourist traffic from South America to India and Minister of Communications visited Buenos Aires during March 1994 to attend the first World Telecommunication Development Conference organised by the ITU. The then Chief Justice of India visited Buenos Aires in August 1994 as the leader of the Indian delegation to the International Law Association Congress. The Embassy in Bogota which was closed down in 1993 was reopened in October 1994. Both India and Colombia have expressed a desire to have close cooperation and similarity of views in relations to the Non-Aligned Movement and the next Summit. Venezauelan Minister of State for Foreign Trade participated in the G-15 Conference held in New Delhi March 1994. Minister for Legal Affairs of Jamaica participated in the G-15 Conference held in New Delhi in March 1994. During the year, a few Indian companies signed Memoranda of Understanding with Guyanese companies for establishment of joint ventures, ITPO participated in the international fair, EXPOCOMER' 94, held in Panama and diplomatic relations were established with Honduras.

Vice President and Foreign Minister of Suriname, where 40 per cent of the population is of India origin, paid a State visit to India during November 1994 and held bilateral discussions with Indian leaders. India agreed to donate an agricultural project, a home gardening project and 10,000 bicycles to Suriname. The first Joint Commission meeting between India and Suriname was held in November 1994.

APEC organised a buyer-seller meet in May 1994 in Chile. Supreme Court Justice Kuldip Singh and Delhi High Court Justice Y.K. Sabharwal visited Chile in

August 1994 to attend the post-meet of the International Law Conference.

Minister of Planning and Development of Trinidad and Tobago visited India and discussed matters of bilateral interest with Indian leaders. Government of Trinidad and Tobago has given five acres of land on a 99-year lease to Government of India for setting up Mahatma Gandhi Institute for Cultural Cooperation. ITPO arranged participation of 19 firms at the third International Exposition 94, held in Port of Spain in April 1994.

Cuban Foreign Minister visited India in March 1994 and held discussions with Indian leaders on ways of expanding bilateral cooperation and trade. Minister of State for Non-Conventional Energy Sources visited Cuba in June 1994 to attend Solar Energy International Conference. India has donated a 11 kw solar energy plant to Cuba to electrify a village. Minister of State for Commerce led the Indian delegation to the second session of the Indo-Cuban Joint Commission held in June-July 1994 in Havana. A four-member delegation from Cuba visited India for exploring possibilities of import of sugar mill machinery and spares from India. A four-member CSIR delegation also visited Cuba to discuss nickel extraction.

Africa (South of The Sahara)

India enjoys warm relations with the African countries and has always attached special significance to her relations with Africa. Africa continues to be a major thrust area under the Indian Technical and Economic Cooperation (ITEC) and Special Commonwealth African Assistance Programme (SCAAP), executed by the Ministry of External Affairs. Out of a total of 1,350 slots allocated for training in Indian civilian institutions under

ITEC for 1994-95, 768 (more than 50 per cent) were reserved for countries in Africa. Twenty-eight Indian experts are also in station in various African countries as of December 1994. Out of 250 slots offered to friendly developing countries for training in Indian defence establishments under the ITEC Programme, more than 150 were allotted to countries in Africa.

The changed politicl scenario in Southern Africa, the integration of South African and Namibian economies, the entry of South Africa into Southern Africa Development Community (SADC), the revival of the Eastern Africa Community among Kenya, Tanzania and Uganda, and greater cooperation among countries of the southern and eastern regions are positive developments and could be expected to play a vital role in the economic regeneration and development of Africa.

Vice President, Shri K.R. Narayanan accompanied by Smt. Usha Narayanan, Smt. Sonia Gandhi and Minister of State for Commerce, represented India at the inauguration of Dr. Mandela as the first President of the new South Africa. Dr. Mandela paid a State visit to India January 1995 and was the Chief Guest at the Republic Day celebrations. During his visit, India and South Africa signed a Treaty on Principles of Inter-State Relations and Cooperation, an Agreement to set up a Joint Commission and a Protocol providing for regular consultations between the Foreign Ministries of the two countries. The Indian Emabssy established in Pretoria in May 1994 was redesignated as High Commission with South Africa joining the Commonwealth on 1 June 1994. India also established a Consulate General in Durban in May 1994, and the Indian Cultural Centre in Johannesburg was converted into a Consulate General Indexpo '94, the largest single country trade exhibition ever organised in South Africa was held in Johannesburg in August 1994. The Indian naval ships, *INS Gomati* and *INS Khukri* visited Durban and Simonstown in December. The South African Deputy Foreign Minister visited India in November 1994. A bilateral agreement to set up the India-South Africa Joint Commission and a Protocol providing for regular consultations between the Foreign Offices were initialled.

During the visit of President Mugabe in March 1994, India agreed to cooperate with Zimbabwe in the informal sector particularly in the development of small and middle enterprises. Smt. Sonia Gandhi attended the ceremony to mark the reintegration of Walvis Bay and the off-shore Islands into Namibia as Special Guest of President Sam Nujoma. A Namibian Parliamentary delegation led by the Chairman of the National Council visited India in September 1994 followed by Defence Minister for purchase of defence equipment. The visit of Finance and Communication Minister of Seychelles in January 1994 has raised hopes of improved trade relations between India and Seychelles. Two Indian navalships-*INS Gomati* and *INS Khukri*-paid a goodwill visit to Port Victoria from 23 to 26 November 1994. India deputed seven experts to Seychelles under the ITEC Programme.

Following the death of President Juvenal Habyarimana of Rwanda in an air crash on 6 April 1994 and the outbreak of ethnic violence in that country, all the Indians there (300 in number) migrated. India supplied relief materials worth Rs. five lakh to Rwandese refugees in Tanzania. An Indian army battalion to United Nations Aid Mission in Rwanda (UNAMIR) reached Kigali on 10 Novermber 1994. Rwanda has shown interest in increasing and strengthening economic and technical cooperation with India. The Angolan External Affairs Minister paid an official visit to India in April 1994. Compaore, President of Burkino Faso paid a visit to India in July 1994. India announced a grant of Rs. 15 crore approximately for setting up an agricultural development project in Burkina Faso.

The traditionally close and friendly relations between Mauritius and India have deepened further during 1994-95. Vice President leading a high-level delegation visited Mauritius for one day in May 1994. Other visits included those of Mauritian Vice President, and Ministers of External Affairs and Finance. Bilateral trade has increased by almost 30 per cent in 1994 and a number of new joint ventures in different fields were established. Mauritius has emerged as the main centre for channelising investments into India through off-shore funds as a result of the advantageous provisions of the treaty for Avoidance of Double Taxation. Twenty-nine civilian training slots were utilised by Mauritius under the ITEC Programme during the year.

Indo-Kenyan relations continued to be warm and friendly, characterised by mutual regard. President Moi stopped over in Delhi on his way to Beijing in May 1994. India donated 476 metric tonnes of rice to Kenya for the drought-affected areas. A Cultural Exchange Programme was signed between the two nations in May 1994. Minister of Civil Aviation and Tourism visited Tanzania in January 1994 and the Tanzanian Home Minister-cum-Deputy Prime Minister visited India. Tanzania utilised 23 civilian training slots under the ITEC Programme. India's relations with Uganda witnessed positive developments during 1994-95. President Museveni led a high-powered trade and investment delegation to India in September 1994. In

December, Ugandan Minister of Education and Sports visited India while several Indian business delegations visited Uganda.

General Gnassingbe Eyadema, President of Togo, paid a State visit to India in September 1994. This opened a new chapter in mutual relations and added an impetus to bilateral cooperation between the two countries. India also announced a grant of Rs. 10 crore approximately for setting up of an agricultural project in Togo and agreed to cooperate in the fields of city transportation, healthcare, scientific research, trade, industry and agriculture. India and Togo also decided to set up a Joint Commission and signed a Memorandum of Understanding on Economic and Technical Cooperation. General Sani Abacha, Head of State of Nigeria visited India in March-April 1994 to attend G-15 Summit and also held bilateral discussions with Indian leadership. Nigeria utilised 10 civilian training slots under the ITEC Programme during 1994-95.

President Diouf of Senegal visited New Delhi in March 1994 to attend the G-15 Summit and had wide-ranging bilateral discussions with the Prime Minister. Foreign Minister also attended the G-15 Troika and Ministerial level meetings. An eye clinic in Ghana is under execution by India. Ghana utilised 13 civilian training slots while two Indian experts were deputed there under ITEC Programme. In Mozambique, after decades of civil war, the ruling Frelimo Party and the main opposition Renamo signed a Peace Accord in 1992 and participated in the country's first multi-party elections in October 1994 under UN supervision. Frelimo Party leader, Joaquin Chissano was re-elected as President. India welcomed this development.

East Asia

India-China relations in 1994-95 continued to improve steadily and to expand into new areas of cooperation. The momentum of high level political dialogue was maintained in 1994 to expand cooperation and create a favourable climate in which the two countries can work for the resolution of outstanding issues. There were several exchange of visits between China and India. The situation along the India-China border remained peaceful during the year. The seventh meeting of the India-China Joint Working Group (JWG) held in Beijing in July 1994 continued discussions on the boundary question and on the implementation of the Border Peace and Tranquility Agreement while the India-China Expert Group (EG) set up under the above Agreement held two meetings is February and April 1994. The two countries also agreed in principle to open more points for border trade and trade through Shipkila in Himachal Pradesh started on 16 July 1994. In the first nine months of 1994, the total volume of bilateral trade was US dollar 593 million, an increase of 29.5 per cent over the corresponding period last year. The Vice President during his visit to China in October 1994, emphasised the need to further increase cooperation in economic and scientific-technological fields and agreements in several fields were signed. The Festival of India was held in China during May and June 1994. The two countries also celebrated the fortieth anniversary of *Panchsheel* or the Five Principles of Peaceful Co-existence.

The economic and commercial relations between India and Japan continued to grow and Japan remained the largest bilateral donor of development assistance to India. It has pledged 1,25,765 million yen, approximately equivalent to Rs. 3,920 crore as ODA to India for 1994-95, a five per cent increase over the previous year. This year's ODA loan package comprises twelve projects covering power, transport, drinking water and sewage system, environment and afforestation sectors. The Japan International Cooperation Agency (JICA) conducted a feasibility study on the setting up of an Industrial Model Town in Haryana. India's trade with Japan during 1993-94 was Rs. 10,231.13 crore of which India's exports were worth Rs. 5,482.21 crore and imports were worth Rs. 4,748.92 crore. During April-July 1994 India's total trade with Japan was Rs. 3,636.22 crore, exports being Rs. 1,904.82 crore and imports being Rs. 1,731.40 crore. Japanese investors are showing considerable interest in the new economic policies of the Government of India.

India's relations with the Republic of Korea (ROK) continued to expand rapidly during 1994-95. The third round of Foreign Office Consultations was held in New Delhi on 6 April 1994 while the Union Minister for Surface Transport visited Seoul in October 1994 along with a delegation of the shipping sector that made series of useful presentations on investment attractions in India to major ROK business conglomerates such as Hyundai, Daewoo, Samsung, Hallu and Kookdang. DCM-Daewoo have agreed for a joint collaboration to produce passenger cars in India. The two-way trade betweeen India and ROK exceeded US dollar one billion for the first time in 1993. ROK's direct investment approvals to India by September 1994 amounted to Rs. 474.6 million. There were exchange of other visits between the two countries on various fields.

India maintained friendly relations with the Democratic People's Republic of Korea (DPRK) and India expressed profound sorrow and grief at the passing away of Kim II Sung on 8 July 1994. Bilareral consultations at Secretary-level were held on 23 March 1994 wherein important interantional issues and bilateral relations including economic cooperation and cultural exchange programme were discussed.

India enjoys a friendly relationship with Mongolia which was further cemented during 1994-95. President P Ochirbat paid a State visit to India in January 1994 when a Treaty of Friendly Relations and Cooperation was concluded, besides agreements on establishing a Joint Committee on Cooperation and on Avoidance of Double Taxation. Agriculture Minister and Commerce Minister visited Ulaan Baator during 1994. India participated in the fourth Mongolia Assistance Group meeting in Tokyo in November 1994. Chartered flights from India to Mongolia opened during 1994.

Central Asia

India is actively engaged in promoting her friendly relations with Central Asian countries as well as with Azerbaijan and Turkey. Minister of State for External Affairs, Shri Salman Khurshid led a delegation and had detailed discussions with the Kazakh leadership on international issues and bilateral relations. In August 1994, the new Foreign Minister of Kazakhastan had detailed discussions with Minister of State for External Affairs, Shri R.L. Bhatia in New Delhi, and their Defence Minister visited India in February 1995. Kazakh Airways has started regular commercial flights between Almaty and New Delhi and the Kazakh Chamber of Commerce and Industry has established a Joint Business Council with Federation of Indian Chambers of Commerce and Industry in November 1994.

The first Indian resident Ambassador to Kyrghystan credentials to President Askar Akaev in June 1994. Minister of State for External Affairs, Shri Salman Khurshid who visited Bishkek in June 1994 had discussions with the Kyrghyz leaders who welcomed greater Indian presence in Central Asia. India's relations with Tajikistan also received considerable stimulus with the visit of Minister of State for External Affairs, Shri Salman Khurshid in June 1994. An Indo-Tajik credit Agreement for extension of an Indian credit line of US dollar five million was signed during the visit. The first resident Indian Ambassador in Dushanbe is in position since December 1994. The Tajik Government is presently represented in India by an Honorary Consul.

Bilateral relations between India and Uzbekistan are marked by close mutual understanding and support.The second sessio of the Indo-Uzbek Joint Commission was held on 22 November 1994 in India. An agreement was signed to use the second tranche of the US dollar 10 million credit which was announced by the Prime Minister during his visit to Uzbekistan in May 1993 after the finalisation of contracts for the first tranche. The Director of India Cultural Centre in Tashkent has been functioning since May 1994 and Doordarshan programmes are directly telecast there. Embassy of Uzbekistan has been upgraded to the level of Ambassador in September 1994 and India has a resident Ambassador in Ashgabat (Turkmenistan) since June 1994. Turkmenistan has opened a resident mission in New Delhi.

India has opened Consulate General in Istanbul and India's External Affairs Minister and some other dignitaries visited Turkey in 1994. The President of Turkey, Suleyman Demirel paid an official visit to India from 30 January to 2 February 1995 and had discussions with President, Prime Minister and other Indian leaders on cooperation in international fora and on bilateral cooperation in diverse fields. Agreements on tourism and avoidance of double taxation were signed during the visit.

The Gulf, West Asia and North Africa

Historically, India and the neighbouring Gulf region have a close interaction based on trade routes and Islam. In recent times, these ties have acquired a significant socio-economic dimension. Currently, India imports nearly two-thirds of her oil from this region and trade with the Gulf countries stood at over Rs. 20,206 crore in 1993-94 (Indian Exports: Rs. 6,260 crore; Indian imports: Rs. 13,946 crore). During this year total value of Indo-Gulf trade grew by 23 per cent. Over 20 lah Indian nationas are estimated to be living in these countries most of whom are gainfully employed. The inward annual remittances from these Indians through banking channels are currently estimated to be Rs. 7,800 crore. The Gulf region is one of the largest markets for the Indian exports. India has, therefore, consistently called for peace, stability and security in this region.

Indo-Bahrain relations continued to develop in various fields. A 22-member delegation of Bahrain Chambers of Commerce and Industries visited India in April 1994 and signed an agreement with FICCI for setting up a Joint Business Council.

Even as India's relations with Iraq have remained restricted by the UN economic sanctions on that country, there was gradual upgradation in bilateral contacts. India has consistently advocated phased lifting of the UN economic sanctions in tandem with Iraqi compliance with the terms of the relevant UN Security Council resolutions. Iraqi Foreign Minister visited India in April 1994 as Iraqi President's Special Envoy.

During 1994-95, Indo-Kuwait relations continued to be on the upswing. On a number of occasions, India reiterated her commitment to Kuwaiti independence, sovereignty and territorial integrity. The Minister of Communication, Electricity and Water of Kuwait and a

15-member Kuwati Multi-Disciplinary Economic delegation visited India during 1994 to explore possibities of boosting bilateral economic cooperation. Kuwaiti Oil Minister paid an official visit in January 1995 and held extensive talks with Minister of State for Petroleum and Natural Gas for bilateral cooperation in oil sector.

The Minister of Chemicals and Fertilizers paid an official visit to Oman in July 1994 and a Memorandum of Understanding envisaging preparation of feasibility report for US dollar 900 million fertilizer joint venture was signed. The Omani Minister of State for Foreign Affairs paid an official visit to India in August. An Indo-Omani Agreement setting principal conditions of the long-term gas supply contract for the import of Omani natural gas through a pipeline across the Arabian Sea was signed in Muscat, Oman on 28 September 1994.

India endeavoured to strengthen economic-commercial relations with Qatar and has recently emerged as a major buyer of ammonia from Qatar. The Minister of State for External Affairs, Shri R.L. Bhatia visited Qatar in July 1994 called on the Amir and held extensive talks with his Qatari counterpart on regional issues and bilateral matters.

India's substantive ties with the kingdom of Saudi Arabia developed satisfactorily during 1994-95 with the bilateral trade reaching the record level of US dollar two billion. The Finance Minister led the Indian delegation for the Fourth Session of the Indo-Saudi Joint Commission held in Riyadh in December 1994 and had meetings with Saudi Ministers of Foreign Affairs, Oil, Finance and Commerce. He also addressed the members of Saudi Chambers of Commerce and Industry, who evinced great interest in economic ties with India.

India's multi-faceted relations with the United Arab Emirates (UAE) continued to grow during the year. In the UAE, a trade fair titled 'India in Dubai' was inaugurated by the Minister of Commerce in September 1994. Around 163 participants attended the fair and orders worth US dollar 55 million were booked. The Eighth Session of the Indo-UAE Joint Commission was held in Abu Dhabi in September.

India's relations with Yamen have been marked by friendship and cordiality. India had to evacuate around 1,700 Indian and some foreign nationals from Yemen. Ali Abdullah Saleh was re-elected as the President of the Republic of Yemen on 2 October. Abdo Rabbo Mansoor Hadi was appointed the new Vice President. Dr. Abdul Karim Iryani was appointed as Deputy Prime Minister of Foreign Affairs. The President, the Prime Minister and the Minister of External Affairs sent congratulatory messages to their newly appointed Yemeni counterparts.

Efforts to strengthen the bilateral relationship with Iran were further pursued during 1994-95 with exchange of high level bilateral visits. External Affairs Minister paid an official visit to Tehran in March 1994 to attend the Seventh Session of India-Iran Joint Commission. The Foreign Minister of Iran visited New Delhi in January 1995 in connection with the Eighth Session of the India-Iran Joint Commission. the Session reviewed the status of bilateral functional cooperation and gave directions for strengthening cooperative activities. A Memorandum of Understanding was signed for a US dollar 300 million joint venture fertilizer project in the Qeshm Island in Iran and a US dollar 45 million project was awarded to Hindustan Machine Tools for supply of equipments and auxiliary vehicle for the Tehran Metro Workshop. IRCON secured a US dollar 25 million project for the execution of Ahwaz-Bandar-e-Imam Signalling Project.

India maintained satisfactory contacts with Algeria. An Indian Railway delegation visited Algiers in July-August 1994 for further cooperation in transport sector. Engineers India Ltd signed a fresh contract with Alteria's state-owned oil and gas company (SONATRACH) worth US dollar five million for providing consultancy services.

The Secretary-General of the Ministry of Foreign Affairs of Djibouti visited India in June 1994 for bilateral talks. It was decided to set up a Joint Committee at Secretary level. India supplied 23 tonnes of milk powder worth Rs. 10 lakh in September 1994 and has also agreed to offer technical assistance under ITEC and slots under the General Cultural Schlorarship Scheme (GCSS) to students from Djibouti wishing to pursue studies in India.

India and Egypt made renewed efforts to impart greater dynamism to the existing friendly and cordial relations which were reflected in the close interaction with various interantional fora. A 9-member Egyptian Parliamentary delegation led by Speaker of the People's Assembly of Egypt visited India in May 1994 and Egyptian Minster of State for Population and Family Welfare visited in January 1995. Foreign Secretary visited Egypt in August 1994 for mutual consultations on matters of common interest and concen. An Indian delegation led by the Health and Family Welfare Minister participated in the UN-sponsored International Conference on Population and Development (ICPD) held in Cairo in September 1994. Two-way trade with Egypt improved considerably during the year. Seventeen Indian companies and an official delegation led by Telecommunication Miniter participated in th Africa Telecom Exhibition held in Cairo in April 1994.

The year witnessed a number of high level exchanges between India and Israel. There Memoranda of Understanding each were signed between Indian and Israeli educational institutions during the visit of the Indian Minister of Human Resource Development and between the Indian enterprises and the Israeli companies during the visit of Chief Minister of Haryana. Some of the agreements signed during visits by Israeli delegations are an Air Transport Agreement signed during the visit of the Israeli Deputy Foreign Minister, a Memorandum of Understanding in telecommunications during the visit of Minister of Science, Arts and Communications and a Trade Agreement signed during the visit of Trade and Industry Minister. The year witnessed a quantum jump in the bilateral trade between Israel and India. Progress was achieved in cooperation in bio-technology, agriculture, dairy industry, drip irrigation and solar energy.

Relations with Jordan continued to remain friendly and were marked by high level contacts. India welcomed the Jordan-Israel agreement signed at Wadi Araba on 26 October 1994 and an Indian delegation led by Shri Salman Khurshid, Minister of State for External Affairs was present during the signing ceremony. Minister of Agriculture visited Jordan in June 1994 and Foreign Secretary held bilateral discussions on 23 August 1994 with Secretary General of the Jordanian Ministry of Foreign Affiars.

Following the end to the civil war in Lebanon there has been widening of bilateral contacts. With the visits of Minister of Agriculture in June and Foreign Secretary in August 1994 to Lebanon for bilateral discussions, commercial and cultural contacts with Lebanon have been resumed.

India's relations with Morocco were marked by

cordiality, cooperation and understanding. The Indian delegation led by Sh. R.L. Bhatia, Minister of State for External Affairs participated in the first Middle East/ North Africa Economic Summit held in Casablanca in October 1994.

India's relations with the PLO continue to be marked by cordiality, close understanding and a complementarity of views. India has been a consistent supporter for the legitimate aspirations of the Palestinian people and welcomed the Israel-PLO agreement signed in Cairo on 4 May 1994, which set up the Palestinian National Authority (PNA) and put into process the withdrawal of Israeli tropps from Gaza and Jericho. An Indian delegation led by the Minister of State for External Affairs, Shri R.L. Bhatia was present during the signing ceremony. India has been a strong supporter of and has enthusiastically participated in the Middle East Peace Process (MEPP) meetings. India has regularly contributed to the United Nations Relief and Works Agency (UNRWA) budget and has also offered to train 15 para-medical staff from Gaza and Jericho. India has proposed to send a team to conduct feasibility studies for setting up a Hi-Tech Centre on Computers and Electronics that will train Palestinian youth and help address the unemployment problem of Gaza and Jericho and has also decided to send 100 metric tonnes of tea to the region.

India sent medicines and seeds worth Rs. 10 lakh to Somalia. Both India and Sudan have sought to widen the scope of their bilateral cooperation and re-establish their multi-dimensional links. First Under Secretary of the Sudanese Ministry of Foreign Affairs visited India in April 1994 to discuss various issues of mutual concern. It was also decided to increase the share of Sudan in the ITEC programme. An Agreement to set up a Joint Committee at the Secretary-level was signed during the visit of Secretary (East) to Sudan January 1995.

Bilateral relations with Syria continued to get warmer. The Minister of Agriculture visited Syria in June 1994. A Programme of Cooperation in the field of agriculture and allied sectors was signed between the two sides. Foreign Secretary visited Syria in August 1994. The 7th session of the Indo-Tunisian Joint Commission took place in New Delhi in September 1994. A Commercial Agreement was signed between the two sides and have exchanged draft treaties on extradition. India maintained traditionally close relations with the League of Arab States and values the efforts made by the League to develop and strengthen friendship between India and the Arab countries.

India made sincere attempts to persuade the Organisation of Islamic Conference to adopt objective and unbiased views on India-specific issues. The Seventh Extra Ordinary Islamic Foreign Ministers Conference held in Islamabad in September passed a resolution for establishing an OIC Contact Group on Kashmir at the UN. India regretted the resolution. Subsequent attempts by the OIC Contact Group to table an India-specific draft resolution in the First Committee of the UNGA had to be given up due to lack of support from the member countries themselves following India's extensive demarches to the concerned countries to explain her position in this regard. While the Seventh Islamic Summit held in Casablanca (Morocco) in December 1994 passed the customary resolution on Jammu and Kashmir dispute, there was a pronounced shift away at the Summit from the bilateral disputes.

International Relations and Regional Co-operation

Certain developments have consolidated themselves and others are becoming visible in the international system following the end of the Cold War. Considered from the perspectives of politics, economics and strategy the common threat running throuhg them is greater centralisation and decentralisation simultaneously in the international polity. The parallel with the centrifugal forces, which distinguished South Asian polity in the historical frame work, is too obvious to be missed. But the difference between the processes familiar to South Asia and what is happening in the world today is that these dialiectically opposed forces are working conjointly in the international system.

The disintegration of the Soviet Union has unleashed forces of heightening divergence: growing ethno-political differences in the former Republics presage the emergence of further political entities. For that matter what is happening in the former Yugosalavia could also inspire similar developments in Eurasia. A fillip has been provided to subnational, centrifugal forces within nations that could disrupt national entities, although they could be represented as anti-status quo forces that challenge the existing power hierarchies and obtaining political systems. This, too, would strengthen beliefs that centrifugal developments are on the ascendancy in the international system.

However, strong intimations are also present favouring the construction of larger politico-economic structures to derive the advantages and benefit from greater unity in cooperative action. The new role assumed by the United Nations is a pointer in this direction. The Commonwealth of Independent States is an example of the efforts to retrieve as much as possible from the debris of past politics and economics. Attempts to construct similar structures in East Asia and to invigorate existing multinational arrangements, especially in the spheres of trade and economic cooperation, emphasize the reality that forces encouraging the convergence of polities are simultaneously obtaining in the world.

Similar divergent and convergent movements are taking shape in the area of international security. Although the Warsaw Pact has broken up, desperate attempts are afoot to keep NATO alive, despite the Soviet threat having disappeared. Consequently, operational tasks are being discovered for NATO outside its traditional areas of operations which, incidentally, include Asia and Africa. Developments within Russia and Ukraine/C.I.S. are also believed to require the Western Alliance's continuance. Areas of tension and instability also continue in existence across Eurasia, ranging from the Korean peninsula to Bosnia and Georgia, that could presage external intervention. But there are signs of peace and stability descending upon the war-torn Middle East with the recent agreement signed by the bitterly hostile leaders of Israel and the P.L.O. And, of the end of apartheid coming near with the evolution of democratic processes in that country based on universal franchise.

The area of proliferation of weapons of mass destruction is similarly witnessing strong efforts by the nuclear weapons powers and their allies to constrain the emergence of further nations that would either acquire nuclear weapons or ballistic missiles. These efforst would gain further urgency and momentum as the NPT Review Conference, scheduled for mid-1995, draws nearer. On the other hand, several international developments have occurred as in the former Soviet Republics, North Korea and South Africa that suggest the likelihood of a more largely proliferated world coming into being.

Turning to South Asia's immediate neighbourhood, ASEAN has reached a stature that commends emulation by SAARC. Indeed, the growth of greater economic/ political linkages between the countries of East Asia and South-east Asia might consign South Asia to the backwaters of the global economy. NAFTA and EEC, despite recurrent problems, are on the way to consolidating their likages, that could have the practical effect of shutting out the developing countries, or in allowing them some limited access for specific purposes, but with non-economic conditionalities attached. This is becoming increasingly apparent in the sphere of technology transfers, especially high technologies, that are being denied on the grounds that they could serve imaginatively presumed non-civil purposes.

South Asia must seek its destiny in this complex international milieu. The choices before it are stark and clearly evident, it could proceed by wise diplomacy and sincere efforts to sink differences and mutual suspicions and increase trade, economic, cultural, social and other ties to recreate the sense of kinship that has always distinguished the South Asia clan. Or, it could dissipate its energies in sterile controversies and disputes, leading to the need for maintaining costly military machines with their significantly high opportunity costs.

Looking Ahead

The fifth decade of Independence has triggered investment interest in India as never before. Policymakers should now bring in a lot more clarity on their objectives.

The rules of international trade have changed. Witrh trade barriers getting dismantled by the day, there is need to infuse a very high degree of competitiveness. A major development is the evolution of regional trade groupings like the European Community (EC), the North American Free Trade Association (NAFTA), ASEAN, APEC etc.

Though the south Asian countries have formed the SAARC, progress achieved in free trade among these has been slow. Apart from mere trade flows, potential benefits in terms of the phasing out of poliltical animosities and more cohesive regional developments are immense.... The EC experience proves this. Over the last 50 years Britain, France and Germany, who have been bitter adversaries for centuries, have been bonded together on the strength of mutuality of economic interests. The SAARC union could grow to include China, the Central Asian Republics and the Indian Ocean rim countries, including South Africa, and forge close links with ASEAN and APEC in course of time. The comparable levels of economic development of most of the countries in this region would help in co-ordinated growth.

There is a huge market for such equiptment: there are capabilities in these countries to produce entire range of such equipment–generators, turbines, boilers, transformers, switchgears, motors et al.

The Korean automobile manufacturers—Daewoo Motors and Hyundai—indicate plants for developing India as a major centre for their global operations. Like we did in regard to Maruti, in the assimilation of mass production technology, India should attempt absorption of the high productivity levels of the Koreans, Americans and others; combine this with the strength of the massive availability of skilled manpower to win global markets.

United Nations and International Organisations

The United Nations (UN) is presently in the process of restructuring and reforming both in terms of institutions and concepts. India's efforts during 1994-95 were directed at influencing these changes in accordance with her world view and her perceptions of the role of the UN. India put forward concrete and forceful proposals at the Economic and Social coucil (ECOSOC), World Hearings on Development and at the General Assembly. The revised Agenda for Development represents a success of the Indian diplomacy.

India constituted a National Committee for Commemoration of the Fiftieth Anniversary of the UN and undertook a substantive year-long programme to mark the event. The celebration was inaugurated on 30 October 1994 by Prime Minister's address to the nation and a cultural programme, couped with a photographic exhibition.

During his visit to India in September 1994, the UN Secretary General, Boutros-Boutros Ghali expressed his gratitude for India's contribution to the UN Peace-Keeping activities. The President of the 48th Session of the General Assembly also visited India.

India continued to play a leading role in UN Peace-Keeping activities. Indian battalion to UN Operation in Mozambique (ONUMOZ) has returned home. India's 5,000 strong contingent to UN Operation in Somalia (UNOSOM II) whose commendable performance was acknowledged by the UN, the various factions in Somalia, the NGOs working for humanitarian relief, and the people of Somalia, returned home after their successful mission. India has provided a battalion to the UN Assistance Mission in Rwanda (UNAMIR) and has also agreed to contribute a brigade group to UN Standby forces, and to provide 100 doctors, engineers and trainers to UN Mission in Haiti (UNMIH), Phase II, in addition to a company of paramilitary forces.

At the 49th session of th UNGA, Commerce Minister stated that India deserve to be a permanent member of the Security Council and also announced her candidature to the non-permanent seat in the Security Council for the year 1996-97.

Pakistan move for an increase in the strength of UNMOGIP observers on both sides of the Line of Control has not found support in the Security Council. The UN Secretary General stressed his willingness to exert every possible effort to facilitate a search for a solution to the outstanding problems between India and Pakistan. India has made it very clear that she remains committed to the Shimla Agreement, which calls for resolution of all outstanding issues bilaterally. Pakistan tried to table a resolution against India in the First Committee of the UNGA through an OIC Contact Group, however prompt and effective counter-measures initiated by India forced Pakistan to abandon the move.

India had played a major role in the negotiations leading to the agreement related to implementation of Part XI of the UN Convention of the Law of the Sea concerning deep sea-bed mining and exploration, which was adopted unanimously by the resumed 48th session of the UNGA in June 1994.

In keeping with her long-standing approach to nuclear disarmament as the first step towards general and complete disarmament, India was actively associated with global measures for the elimination of nuclear weapons. In January 1994, an Adhoc Committee of the Conference on Disarmament on Nuclear Test Ban (NBT) with a full negotiating mandate to conclude a Comprehensive Test Ban Treaty (CTBT) was established. The Indian delegate is the Friend of Chair (FOC) on Seismic Methods under the Working Group on Verificat' on. A draft 'rolling text' of the CTBT was finalised in September 1994. India tabled a resolution on the subject of a Convention on the Prohibition of the Use and Threat of Use of Nuclear Weapons which the First Committee of the UN adopted with 98 votes in favour. India also co-sponsored a new resolution calling for a step-by-step reduction of the nuclear weapons which was adopted by the First Committee with 91 votes in favour. India's proposal for the convening of a Fourth Special Session of the General Assembly devoted to Disarmament (SSOD-IV) taken up enthusiastically by NAM and presented as a NAM initiative at the last session of the UNGA. A consensus resolution agreeing to the convening of such a session of the UNGA. A consensus resolution agreeing to the convening of such a session in 1997 was adoped by the First Committee of the UNGA.

India was also actively involved in UN expert groups on the Register on Conventional Arms, the Inhumane Weapons Convention, and Verificaion in All Its Aspects. India continued her principled opposition to ad hoc export control regimes such as the Australia Group, Nuclear Suppliers Group (NSG) and the Missile Technology Control Regime (MTCR) in various international fora and called for their conversion into universal, transparent, non-discriminatory treaties which clearly distinguish between civilian and military applications. An MTCR Quad team consisting of representations of Switzerland, US, UK and Australia visited India on 30 August 1994 for official level discussions.

A Special Conference of the States Parties of the Biological Weapons Convention (BWC) was held at

Geneva in September 1994 in which India participated actively as one of the Vice Presidents. An ad hoc group of experts was set up to consider verification measures for the BWC.

India continued bilateral dialogues on disarmament, non-proliferation and security-related issues with the USA, France and Germany. Bilateral initiatives resulted in (i) the issuance of a joint statement by Prime Minister Shri P.V. Narsimha Rao and President Clinton in May 1994 offering their strong support for efforts towards non-proliferation of weapons of mass destruction and their means of delivery and towards the progressive reduction with the goal of elimination of such weapons and (ii) a joint declaration issued by prime Minister Shri P.V. Narsimha Rao and President Yeltsin reiterating their commitment to all measures aimed at the complete and universal elimination of the weapons of mass destruction. India also utilised these dialogues to effectively project her position that her security concerns cannot be addressed in the narrow framework of India-Pakistan relations but as part of a global problem which would require a global solution.

Regarding human rights, India's consistent stand in the UN fora was that it should be pursued in the Vienna spirit of cooperation and consensus. During 1994-95, the National Human Rights Commission was established through an Act of the Parliament. A number of envoys visited Jammu and Kashmir which reflect India's policy of transparency in protection and promotion of human rights. During the 50th session of the Commission on Human Rights in Geneva in March 1994, a resolution on Human Rights and Terrorism was adopted by consensus. India participated as an observer in the 46th session of the UN Sub-Commission on Prevention of Discrimination and Protection of

Minorities in August 1994. Pakistani moves to float a resolution were successfully thwarted, while the adoption at the 49th UNGA Declaration on Measures to Eliminate International Terrorism was an achievement of India's diplomacy in the United Nations. It called upon all States to take effective measures to prevent, combat and eliminate terrorism.

India continued to play an active role in the ECOSOC, the Governing Boards of the specialised agencies, various international meetings on the issue of promotion and protection of environment, and in the Second Committee of the United Nations.

The Second Session of the Commission on Sustainable Development (CSD), including the High Level Segment, held in May 1994 in New York was attended by the Minister of State for Environment and Forests. India was elected to the Bureau and became a Vice Chairman, representing Asia. India was also elected as the Chairperson of the Working Group I of the CSD.

India signed the Convention to Combat Desertification with Special Reference to Africa which was finalised at the Fifth Meeting of the Intergovernmental negotiating Committe in Paris in 1994.

In the second session of the Inter-governmental Committee on Convention on Bio-Diversity held in Nairobi in June 1994, India was able to seek endorsement from the G-77 and effectively project her views on the issue of conclusion of a Protocol on Bio-Safety, Farmers' Rights and *ex-situ* collections, collections of CGIAR system, criteria for selection of the Secretariat.

As a recognition of the prominent role played by India, the Indian member was unanimously elected as the first Chairman of the GEF Executive Council. India is a donor and recipient nation and has contributed SDR six million (US dollar 8.5 million approximately) to the total GEF corpus of US dollar two billion. India hosted the 50th session of the ESCAP in New Delhi in April 1994, and also continued to take an active part in various activities for the Asia and Pacific region organised by ESCAP.

At the third International Conference on Population and Development held in Cairo in September 1994, India pointed out that the problem of demographic growth could only be addressed through integrated solutions, encompassing health, family welfare, education, women empowerment, employment and eradication of poverty. India participated actively in the discussions in the second and the third sessions of the PREPCOM for the World Summit for Social Development held in New York in August September 1994 and in January 1995.

India was a member of the Ad hoc Group established to investigate fraud within the UN system, and also remained a member of the Board of Auditors of the UN and voiced concern over the mounting expenditure on peace-keeping operations and the delayed or non-payment of assessments by the member States. It was elected/nominated to the Commission on Transnational Corporations; the Inter-governmental Working Group of Experts on International Standards of Accounting and Reporting; the Committee on Non-Government Organisations; the Executive Board of UNICEF; the Committee for UN Population Award; the UN Administrative Tribunal; the Commission on Human Rights of ECOSOC; the Postal Operations Council and Consultative Council for Postal Studies of the Universal Postal Union; the Administrative Council of the International Telecommunications Union; the Human Rights Committee of the International Covenant of Civil and Political Rights (ICCPR); and the Economic and Social Council (ECOSOC). India was also elected as the Vice Presidents of the 49th Session of the UN General Assembly and the Commission on Sustainable Development and as the Chairman of several of the international meetings held in the region under ESCAP.

India participated actively in the NAM meetings and took active interest in the work of the Coordinating Bureau of the Movement in New York. The Fifth Conference of the Labour Ministers of Non-Aligned and other Developing Countries inaugurated by the Prime Minister on 19 January 1995, adopted the Delhi Declaration and a Plan of Action.

India continued to participate actively in meetings of the Commonwealth's over-arching governance mechanisms. The Commonwealth Secretary General who officially visited India in December 1994 paid tribute to India's contribution to the concept of a modern Commonwealth which had allowed it to outgrow an Anglo-centric past and expressed the hope that the Commonwealth philosophy of mutual help and Jawarhar Lal Nehru's legacy of the 'healing touch' would held the Commonwealth to serve members better.

India participated in the 46th Session of the International Law Commission (ILC) which was held at Geneva in July 1994 and the 27th session of the United Nations Commission on International Trade Law (UNCITRAL) held at New York. India also actively parcipated in the deliberations of the Sixth (Legal) Committee at the 49th Session of the UNGA, the annual session of the Legal Sub-Committee of the UN committee on Peaceful Uses of Outer Space at Vienna in March/April 1994 and the meeting of legal experts of States signatory to the Antartica Treaty, held at The Hague in November 1994. India became a party to several multilateral Conventions.

International Economic Environment

1. With the progress of economic reforms in many countries of the world and deregulation of financial markets, the importance of private capital flows into Asia has increased from US $ 76.8 billion in 1994 to US $ 98.0 billion in 1995, while net official flows increased marginally from US $ 5.6 billion to US $6.4 billlion during the same period. Similarly, while there were considerable official flows to Mexico and the transition countries in 1995 in support of their comprehensive adjustment programmes, net private capital flows to the developing countries increased from US $ 140.4 billion in 1994 to US $ 166.6 billion in 1995. India has has modest, but increasing, success in attracting a growing part of these private capital flows. Furthermore, much of these private capital inflows into India has been of the non-debt creating variety, and helped to boost the balance of payments as well as the availability of investible resources in the economy.

2. The international financial community is appreciative of India's economic performance in the last years, but concerns continue to be expressed about the high fiscal deficit, the slowing down of structural reforms, continued restrictions on consumer goods imports, and tariff levels considerably higher than in other countries. Also, references are often made to India's move towards capital account convertibility (with some observers advocating a cautions approach), high level of

subsidies, inadequate disinvestment in the public sector, need for further relaxation of rules to attract foreign investment and the continued high stake of the government in the public sector banks. On the whole, the international community is very positive about India's effort to achieve a high rate of growth.

3. Participants in the India Development Forum (IDF) meeting in September 1996 acknowledged the strong performance of the Indian economy and appreciated the new Government's declaration to continue reform measures to strengthen the social programmes as set out in the Common Minimum Programme (CMP). Various delgates stressed the importance of (i) fiscal consolidation, (ii) sustaining programmes in the social sectors, (iii) infrastructrue, (iv) provety eradication, (v) reforms in agriculture, public sector, and financial sector, and (vi) strengthening of legislation against child labour. In support of India's economic development, the donor countries pledged official assistance in 1996-97 of US $ 6.7 billion. Inclusion of US $ 400 million in long-term finance, promised on a bilateral basis at market rates, will raise this total to above US $ 7 billion. About 33 per cent of the total could be in the form of grants and interest-free loans.

4. With effect from January 1, 1997, India subscribed to the Special Data Dissemination Standards (SDDS) of the International Monetary Fund (IMF). by subscribing to the SDDS, India ha committed itself to streamilining the tatistical system of the country to produce most of the data categories with a much shorter time lag, improved quality and coverage by December 31, 1988.

Foreign Economic Relations

Government of India continued to give special and focussed attention to economic diplomacy at the bilateral, regional and multilateral levels. Government's efforts is to expand existing opportunities and create new ones for trade, investment and technological cooperation with the industrialised, newly industrialising and developing countries.

India's engagement in economic cooperation among a trans-regional group of developing countries in Asia, Latin America and Africa assumed special significance. The 4th Summit of the G-15 was held in New Delhi from 28 to 30 March 1994. It was decided to broaden the scope of intra G-15 cooperation through the establishment of a Committee of Trade, Investment and Technology to work towards evolution of trans-regional arangements for liberalisation, facilitation and promotion of trade, investment and technology transfer. The Summit decided to harness the information and communication revolution to promote better understanding and knowledge of capabilities, potential and experiences of G-15 countries among each other and extend full support through appropriate projects for expanding cooperation in setting up of small scale industreis.

At the 30th Anniversary commemoration meeting of the Group of 77 held in New York in July 1994, India reaffirmed the historical validity of the concept, purpose and endeavours of the Group of 77. By inserting a development dimension and consensus in international institutions and policies, the G-77 had acted as a development conscience of the world and recorded some gains in this respect.

Progress has been made in establishment on an ASEAN-India Trade and Investment Information and

Promotion Centre, collaboration and joint ventures in India, ASEAN and third countries; cooperation in tourist destination, development and exchange of information and technology.

In July 1994 India gave a detailed presentation to OECD on economic reforms inititated by India, which was followed by a visit by the President of the OECD Development Centre to India. A break-through in closer association with the OECD was achieved in December 1994 when the OECD Council approved inclussion of India along with Indonesia and China in their OECD Policy Dialogue framework with Dynamic New Major Economies (DNMEs). India continued to further fine tune, adapt and expand her ECDC and TCDC programmes under the ITEC programme and the SCAAP for the benefit of developing countries mainly in Africa, Latin America, Caribbean and South East Asia. During 1994-95, 875 slots have been allocated for training of foreign nominees in Indian civilian institutions and 65 regular courses are being held in 30 prominent institutions in banking, small scale industries, finance, tool research, etc. India also offered military training to nominees from friendly foreign countreis.

Under the ITEC programme, projects are executed in partner countries, among other things, such projects serve as demonstration models highlighting India's technology and potential in specific areas. Under execution are Vocational Training Centres in Vietnam and Mongolia, Solar Photovoltaic Plants in Oman and Cuba, a Remote Sensing Centre in Mauritius and a Mobile Eye Clinic in Ghana. Execution of feasibility studies/extension of consultancy services in partner countries are also undertaken under ITEC.

The SCAAP programme is aimed at providing technical assistance by India to 15 African counries which are ex-colonies of UK. In 1994-95, a total of 475 slots were allocated to nominees from Ghana, Nigeria, Mauritius, Tanzania and Zambia. A new dimension was attempted to be given to Indian's policy of South-South Cooperation through the Special volunteers Programme (SVP). The SVP envisages the sending of special volunteers to developing countries in Africa and Asia to assist them in their development programmes. During 1994-95, disaster relief assistance has been/is being extended to Armenia, Tanzania, Mozambique, Afghanistan, Uzbekistan, Rawanda, Somalia, Madagascar, Djibouti, Mauritius, etc. Such humanitarian gestures strike a positive chord amongst the people of these countries and create goodwill for India.

Trade and Investment Promotion

One of the most important forces current developments today is the emergence of a truly global economy. India's economic reforms programme reflects her determination to build an economy that is internationally competitive and integrated into the global economy.

Investment promotion seminars have been organised in Japan, Germany, singapore, Thailand, Australia,l Italy and USA, wide publicity was given to international fairs organised in India like IITF'94, International Seminar on Mineral and Mineral-based industries in ESCAP Region'94, MANTECH'95 IETF'95, AGROEXPO'95, Gifts and Handicrafts Fair'95 and 22nd World Marketing and Management congress'95. Special efforts were made to reach out to business journalists in foreign countries by arranging their visits to India in order to enable them to see first hand the changes in the business environment. Prime Minister's visits to the UK, Russia, USA, Vietnam and Singapore, as well as visits by Ministers and prominent economic personalities were utilised to highlight the opportunities for economic collaborations and business tie-ups with India. In the course of the Prime Minister's visit to Singapore in September 1994, 12 agreements were signed between Indian and Singaporean companies in diverse fields.

Various investment promotion seminars were also organised in India.Prominenet among these were INVESTMART organised in April 1994 by Ministry of Industry in collaboration with UNIDO. The entire forum was focussed on promoting 250 specific projects identified in specific sectors by Ministry of Industry. France, Italy, UK, USA and Singapore participated. About 70 Letters of Intent for identified projects were signed between Indian entrepreneurs and foreign collaborators.

Trade Scenario in Post-Independence Era

By virtue of the radical shift from a highly-regulated to an outward-oriented economy, India has generated immense interest abroad, but it has a long way to go before emerging as a strong global player, opines the author.

India's development strategy launched in the 1950s, soon after Independence, aimed mainly at strengthening the industrial base of the country, especially in basic goods and heavy machine-building, and adopted the import-substituation model to achieve self-reliance. Rxports were not viewed as an integral part of overall economic development, and such imports as became unavoidable were financed by drawing down foreign exchange reserves that had accrued to India at the time of Independence, in the form of sterling balances held in its favour for goods and services provided by this country during the Second World War.

Export pessimism dominated the mood of the early planners as it was rightly assumed then that until India's manufactures began to be diversified, there was little possibility of exporting manufactures while primary products and traditional manufactured goods faced poor demand prospects in the world market. It was during the later half of the fifties, when the Second Five Year Plan was under way with its emphasis on heavy industry, largely in the public sector, that it began to be realised that India needed to export to be able to finance at least part of the maintenance and developmental imports.

The foreign exchange crisis that was looming by mid-1957 reinforced the importance of export growth as part of planned development. *The pessimistic view about the potential for export earnings gave way to a more positive approach in the Third Plan (1961-66) with the introduction of export promotion measures without deflecting from the thrust of import subsitution and industrialisation.* It was clear by mid-estimated the import content of the inward-looking path of development opted by India. Pressures on balance of pyaments had already brought into existence the Aid-India-Consortium comprising the World Bank and developed countries interested in providing assistance to India. Renewed emphasis on exports was laid in the Fourth Plan (1969-74) which envisaged porogressive elimination of dependence on foreign aid while the Fifth Plan (1974-79) identified certain sectors such as engineering goods, garments, leather manufacture and marine products for achieving increases in exports.

Thus, as agianst virtual stagnation in the 1950s, export performance improved to an average growth of 3 to 4 per cent in the 1960s, and was more impressive in 1970s with an average growth of 6.3 per cent in volume and 15.9 per cent in value terms.

But in the three decades, India's share in world exports had declined throughout from about 2 per cent in 1950 to 0.65 per cent in 1970 and dropped further to 0.42 per cent in 1980. This was the period when there was impressive grow thin world trade and the opportunities were seize by many smaller Asian developing countries as well as the industrialising economies in Latin America to great advantage.

Paradoxically, even as india's export growth was being maintained or marginaly improved upon, her share of world exports was declining. Over the three decades ending the Seventies, the share of exports in Gross Domestic Product (GDP) ranged from 4 to 6 per cent. *In a continental economy of India's size, the role of external sector in the development process was under-played so much that it took a successions of droughts, oil price shocks and balance of payments difficulties in the first two and a half decades of planning before the country could begin to see import substitution and export promotion as two sides of the same coin.* But heavy reliance on quantitative restrictions on trade through import and export controls and detailed industrial licensing kept India a closed economy.

Over the years the Government of India has been adopting various measures for the liberalisation of the Industrial Policy, for streamling the licensing and foreign collaboration procedures, for reducing the number of agencies which the prospective investors have to approach to get the necessary approvals, etc., with the objective of attracting more investment and technology transfer. On the 24th July, 1991 the Government tabled before Parliament the Statement on Industrial Policy, 1991, which was followed by the issuance of a Notification by the Department of the Industrial Development to implement the Policy Statement and a series of Press Notes to set out the changes in the existing system and procedure for obtaining industrial licenses and approval of proposals for foreign and for foreign testing of indigenous raw materials and products and indigenously developed technlogies.

Industrial Licensing Policy

The new Industrial Licensing Policy of the Government of India has exempted form the requirement of obtaining industrial licence all industries, except those reserved for the Public Sector (Schedule I to the the Notification), those in respect of which Idustrial Licensing is compulsory (Schedule II to the Notification) and those relating to the items reserved for exclusive manufacture in the small scale sector (Schedule III to the Notification).

The exemption from Industrial licensing is also subject to:

* The proposed project (except in the case of a project relating to electronics, computer software, printing industry, industry located within an area designated as 'industrial area' by a State Government before the 25th July, 1991 or the small scale or the ancillary sector) being not located with 25 kilo meters form the periphery of the standard urban area limits of a city having a population of more than one million according to the 1991 census; and
* Of the Central and the State environmental laws and regulations including local zoning and land use laws and regulations.

Units qualifying for exemption from industrial licensing in accordance with the foregoing conditions are required only to file a Memorandum in the prescribed form, before establishement of the project, with the Department of Industrial Development

(Secretariat for Industrial Approvals) together with a crossed demand draft for rupees one thousand in favour of the Pay and Account Officer, Department of Industrial Development and another Memorandum in the prescribed form at the time of commencement of commercial production.

Small scale and ancillary units are required, as before, to be registered with the Director of Industries of the concerned State. Manufacturing units with an investment in plant and machinery up to Rs. 60 lakhs, ancillary units with an investment in plant and machinery up to Rs. 75 lakhs and units which are willing to undertake an export obligation to the extend of 30 per cent of their annual production by the third year with an investment up to Rs. 75 lakhs are eligible for small scale registration.

Foreign Investment Policy

The new industrial policy of the Government of India has announced major liberalisation for attracting foreign investment in respect of a list of high priority industries (Annexure III to the Statement of Industrial Policy, 1991). Foreign equity investment up to 51 per cent will be allowed subject only to the condition that:

The requirement of imported capital goods should be covered by the foreign equity;

Remittance of dividends should be covered by earnings of the company from export of items in Annexure III to the Statement of Industrial Policy, 1991. The amount of dividend payment may be converted by export earnings of such items recorded in Years prior to the payment of dividend or in the year of payment of dividend. This will be monitored by the Reserve Bank of India. However, such balancing will not be required beyond a period of seven years from commencement of production.

In all such cases the Reserve Bank of India has been authorised to issue automatic approvals of foreign investment and also grant exemption from the operation of the relevant sections of the Foreign Exchange Regulations Act, 1973.

The Primary issuance of securities has a long history in India. The Indian bond market, measured by the estimated value of bonds outstanding, is next only to the Japanese and the Korean bond market in Asia. By January 31, 1995, the outstanding value of the Indian securities market was estimated to have reached Rs.3000 billion, almost 3.5 times its size in 1986. The size is deceptive as, despite attractive yields, secondary market trading has remained poor with virtually no quotation even in respect of listed securities. The estimated outstanding amount accounts for about 42% of GDP, as at the end of January 1995. Partial deregulation of interest rates in the early nineties and increasing emphasis on monetary policy in stabilization are the first major steps towards the emergence of an active debt market, with government securities spearheading the process. With the issuance of government securities at market determined coupon rates and the use of innnovative products, it has become possible, for the first time, for other issuers to offer debt products priced off the yield on government securities.

The process of financial sector reforms initiated in 1991, is far from complete. The Growth of the Indian Capital Market since Independence has been phenomenal. The number of stock exchanges increased from 7 in 1947 io 23 in 1994. Likewise the number of listed companies on stock exchanges grew from 1125 in 1946 to 7811 at the end of 994. Similarly, the quantum of listed capital registered a growth of about 565 times from Rs.270 crore in 1946 to Rs.152,322 crore at the end of March, 1994.

The basic objective of financial sector reforms is to promote a diversified, efficient and competitive financial system by a policy shift from detailed regulation and controls to one based on market forces. Alongwith dismantling administrative regulation, the goal is establishment of a system of prudential regulation, supported by a mechanism for reporting, monitoring and supervision of the compliance.

Another major plan of reform is injection of new competition into a hitherto virtually government owned financial system. For the first time in many years, six new banking licences have been granted to the private sector all of which have been implemented. The new banks are permitted to have financial joint ventures with fgoreign baks, particularly for accessing modern systems and technology. There has been a mushrooming of Non-Banming Finance Companies (NBFCs), some of whom have already built up a large net-work. Several well known investment banks have established a presence in India. Since April 1993, nearly 300 Foreign Institutional Inestors (FIIs) have been registered with the regulatory authority and quite a few are active investors in the domestic capital market which has been opened up to foreign portfolio investment in a limited way. Several new mutual funds have been set up by the private sector including some by global fund managers. The most spectacular growth has been registered when we compare the share of market capitalization to gross domestic products (GDP) which was 12.9% in 1946, while in 1991-92 it was 57.2% and further increased to 68.8% during 1993-984.

Side by side with the announcement of New Industrial Policy for Promoting Small Tiny and Village Enterprises, the Government have also announced major reforms in the Trade Policy. The main objective of the trade policy have been to progressively reduce the system of administrative controls and lilcences and to link import except in the case of essential items. The major reforms in the Trade Policy are given below:

Exports were in the past allowed replenishment to providc for essential inputs required for the manufacture of products exported. To allow flexibility to enable diversification of export products and also as an incentive for exports, the REP licenses so issued, were allowed to be freely sold. The entitlement for REP licenses also varied from item to item. In view of the flexibility of the REP Licenses Government realise that to treat it as licence is an misnomer, under the new policy the REP licences have been replaced by a new instrument named 'Eximscrips'. Eximscrips will be issued on the basis of FOB value of exports or Net FOreign Exchange (NFE) earnings from exports as indicated below. The main features of the new systems are:

(i) The basic rate at which Eximscripts will be issued against exports will be 30% of FOB value. Exports to hard currency areas will be eligible for Eximscrips valid for hard currency imports while exports to rupee payment areas will be issued Eximscrips valid for imports from these areas only. However, as a measure of transition, exports to rupee payment areas may continue to avail of REP licences valid for hard currency imports at the rate prevailing prior to 4th July, 1991. This transition facility will be available only for exports effected upto 31st December 1991.

(ii) Products such as gems and jewellery, handcrafts, newspapers, journals and periodicals and cinematographic films, which enjoyed higher rated of REP will receive Eximscrips at the same rates as before.

(iii) The Basis rate of 30% is inadequate for exports of certain products such as value-added agricultural projects, electronics, bulk drugs and marine products, formulations and certain categories of advanced engineering goods. These products will be eligible for an additional Eximscrips entitlement of 10 percentage points, taking the total Eximscrips rate to 40% of FOB value.

For exports made on the basis of duty free imports obtained against Advance Licences, Eximscrips will be available at the general rate of 30% but this will be applied to the net foreign exchange earnings. On the same principle. Eximscrips at 30% of NFE will also be available for all EOU and EPZ units.

(iv) The 30% of NFE rate of Eximscrips is also applicable to service exports, including software exports which is a thrust area. The definition of services covered under this category is being ratinallized and extended to include other services such as services of architects, textile designers, artists, management consultants, lawyers etc. The benefit will be available to services exported by resident Indians for which remittances are made to India. The details are being notified separately.

Eximscrips issued to exporters will be tradeable and can be used to import any item in the limited permissible list (Appendix-3), the non-sensitive canalised list (Appendix-5A) and for all OGL, items for actual users (Appendix-6, List 8, Part I and List 10). Eximscrips earned by exporters on their own exports can also be used to import non-OGL capital goods other than those on the restricted list (Appendix-1A). All REP licences issued against exports prior to 4th July, 1991 will continue to be valid for the life of the licence and will have the same import entitlement as the new Eximscrips. Additional licences issued to export houses/trading houses, which were earlier valid for a more limited range of imports, will also be valid for the same range of imports as Eximscrips.

With the introduction of Eximscrips, the system of issuing supplementary licences of raw material, components and spares listed in Appendix-3 will be discontinued except for small scale industries and for manufacturers of specified life saving drugs and equipment. In future, all import requirements of these items (with the exceptions indicated above) will be made through Eximscrips, Similarly items in Appoendix-4 and Appendix-9, which were earlier importable against supplementary licences, will henceforth be importable only against Eximscrips. Import of items appearing in Appendix-2 Part B (list of Restricted Items) and Appendix-8 (List of Scientific and Measuring Instruments Restricted for Import) of the Import-Export Policy 1990-93 will continue to require licences. Such licences as well as licences required for small scale industries and manufactures of life saving drugs/equipment will be called Special Licences as these will be limited and include special cases.

As a measure of import compression and to strengthen the linkage between import capability and exports, two further changes have been made. The category of unlisted OGL has been abolished and these items have been shifted to Appendix-3. They are now importable only against Eximscrips (except for SSI and manufacturers of life saving drugs and equipment). In the case of units subject to the Phased Manufacturing Programme (PMP), many of which benefit from concessional duty on their imports of OGL items, all such items will henceforth be importable only against Eximscrips.

Eximscrips will be issued only after export proceeds have been realised. The procedure for issue of Eximscrips has been streamlined and Government will ensure that Eximscrips are issued within 48 hours of the receipt of the application accompanied by single document, namely, the bank certificate for the realisation of export proceeds.

Advance Licences

The system of advance licences is designed to provide exporters with duty free access to the inputs they need to produce competitively for world markets. This is an important instrument of trade policy especially in our situation where tariff levels are still high. The Government has taken the following steps to strengthen the system of Advance Licences as an instrument of export promotion:

(i) The procedures for considering Advance Licence applications have been simplified to ensure that advance licences will be issued within 15 days of application in all cases where input-output norms have been fixed. Where norms have not been fixed, the licence will be issued within 45 days.

(ii) The number of documents accompanying an Advance licence application has been reduced from 9 to 3 where norms are prescribed and to 4 where they are not prescribed.

(iii) Ar present norms have been prescribed for 540 items. This will be increased to over 1000 items by 31st October, 1991 and more items will be covered thereafter.

(iv) Substantial Manufacturing Activity as a necessary condition under the Advance Licence Scheme will no longer be applicable for exports to the general currency area. However, the value addition norms will remain in force. A large number of exporters will benefit under this scheme.

(v) A new Scheme of Transferable Advance Licence has been introduced for GCA exports in selected thrust areas, namely textiles, leather goods and engineering industries. Under this scheme exporters can undertake exports based on duty paid inputs obtained from the market and subsequently obtain advance licences for replenishment of these inputs by duty free imports. These advance licences will be freely transferable. The coverage of the scheme will be extended on merits.

(vi) Advance licence will specify values in free foreign exchange both for the purpose of import and export. The currencies in which such values are denominated will be limited to those notified for this purpose by the RBI.

(vii) The Existing procedure for obtaining Bank Guarantee (BG) and Legal Undertaking (LUT) from different categories of exporters in being streamlined and liberalised as follows:

(a) Export/Trading/Star Trading House and Public Sector Undertakings will have the facility of obtaining advance licence against LUT only without any monetary limit.

(b) All manufacturing units having an annual turnover of at least Rs. 5 crores (including both domestic and exports turnover) during the previous 3 year would also be able to avail of the LUT facility up to a value limit of 50% of their annual production.

(c) A new unit without any production or export performance to its credit would also be allowed LUT facility provided it is promoted by an existing company with an annual production of Rs. 5 crores for more than three years. In such a case, both the new company and the promoting company would have to provide LUT.

(d) Bank guarantee and/or LUT obligation will be concurrent to the fulfilment of export obligation.

(viii) Exporters would be allowed to dispose of the materials imported against advance licences by way of replenishment without seeking prior permission of the licensing authority in cases where no MODVAT facility has been availed of on the domestic material used in exports.

(ix) Adjustment needed on account of fluctuation of prices of imported individual items would be permitted within the overall CIF value of advance licence.

(x) The power of revalidation which presently vests in the Licencing Committee at the

Headquarters has been delegated to the Licensing Authorities.

(xi) In case where applications for an advance licence are turned down, the exporter will be permitted to convert to the Duty Drawback regime by the Collectors of Customs so that shipments made in advance can be imported on payment of duty subsequent claims of duty drawback.

(xii) Exporters can obtain advance release orders for domestic supply against advance licences under which the domestic supplier gets the benefit of deemed exports. Henceforth, release orders will be issued across the counter without requiring the name of the domestic supplier, which could be given later.

The adoption of these procedures would reduce discretionary controls and delays and afford much greater freedom to exporters in procuring essential duty free raw materials to maintain their competitiveness in the would market thereby promoting exports from the country.

The export Processing Zone scheme and the 100% EOU scheme were introduced to provide for duty-free enclaves, which would enable entrepreneurs to concentrate on production exclusively for export. However, with increasing liberalisation in the DTA, the duty advantages enjoyed by EPZs/EOUs have become less important. While the procedures of Customs Bonding are very onerous. The schemes have not therefore taken off as expected and they have also not attracted foreign investment aimed at tapping export markets to the extent that was expected. The working of these schemes has been reviewed and the following changes made:

(i) All EOUs/EPZ unit will be eligible for Eximscrips at the basic rate of 30% applied to net foreign exchange earning.

(ii) The duty applicable on DTA sales from EOUs/EPZ units is being reduced to 50% of the normal customs subject to the duty payable not being less than the excise duty on the same product. The extent of DTA sales allowed will be accordance with their entitlement. DTA sales will be permitted in the ratio of 25:75 in relation to export sales in case of units while use of indigenous raw material is more than 30% of production. In all other cases the ratio of permissible DTA sales to export sales will be 15:85. The procedures for clearing goods from the EOU/EPZ units for DTA sales are also being streamlined.

(iii) In order to encourage exporters to set up EOUs or EPX units the net foreign exchange earned by EOUs or EPZ units can be clubbed with the earnings of their parent/associated companies in the DTA for the purpose of according Export House. Trading House of Star Trading House status for the latter.

(iv) The IPRS scheme for supply of steel to exporters will also be extended to EOUs and EPZ units. The Development Commissioners are being empowered to issue "payment authorities" in lieu of JCCI & Es.

Under the New Industrial Policy, most industries do not require an industrial licence except for a defined list. With a view to bringing about comparable streamlining in the procedure for EOU/EPZ approvals, a systems of automatic approvals is being established for all proposals which fall within certain parameters.

Capital goods imports will be allowed under the automatic approvals procedure if they are fully covered by foreign equity or if they do not exceed 50% of the value of plant and equipment subject to a ceiling of Rs 3 crores. All proposals within the automatic approval parameters will be cleared within two weeks. All other proposals will be submitted to the Board of Approvals for consideration and decisions including issue of licences will be taken within 45 days.

A large number of issues relating to the operation of EOUs/EPZ units required centralized clearance in the Ministries of Commerce and Industry. Powers are being delegated to the Development Commissioners so that these approvals can be given on a decentralised basis. The specific approval of the Development Commissioner would not be required in cases of broad banding by EPZ units, where value addition is being maintained. The unit concerned would need only to provide relevant information to the Development Commissioner.

The following specific concessions to EOUs/EPZ units have also been extended:

(i) Allowing wntry of imported raw material on "Provisional Assessment" basis, to expedite customs clearance.

(ii) Permitting units under the EPZ and EOU schemes to supply/transfer finished goods among themselves.

(iii) Replacement of multiple bond by a single bond, for obtaining import clearance.

(iv) Increasing the list of items under the "Special Imprest Licence Scheme" on selective basis.

(vi) Clarifying that containers stuffed in EPZ and

EOUs are not to be reinspected at other points, as long as seals are intact.

Government have also decided to allow private parties to establish bonded warehouses within EPZs for stocking and sale of duty free raw materials, components, consumables and spares to EPZ units and EOUs. This will cut down delay in obtaining supplies of duty free materials which are in constant and regular demand by exporters. The details of this scheme will be notified shortly.

Other steps announced in the new Trade Policy have been the simplification of procedures for import of capital goods, decanalisation of number of items which were previously canalised, permission to allow established exporters to open foreign currency accounts in approved banks, raise external credits, pay for export related imports from such accounts and credit export proceeds to such accounts, its decision to re-designate the office of the Chief Controller of Import and Exports as Directorate General of International Trade with the principal function being to promote of exports, and facilitation of imports to promote export trade.

The policy changes now being implemented imply substantial reduction in the extent of licensing and in the number of types of licences. Supplementary licences for import of items in Appendixes-3 (except for SSI and manufacturers of life saving drugs and equipment), 4 and 9 of the Import-Export Policy 1990-93 have been abolished. Additional licences which were issued as an incentive to Export Houses and Trading Houses will stand abolished with effect from 1st April, 1992 and the incentive will take the form of an additional Eximscrip entitlement.

To achieve optimal import containment in the

context of the present Balance of Payments situation, several steps have been taken. One of these is the shift of many items which are on OGL to the limited permissible list.

With these changes, the policy for import of raw materials components and other inputs needed for production has been simplified. Most raw materials and other inputs (except for those on the Restricted List) can be freely imported either against Eximscrips or on OGL. Some raw materials continue to be canalised but in more of these cases requirements beyond those provided by the canalising agencies can be met through Eximscrips.It is the policy of the Government to move to a situation where imports of essential raw materials and components needed for industrial production are regulated through appropriate tariffs. However, in view of the Balance of Payments position which necessitates continued import containment, this cannot be done immediately. Many items must therefore remain on the limited permissible list, with imports permitted only against Eximscrips.

The medium term objective of the Government is to progressively eliminate licensing and quantitative restrictions on capital goods and raw materials/components so that all these items can be placed on OGL save for a small carefully defined negative list. This shift is proposed to be achieved over a 3 to 5 year period. The Government will appoint a High Level Committee to work out the modalities of achieving this transition keeping in mind the Balance of Payments position and the need to rationalise the reduce tariffs progressively to provide Indian Industry with an appropriate environment to develop international competitiveness.

International Trade and India

1. The important place commanded by India in world trade in coffee, tea, leather and spices on a historical basis has continued in recent years as wll. In 1994, India accounted for 2.4 per cent, 13.6 per cent, 2.5 per cent and 9.1 per cent of world trade in coffee and coffee substitues, tea and mate, leather, and spices, respectively. Furthermore, there has been a significant progress in export diversification, and India has emerged as an important exporter of iron ore and concentrates, and pearis, precious and semi-precious stones. In 1994, India accounted for 6 per cent or world exports of iron ore and concentrates and 10.9 per cent of world exports of pearls, precious and semi precious stones (Source: 1994 United Nations International Trade Statistics Year Book, 1995).

2. During 1950, India accounted for about 1.8 per cent (1.85 per cent of exports and 1.71 per cent of imports) of world trade. After gradually declining to 0.57 per cent by 1980, India's share improved marginally to 0.63 per cent by 1985. The reason for improvement in the share was that while world trade declined in the period 1980-85, India's trade continued to grow. However it came down again to 0.53 per cent by 1991. The first half of the nineties witnessed a sharp increase in India's exports and imports have grown in dollar terms annually by 12.4 per cent and 9.4 per cent, respectively. The corresponding growth rates of world trade was about 5.7 per cent. The secular decline in India's share in world trade has been arrested and reversed, and the years ahead are likely to see a continuation of this increasing trend.

3. The trade policy components of the reform process

undertaken since July 1991 have been motivated by a full recognition of the important role that trade can play in promoting growth. The utilisation of the expanded scope for specialising in areas of comparative advantage is manifest in the improved growth performance of the economy. Furthermore, while exports have vigorously responded to the removal of the anti-export bias of a protectionist environment, domestic industry appears to have been stimulated by the expended availability of imported inputs and capital goods as well as the challenge of competing in the international market place. The positive response of Indian industry to liberalisation is amply demonstrated by the capital goods sector. The tariff on capital goods was as high as 85 per cent in the pre-reforms period. This has been reduced to about 25 per cent covering about 80 per cent of capital goods in 1995-96. The capital goods industry which witnessed a negative growth of 12.8 per cent in 1991-92, registered an average growth of about 23 per cent during 1994-96.

Terms of Trade

4. The terms of trade, which measure the terms of exchange between a unit of exports and a unit of imports, have been improving in the post-reform period. Two common ways of measuring the terms of trade are the net terms of trade (NTT) and the income terms of trade (ITT). A time series indicating all parameters of terms of trade (TOT) for India since 1969-70 with the base of 1978-79 = 100 Indicates that there have been wide fluctuations in the TOT. The NIT (1978-79=100), which is an index of export prices divided by an index of import prices, improved from 109.3 in 1990-91 to 152.4 in 1994-95. It is

5. it may be mentioned that India s purchasing power of exports as reflected thorough ITT has been improving continuously since 1985- 86. The value index of exports at 484 stands much higher than that of imports at 351 and hence, in terms of value, india has gained.But in terms of volume, the index of exports has been much less at 384 in comparison to that of imports at 515. This means that the volume of imports is increassing faster, though India is getting a better price for her exports.

6. Compared to the experience of other developing countries, the improvement in the terms of trade for India has been very impressive.

7. Developing economies, with exports dominated by primary products, lost out to developed economies. Relavtive abundance of supply of primary products as well as the superior bargaining strength of developed countries have often ben adduced as two major reasons for the deterioration in the terms of trace. Gains in the terms of trade for India in the comparable period perhaps reflects her diversified export base as well as the relatively low international prices of oil in the relevant period.

India is committed to further liberalisation of its import regime, notwithstanding the dismantling of licensing controls over a wide area. At the same time, there are concerns whether developed nations of the world are implementing in letter and spirit their part of the obligations under the Uruguay Round Agreements. Many contries are resorting to protectinist devices in the guise of environmental hazards and exploitation of labour such as child labour. The obligations of providing access to imports of developing countries, especially textiles and garments, are being circumvented under one pretext or the other, even under the back-loaded integration of Textiles and Clothing into the World Trading System. Such restrictions are designed to keep out cheaper imports.

By virtue of the radical shift from a highly-regulated to an outward-oriented economy, India has attracted immense interest abroad, at both Governmental and private investor levels. India is one of the largest emerging markets, second only to China's, and the country has been experiencing inflows of foreign portfolio and direct investments—thought not as large as in China and a few other countries—which were unthinkable in the world of even 1980s. Economic strength has become the principal determinant of a nation's standing in the international community, and even the most powerful country, the United States of America, looks for market opportunities all over, more especially in the dynamic Asia-Pacific region, as the best shield of security.

With the end of the Cold War, the East-West barriers have broken down. The rapid spread of liberalisation and globalisation is a historic development which has blurred both East-West and North-South divisions. Developing countries have been compelled to adapt themselves to conditions of global interdependence although in the process they run grave risks in the medium-term and rare not assured of international safety nets.

In the rapidly changing world environment, each developing country must certainly concentrate on building its inherent strength and developing areas of comparative advantage and forge alliances with neighbours and, where promising, enter regional blocs which offer greater opportunities of trade and other exchanges to enhance national arena, disadvantaged nations must make common cause and unite to advance their pressing needs more effectively than what has been witnessed over the last fifty years in the post-decolonisation era. This is the only way of securing a post-cold war order which is just and equitable.

India has a long way to go before it could emerge as a strong global player, as currently it occupies the 32nd place as a leading exporter of merchandise, well below several countries in East and South-East Asia. It has to make up for the time lost in its inward-looking route to development which left the cuntry far behind in the international league, despite building a strong industrial base and possessing highly technical manpower, the third largest in the world. Indian planning did not take sufficient note of the gathering pace of global intergration with the frowth of merchandise trade exceeding the growth of output in virtually every year of the post-war period.

In recent years, India has begun to look East, is now a full dialogue partner in ASEAN (the 7-member Association of South East Nations) and excepts to find a place in the Asia Pacific Economic Forum (APEC) by 1999. These should promote greater intra-Asian trade and investment flows even as India strives to gain an increasing share of exports into developed economies of the West such as the European Union and North America. Trade with Russia and Eastern Europe as well as Central Asian States holds prospects of considerable expansion over present levels and a more promising development is the initiative taken by 14 states of the Indian Ocean Rim for an economic cooperation grouping with a Charter expected to be signed in March 1997.

The bilateral and pluralistic approaches cannot, and should not, in any way dilute India's firm commitment to multilaterialism which is the best safeguard against domination of the global economy by a few powerful nations. India's immediate responsibility is to solidify South Asian cooperation through SAPTA and ensure its early graduation to becomes SAFTA (South Asian Free Trade Area) to make it a region of good neighbourliness less prone to conflilcts than at present. With 16 per cent of the world's population, India's weight in the international economy remains negligible, and the building up of internal strength with determination through higher saving, and investments and greater efficiency in the use of resources is a pre-requisite for the country to claim its due share in the global market-place.

The Indian consultancy scenario is a rich blend of both "self-developed" technology on one hand and "acquired" know-how on the other. When the country emerged into freedom in 1947 the Indian Economy was at a low ebb with impoverished resources, processes and infrastructure designed to meet vested requirements and an environment wherein the wherewithal for nurturing and training technical and managerial talent was hardly there. The country soon took stock of the situation. National priorities were identified and a well conceived policy of "planned development" was adopted. Economic re-generation & growth forced an important segment in these planning programmes with socio-economic factors, like medicare, education, technical training, employment etc. appropriately dovetailed. It was recognised that for all these programmes or activities it was essential to nurture, encourage and develop an effective cadre of professionals, both technical and managerial. The concept of consultancy was thus ushered in and gathered strength gradually.

In the course of these four score and more years-in an environment of growth and development-the Indian consultant has been sufficiently exposed not only to the technological development and consultancy practices in other countries but also is a part of the indigenous consultancy culture that has evolved as an achievement towards the national objective of self-reliance. India's commitment to self-reliance in engineering skills has ensured a fairly good growth of the consultancy sector. As a part of the overall strategy for industrial development, the utilisation of indigenous design and engineering inputs is one of the key factors. The sixties and seventies witnessed the emergence of several consultancy organisations, with specialisation in various sectors of industry. Some of these were set up in collaboration with foreign organisations while many others were set up totally with local expertise.

According to a survey recently conducted by the Consultancy Development Centre (CDC) and the Federation of Indian Export Organisations (FIEO), Both non-profit institutions set up by the Government of India to service Indian Consultancy-there are more then 1400 consultancy organisations and individual consultants (both management and technical) rendering services in various aspects of industrial and non-industrial sectors of the economy.

The three decades of continues growth have brought maturity to the movement of entrepreneurship development in India. Till the beginning of the 1960s, entrepreneurship remained a topic of academic and philosophical discussion by economist, sociologist and psychologist. The attempt was to accurately define and describe entrepreneurship, its nature and functions. Such description were markedly influenced by respective academic disciplines. Although most of these descriptions were partly true, yet none of them had the quality of describing entrepreneurship as a whole.

Towards the end of the 60s, two very significant contributions were made in the field of entrepreneurship. These were:

(i) Establishment of positive linkages between entrepreneurship and economic prosperity. 1 and

(ii) Emergence of strong hypothese that entrepreneurship can be developed through planned efforts.

The former helped acceptance of entrepreneurship development for achieving economic prosperity and the later facilitated experimentation with various strategies for developing entrepreneurship.

In 70's varieties of strategies and models of developing entrepreneurship were developed, repeated and replicated. As a result entrepreneurship was identified as important vehicle of industrial development which is evident by the emergence of about 1.7 million SSI enterprises creating jobs for more than 10 million workers in the sector. During 80's the structure and functions needed for promoting entrepreneurship become more or less clear and entrepreneurship attained the status of a movement. At national level during 1982-83 National Science & Entrepreneurship Development Board (NSEDB) and National Entrepreneurship Development Board (NEDB) were created under the Chairmanship of the Prime Minister and Union Minister for Industry respectively. Two national resource institutions, i.e., National Institute for Entrepreneurship & Small Business Development (NIESBUD) at New Delhi and Entrepreneurship development Institute of India (EDII) at Ahmedabad were established during the same period. Presently more than 700 organisations including 7 state level entrepreneurship development institutes, 27 SISIs under SIDO, 17 TCOs, 20 Engineering and Technical Institution, 7 STEOs and a host of non-governmental organisations are engaged in developing entrepreneurship. SIDO alone has trained more than 50,000 potential entrepreneurs during 78-88 and one Centre for Entrepreneurship Development of Gujarat trained more than 10,000 potential entrepreneurs since its inception. In this way thousand of people get opportunities to be developed as entrepreneurs. But the coverage is still far less as compared to the potential available in the country. We may have to took into the infrastructural facility, availability and accessibility to information and technology and develop enormously large cader of trainers and poromoters to reach both urban and rural population. To illustrate, during the 8th Five Year Plan, as per the modest calculations, the country needs about 13,000 trainers, promoters for training potential entrepreneurs as against few hundred which are available today.

The mid 70s witnessed the crystallisation of an integrated model for Entrepreneurship Decelopment (EDP), consisting of *stimulatory, support* and *sustaining activities*. This was replicated and very widely with minor variations. The present decade is shaping up to be *"age of entrepreneurial explosion"*. It is visiable as a significant programme in national development plan. During 80s, the structure and function needed for promoting entrepreneurship have become more or less clear. With growing emphasis by the Government and the matching enthusiasm by NGOs, entrepreneurship has now attained the status of a movement.

The movement of entrepreneurship development in India, however, started as part of the total strategy of small industry development. The dynamic SSI policy has strongly supported the cause of entrepreneurship development and both have mutually supplemented each other.

Presently, Small Scale Industries in India are defined by investment limit of Rs. 6 million (Rs. 7.5 million for ancillary units). Besides manufacturing, services, maintenance and processing enterprises are also included in SSI. The tiny sector which has been given the distinctive position is defined as consisting of those units having investment less than Rs. 0.5 million.

The response to such dynamic policy has been very rewarding. The growth of SSI Sector has been one of the most impressive. Between 1973-74 and 1986-87 the number of SSI increased by over 3 folds from 0.416 million to nearly 1.457 million. Presently (1990) their number is estimated as 1.7 million. Employment in this sector has risen more than double from nearly 3.47 million to 10.14 million. The value of Production in terms of current prices increased ten times (Rs. 72,000 million to Rs. 722,500 million). In the field of export, SSI conribution was recorded as approximately 30 per cent of the country's total exports.

More impressive than these statistics is the number crossing 5,000 products which are manufactured in the small scale sector. Beginning with the production of simple consumer goods, the small scale today manufacturs several sophisticated, precision items using latest technology. Some of the sophisticated items precision items using latest technology. Some of the sophisticated items produced in SSI sector include T.V., electronic disk calculator, micro-wave components, electro-medical equipment, miniature bulbs, optical lens, digital measuring equipments, air-conditioning equipments, electric motors, machine tools, authomobile and scooter parts.

Small enterprises in India were also found more economical than large enterprises in terms of capital investment and development generation. Further, small enterprises are providing learning ground for imparting, managerial, entrepreneurial and technical skills. They also provide an outlet for creative urge among individuals to persue excellence in product design and innovations resulting into competitive culture and problem solving orientation which usually lack at the initial stage of development but are basic to socio-economic prosperity.

The most significant aspect of small industry development is that this sector has stimulated vigorously the economic activity of a far reaching magnitude and created a sense of confidence among very large number of small entrepreneurs about their strength and vitality.

In keeping with the cuntry's progress towards a more open economy with greater trade and investment linkages with the rest of the world, Mr. Chidambaram said he would introduce later in the year a new Act to replace the Foreign Exchange Regulation Act. 1973 (FERA). At the same time, he signalled a move toward convertibility of the rupee on capital account with his decision to ask the Reserve Bank to set up an expert group to lay out the road map and work out a time table for achieving the goal. A beginning in agricultural sector reform has also been made with the decision to repeal regulations governing rice milling and ginning and pressing factories. Domestic future trading is to be resumed in ginned and baled cotton, raw jute and jute goods.

In formulating his tax proposals, Mr. Chidambaram set himself a target of increasing the net tax revenues of the Centre by 15 to 16 per cent in 1997—98.

Notwithstanding the rate reductions and reliefs he has extended, the Finance Minister hopes to make up the loss by better collections. For the corporate sector, he has not only reduced the tax rate to 35 per cent but also abolished the tax on dividends in the hands of the share holder. He, however, proposed a 10 per cent tax on profits distributed in order to persuade companies to invest them for future growth.

Mr. Chidambaram rejected the demand for withdrawal of the controversial Minimum Alternate Tax (MAT) he introduced last year but announced exemption of export profits from MAT. He has also revised the manner in which MAT is charged and collected with a provision for tax credit. He has accepted the Corporate Sector's demand for buy—back of shares by companies and said an overall ceiling of 60 per cent will be kept for intercorporate investment and loans. Another proposal to boost the capital market is a one—time permission to stock brokers to corporatise their business without attracting tax on capital gains which will be exempted.

After an interval of one year, Mr. Chidambaram has taken up tariff reform reducing the peak rate of customs duty from 50 to 40 per cent. In the process, he reduced import duty on products which are inputs of the steel industry like coking coal, or on items which would help industries like engineering, textiles, chemicals and host of items related to information technology. The Power sector will get relief with the cut in the duty on non—coking coal from 20 to 10 per cent. In excise duty, Mr. Chidambaram has sought to simplify the structure with three new rates of 8, 13 and 18 per cent, rationalising the existing rates in the process.

The only tax measure in the budget is a tax on

certain services calculated to yield Rs. 900 crore in 1997—98 and Rs. 1200 crore in a full year. The net gain to the Centre will however, be only Rs. 300 crore because of the lowering of the interest tax on banks, which would result in a loss of revenue of Rs. 600 crore.

Despite the burdens thrown by the Fifth Pay Commission recommendations, higher provisions for subsidies, defence and interest payments, Mr. Chidambaram has managed to bring about a reduction in revenue deficit from 2.3 per cent of G.D.P. in the current year to 2.1 per cent next year. He has also increased the budget support for the Central Plan outlay by Rs. 6000 crore.

Mr. Chidambaram has framed his budget against the background of an economy which has been growing at an average rate of 7 per cent during the last three years. He is confident that GDP growth will be sustained at this level or even improved upon in the coming year, though he has listed some areas of concern. These are the sharp decline in crude oil production, poor performance of power sector, the slowdown in export growth, rise in the rate of inflation and volatile capital market. He asserts that his budget proposals are aimed at addressing these concerns. To maintain price stability, he has expressed his determination to adhere toa prudent fiscal policy, contain growth of money supply within 16 per cent and resort to liberal imports of wheat and other essential commodities to counter the pressure on prices. The coming months would show how far the Finance Minister's expectations including price stability (are) are fulfilled. He has indeed given a kick start to an economy which had been widely perceived to have begun to falter in recent months.

Application for Collaboration Approval

All foreign investment proposals and technical license agreements require approval from either the Secretariat of Industrial Approval (SIA) or the Reserve Bank of Inida (RBI) depending on the applicable criteria.

Applications for approval of technical collaborations requiring clearance by Reserve Bank should henceforth be made in form FC(RBI) (10 copies) to the Controller Exchange Control Department, Foreign Investment and Technology Transfer Section, Reserve Bank of India, Central Office, Bombay -400 023. Applications requiring clearance of the Government of India should be submitted in form FC(SIA) (10 copies) to the Entrepreneurial Assistance Unit of the Secretariat for Industrial Approvals (SIA) in the Department of Industrial Development, Ministry of Industry, Government of India, Udyog Bhawan, New Delhi - 110 011. Copies of both the Forms along with the guidelines issued by the Reserve Bank of India have been annexed ot this Update so as to assist the reader in knowing the type of information that would have to be supplied to the Indian Authorities.

Following the statement that permission to bring in technology and/or equity participation has been made 'automatic', several notifications and clarifications have been announced by the Government and by Reserve Bank of India regarding the procedural requirements prior to securing such permission. These announcements and policy changes continue to be announced on a day to day basis. Before advising a client or embarking upon a new foreign investment related project, it may therefore be appropriate to seek professional advice and assistance.

A specially empowered board namely the Foreign Investment Promotion Board (FIPB) has been constituted and has been vested with enough flexibility to examine those offers that do not come under the purviews of either the RBI or the SIA on a case by case basis. This board, located in the office of the Prime Minister has as its Chairman the Principal Secretary to the Prime Minister. The objective of the Board is to invite and facilitate investment in India by international companies in projects which are considered to be of benefit to the Indian economy and do not fall within the parameters of the existing policy for clearance of foreign investment proposals. The Board will provide a single window clearance for all aspects of projects considered by it.

The Investment Week issue of November 16, 1992 reports that the Foreign Investment Promotion Board has recently cleared 23 more foreign Investment proposals, most of which are 100% Export Oriented Units, (EOUS) and in the small scale sector.

The investment proposals to the FIPB can be in the form of a plain letter, without any prescribed format and will be decided on the basis of the relevant details given. According to the Government's statement in the Lok Sabha on 15th July, 1992 the criteria for clearing these cases are export potential, employment potential and other benefits likely to accure from the projects. It has been reported that almost all the cases submitted to the SIA and the FIPB in the last few months have received the necessary approvals expeditiously.

The FITT section was set up in the Central Office of the Exchange Control Department at Bombay on 16th September, 1991.

Till 26th September 1992 the FITT had received 996 applications of which 733 were approved and 221 returned for want of certain prerequisites and stipulated conditions being fulfilled by applicants.

The bulk of foreign investments approved were in the chemicals industry, electricals/electronics, food processing, industrial machinery and scientific and electrical laboratory equipment.

Proposals involving equity investment over Rs. 3000/- million are submitted to and approved by the CCFI which is headed by the Prime Minister.

A new liberalised policy pakage for the garments sector has been approved at a meeting of the CCFI. The new policy will also enable the garments sector unit to raise its capacity through technologies upgradation and increase investment upto Rs. 30 million provided it exports half of its production.

The Reserve bank of India in January, 1992 liberalised the branch licensing policy for foreign banks after nearly two decades. Foreign banks have sought 44 more branches as a result.

Foreign companies engaged in the manufacturing and trading activities abroad are now permitted to open branch offices in India for carrying on certain activities as follows:

- to represent the parent company/other foreign companies in various matters in India eg. as buying/selling agents in India etc;
- to conduct research work in which the parent company is engaged provided the results of the research are made available to the Indian companies;
- to undertake export and import trading activities;
- to promote possible technical & financial collaborations between the Indian companies & overseas companies.

The Government of India has recently notified the electronic hardware technology park (EHTP) scheme for building a strong electronics industry with emphasis on enhancing its export potential. For this purpose, foreign equity upto 100% has been allowed in the case of such units. Such a park can be set up by the Central Government, State Governments and public or privates sector organisations. Multinational companies, setting up manufacturing facilities in computer hardware and peripherals under 100% EOU Scheme will be allowed to sell upto 30% of their production in the domestic market. These companies will be allowed to import, paying upto a maximum of 30% import duty, raw materials, plant and machinery.

The following are the recently announced procedural measures initiated by the Government for the delicensing and decentralising of the Electronics Sector:

- The entire electronic industry has been exempted from the locational limitations imposed on other industries and may thus be located even in urban areas.
- Licensing has been abolished for all industrial undertakings including companies covered under Monopolies and Restrictive Trade Practices (MRTP) and Foreign Exchange Regulation Act (FERA) except the sub-sector of consumer electronics and strategic electronics.
- The system of phased manufacturing programme (PMP) run on case by case basis has been abolished.
- Development of small scale industries is being encouraged. Approvals/registrations have been totally decentralised to the level of State

Directorates of Industries. Investment limit for this sector has been revised upwards to Rs. 60 lakhs and that for ancillary units to Rs. 75 lakhs.

- Existing units are permitted to manufacture any article without additional investment under broad-banding subject to certain conditions.
- As recently as 20th November, 1992 the Commerce Ministry has by a notification significantly liberalised the advance licensing scheme for the electronics sector. The Government has substantially reduced and rationalised the value addition norms as well as input output norms for various electronic items, particularly components, with a view to boosting electronic exports from the country.

As India tries to integrate with the world economy some major changes affecting the Indian Software Industry have been initiated by the Government of India.

- Software industry is a 'high priority industry', thus it qualifies for automatic approval by the RBI for 'foreign technology agreements'.
- In March 1992, the Indian Department of Electronics (DOE) authorised the reproduction of foreign software for distribution within India if the local distribution fulfils certain conditions.
- The new Import-Export Policy has substantially eliminated import licensing, quantitative restrictions and other regulatory and discriminatory controls on the import of software.

In order to boost Software exports, the Government of India in the Union Budget 1991-92 has provided a new section whereby an assessee engaged in the business of export of computer software or rendering of technical software services outside India is allowed a pro-rata deduction for the next 3 assessment years. The pro-rata deduction is computed on a formula which takes into consideration the percentage of revenue earned from the export division. If the total income of a software business is generated from exports only, 100% exemption from income tax would be available. This exemption supplements the deduction available in respect of export profits under section 80 HHC of the Income Tax Act 1961.

The Government of India has consistently been in favour of establishing maintaining and steadily improving economic and technical cooperation among the developing countries and has been adopting all necessary measures for achieving these objectives, duly participating in, and promoting, the global developments of extending the frontiers of international trade and investment.

The problems in industrial development initially faced by India were similar to those faced by most other developing nations, namely, scarcity of capital, low productivity, slow rate of economic growth, absence of infrastructural facilitiess, a rapidly expending population, unemployment, inflation and other socio-economic problems. India has already achieved a considerable measure of success in resolving these during the preceding four decades or so (since the country attained independence) and is tackling the residuary problems with its sagacious economic and industrial policies, modifying in inproving them from time to time, to suit the emerging requirements of the changing times. These resilient and dynamic policies have been aimed at achieving a rapid and orderly industrialisation of the country and a steady improvement in the standard of living of its people. From self-reliance to exporting goods and services India has treaded a long path.

India's achievements on the industrial front by following such policies have been impressive. Besides increase in the volume of industrial output, there has been substantial change in the composition of industrial production over the years. India now produces machinery for textiles, sugar, cement, jute, paper etc. Apart from these, large quantities of metallurgical and heavy equipment and mining machinery are also produced. India has also gone into production of heavy electrical equipment such as power turbines and generators. Substantial capacities have been set up for the production of electric motors of different kinds, as also of various types of machine tools including high-speed lathes, milling machines, radial drills, grinding machines etc. A variety of scientific instruments are also produced.

Top priority accorded to the development of infrastructural facilities over the years has resulted in the establishment of an efficient transportatin and communication network. India has a excellent railway system, which ranks third in the world in terms of route length as well as passenger and goods traffic. There is also a very good network of roads which connects most of the villages and towns. Moreover, the communication system is well-developed and India is connected with most other countries, especially the commercial centres of the world, by modern means of communication.

There has also been tremendous growth in the

financial infrastructure. Commercial banking and financial markets, especially in industrial finance, have expanded at very fast rate.

India is in aposition to offer appropriate technologies to other developing countries which are cost-effective, suited to local conditions, make maximum use of local inputs and provide maximum employment to local persons through labour orientation. Some well-known examples are the export of technology for the manufacture of trucks, three wheelers and two wheelers and pulp and paper plants.

According to reliable estimates, more than one thousand consultancy firms, besides individual professionals, are offering their services in various fields. The services offered range from preparation of market surveys, feasibility reports etc. to basic and detailed engineering services, erection and commissioning of plants, training of personnel etc.

The Indian Consultancy Organisations are today offering their services in divergent fields like engineering industries, electronic industries, ferrous and non-ferrous metallurgical industries, chemical industries, aluminium, pulp and paper, forest-based industries, mining and allied industries, urban development, sewage disposal and effluent treatment, distillation and refinery plants, chemical plants, drugs and pharmaceuticals, generation, transmission and distribution of power, railways, highways and bridges, water supply and town planning architecture and irrigation and flood control management.

The Indian enterprises have acquired necessary capabilities of offering project export services ranging from civil and construction projects to industrial projects. The scope of services varies from subcontracting to execution of turnkey projects. In the industrial sector, the project exports from India range from low level technology areas like structural engineering and power distribution to sophisticated technology areas such as power generation, setting up of chemical plants, cement plants, transportation and tele-communication. In addition to securing a number of project contracts from the countries of West Asia, South Asia, Africa etc., the Indian industry has been able to obtain contracts for projects funded by the World Bank, the Asian Development Bank. The African Development Bank etc. in a process of competitive bidding.

Specialised services from the Indian Consultancy Organisations are available in the fields of Agriculture and Natural Resources, Energy, Oil and Gas Industry, Management Building, Public Health Engineering and Water Supply and Transport.

The Indian technology suppliers have to comply with rigorous requirements regafding import of technology, local content etc. They are thus in an advantageous position to understand the requirements and conditions of other developing countries and to adapt themselves to those conditins. The technologies offered by India will also be suited to the economies of scale of other developing countries, in addition to being of low cost. India is now in a position to export technology and services in the aforesaid areas and have many joint ventures not only in the developing but even in the highly industrialised countries.

As on 30th June, 1991 there are 159 Indian Joint Ventures in operation in 42 countries. Out of this 22 are in Europe, 7 in the United States of America, 56 in South East Asia, 24 in South Asia, 17 in West Asia, 29 in Africa and 4 in the Oceania region. Another 65 joint ventures are under various stages of implementation in these countries. Indian joint Ventures are in operation in the following areas.

(a) *Engineering Industries*

1. Light Engineering
2. Commercial Vehicles

(b) *Metallurgical Industries*

3. Iron and Steel Products

(c) *Chemical Industries*

4. Textiles and Allied Products
5. Chemicals and Pharmaceuticals
6. Oil Seed Crushing and Palm Oil Refining
7. Food Products (including soft drinks)
8. Pulp and paer
9. Glass and Glass Products
10. Leather and Rubber Products
11. Cement Products

(d) *Other Manufacturing Industries*

(e) *Service Sector*

12. Hotels and Restaurants
13. Consultancy
14. Engineering contracts and construction
15. Trading and Marketing

(f) *Other Non-manufacturing Ventures*

An illustrative list of areas where India is capable of offering technologies and setting up joint ventures is given below:

Metallurgical Industries

- Iron and Steel Castings
- Steel Forgings
- Rolling Mill Rolls
- Steel Rolling Mills
- Steel Wires
- Non-ferrous castings
- Aluminium Extrusion

Industrial Machinery

- Rice Mill Machinery
- Sugar Mill Machinery
- Boilers
- Air and Water Pollution Control Equipment
- Power Driven Pumps
- Speed Reduction Units
- Chemical and Pharmaceutical Machinery
- Food Processing Machinery
- Pulp and Paper Making Machinery
- Power Plant Equipment
- Miscellaneous Industrial Machinery

Electrical Equipment

- Electric Motors
- Alternators

- Transformers
- Condenser Bushings/Circuit Breakers/Power Capacitors
- Arc Furnaces and Induction Furnaces
- Voltage Regulators
- Electric Fans
- Household Electric Appliances
- Electric Bulbs
- Cables and Conductors

Electronic Equipment

- Radios, Tape Recorders, "Two-in-Ones"
- Television Receivers
- Components like Resistors, Capacitors, Transistors and Diodes
- Printed Circuit Boards
- Micro/Mini-Computers
- Computer Software

Transportation

- Trucks, Four Wheelers, Three Wheelers, Two Wheelers, Mopeds
- Automobile Ancillaries
- Diesel Engines
- Crawler Tractors/Dumpers/Loaders
- Bicycles and Bicycle Parts

Agricultural Machinery

- Agricultural Tractors and Tillers/Agricultural Implements

Machine Tools

- Lathes
- Drilling Machines
- Milling Machines
- Planning Machines
- Wood Working Machinery
- Machine Tools Accessories
- Small Tools/Hand Tools

Mechanical Engineering

- Structural Fabrication
- Transmission Line Towers
- Pipes and Tubes
- Typewriters
- Cash Registers
- Sewing Machines
- Bolts/Nuts/Screws/Studs
- Drums and Barrels
- Tin Containers
- Cutlery
- Pressure Cookers
- Aluminium and Steel Furniture/Office Equipment
- Steel Almirahs/Vaults/Safes
- Stoves

Other Engineering Industries

- Air Conditioners and Refrigerators

- Solar Water Heaters/Solar Cookers
- Mathematical and Survey Instruments
- Energy Meters/Water Meters

Chemical Industry

- Bricks and Tiles
- Cement
- RCC/PCC Pipes, Poles and Sleepers
- Glass Containers
- Potassium Chlorate/Sodium Chlorate
- Fertilisers
- Carbon Black
- Aromatics and Laboratory Chemicals
- Fine Chemical and Flavours
- Cosmetics
- Soaps and Detergents
- Drugs and Pharmaceuticals
- Dye Stuffs and Dye Intermediates
- Food Processing
- Distilleries
- Soft Drink Bottling Plants
- Vegetable Oil Processing
- Solvent Extraction
- Crockery
- Ceramic Tiles
- Sanitary Wares

- Leather and Leather Products
- Paper, Pulp and Paper Products
- Paints/Enamels/Varnishes
- Rubber Products including Automobile Tyre and Tubes
- Plastic Products
- Viscose Staple Fibre
- Jute Goods
- Textiles/Yarns (Cotton/Blended/Synthetic)
- Readymade Garments
- Wooden Furniture
- Sports Goods
- Stationery Items

Other Sectors

- Setting up of Hotels/Hospitals/Diagnostic Centres.

Environmental Options for the 21st Century

Human activities have pushed our planet to the brink of disaster necessitating a comprehensive global action to retrieve the situation. While exploring newer forms of renewable sources of energy to address the environmental malady, our planners and administrators need to address the most urgent task of improving energy efficiency. The rural areas should depend on minihydel projects and bioenergy as far as possible. A serious and lasting government commitment to the development and use of energy efficient and renewable technologies is the need of the hour.

Like it or not, we find ourselves in a world where

we are responsible for each other's well-being. In the last few years of this millennium, difficult questions of social equality, national sovereignty, and individual rights and responsibilities are emerging. A person may be able to afford a large, energy-consumptive automobile, but can the planet afford it? Indeed, the larger question boils down as to how many carbon-emitting automobilies can the planet tolerate without the habitability of the earth being disturbed. At a more mundane level, a couple may desire and be able to support several children, but can the planet afford several children per family? Does our generation have the right to extinguish plant and animal species that have evolved over millions of years? Do we not have the obligation to preserve our biological heritage for our future generations?

An affirmative answer to these questions depends on restoring and prserving the conditions that make the earth habitable, a place capable of supporting a diversity of life and modern civilization. Human activities have pushed the planet to the brink of disaster.

A comprehensive global action plan to remedy the situation should include: developing energy strategies that have climate protection as their cornerstone; expanding the earth's forest cover so as to prevent global warming; doubling the per capita grain production and lastly, breaking the momentum of population growth.

While these are the macro-level targets for making this globe a sustainable one in the forthcoming century, at the micro-level it amounts to a severe test on the capacity of world leaders as well as the local ones in their efforts in ecological economic betterment of the populations under their jurisdiction.

It is no wonder that the modes of energy production that are in vogue around the world are primarily responsible for the change in the earth's climate. The huge quantities of oil, coal and natural gas that fuel the global economy account for most of the carbon dioxide emissions responsible for global warming through the greenhouse effect. Producing less carbon dioxide requires using less fuel from among the traditional category. This in turn means exploring other non-conventional energy sources, enough to substitute the fossil sources.

4

Organisational Functions

A Military Department was created in the Supreme Government of the East India Company at Calcutta in the year 1776. Its main function was to sift and record orders relating to the army passed in other Departments. It also maintained a list of Army personnel. Although headed by a separate Secretary to the Government from 1776 onwards, it continued to function for many years as a branch of the Public Department.

The Charter Act of 1833 brought about a number of changes in its administrative setup under the East India Company. The Secretariat was reorganised in four Departments, including a Military Department, each headed by a Secretary to the Government. In 1864, the Military Accounts Departments of Bengal, Bombay and Madras Presidencies were merged with the Military Department. The Army, however, continued to function as the Presidency armies till April 1895, when they were unified into a single Indian Army. For administrative convenience, it was divided into four Commands viz., Punjab (including the North West Frontier), Bengal, Madras (including Burma) and Bombay (including Sind, Quetta and Aden).

The supreme authority over the Indian Army was vested in the Governor General-in-Council, subject to the Control of the Crown, which was exercised by the Secretary of State for India. In the Council, there were two members responsible for military affairs, one of whom was the Military Member, who supervised all administrative and financial matters while the other was the Commander-in-Chief who was responsible for all operational matters. After 1909, the Military Department was renamed as the Army Department and was redesignated as the Defence department in 1938. In 1947, the Defence Department became the Ministry of Defence under a Cabinet Minister.

Post-independence organisational setup

On August 15,1947, each Service was placed under its own Commander-in-Chief. Under the Constitution, the Supreme Command of the Armed Forces vested in the President. In 1955, the title of Commander-in-Chief was abolished and the three Service Chiefs were designated as the Chief of the Army Staff, the Chief of the Naval Staff and the Chief of the Air Staff respectively. In November 1962, a Department of Defence Production was set up to deal with research, development and production of defence equipment. The Department of Defence Supplies was created in November 1965 for planning and execution of schemes for substitution of import requirements for defence purposes. These two Departments were later merged to form the Department of Defence Production and Supplies. A Scientific Adviser to the Defence Minister was appointed to advise him on scientific aspects of military equipment, research and design of equipment used by the Defence forces. A Department of Defence Research and Development was created in 1980.

The Government of India is responsible for ensuring the defence of India and every part thereof. The Supreme Command of the Armed Forces vests in the President. The responsibility for national defence rests with the Cabinet. This is discharged through the Ministry of

Defence, which provides the policy framework, and wherewithal to the Armed Forces to discharge their responsibilities in the context of the defence of the country. The Raksha Mantri (Defence Minister) is the head of the Ministry of Defence

Departments

The Defence Secretary functions as head of the Department of Defence and is additionally responsible for co-ordinating the activities of the three Departments in the Ministry. The principal functions of the Departments are as follows:

— The Department of Defence deals with the three Services and with Inter-Services organisations. It is also responsible for the Defence Budget, establishment matters, defence policy, matters relating to Parliament, defence co-operation with foreign countries and co-ordination of all activities.

— The Department of Defence Production and Supplies is headed by a Secretary and deals with matters pertaining to defence production, indigenisation of imported stores, equipment and spares, planning and control of departmental production units of the Ordnance Factory Board, and for Defence Public Sector Undertakings (DPS Us).

— The Department of Defence Research and Development is headed by a Secretary, who is also the Scientific Adviser to the Raksha Mantri. It's function is to advise the Government on scientific aspects of military equipment and logistics and the formulation of research, design and development plans for equipment used by the Services.

The Finance Division of the Ministry of Defence is headed by a Financial Adviser. He is tasked with exercising financial control over proposals involving expenditure from the Defence Budget, and with the responsibility for internal audit and accounting of defence expenditure. In the latter tasks, he is assisted by the Controller General of Defence Accounts (CGDA).

Committees

A number of Committees dealing with defence related activities assist the Raksha Mantri. He holds weekly meetings which are attended by the Defence Secretary, Secretary (Defence Production and Supplies), Scientific Adviser to Raksha Mantri, the Financial Adviser, Principal Secretary to the Prime Minister, Cabinet Secretary, Foreign Secretary and the Chiefs of Staff of the three Services to review important developments and discuss issues concerning national security. The Raksha Mantri also chairs monthly meetings of the Defence Minister's Committee with the Secretaries in the Defence Ministry, Financial Adviser and the Chiefs of Staff of the three Services to review and take coordinated decisions on various key programmes.

The Chiefs of Staff Committee is a forum in which the Service Chiefs discuss matters having a bearing on the activities of the Services and advise the Ministry. The position of Chairman of the Chiefs of Staff Committee devolves on the longest serving Chief of Staff, and consequently rotates amongst the three Services. To facilitate the task of the Chiefs of Staff Committee, a number of sub-committees have been set up.

The principal task of the Defence Ministry is to obtain policy directions of the Government on all defence and security related matters and communicate them for implementation to the Services Headquarters, Inter-Services Organisations, Production Establishments and Research and Development Organisations. It is also required to ensure effective implementation of the Government's policy directions and the execution of approved programmes 2.14 within the allocated resources. A list of items dealt with by the Departments in the Ministry of Defence is given in Appendix-1.

The three Services Headquarters, viz. the Army Headquarters, the Naval Headquarters and the Air Headquarters function under the Chief of the Army Staff (COAS), the Chief of the Naval Staff (CNS) and the Chief of the Air Staff (CAS), respectively. They are assisted by their Principal Staff Officers (PSOs). The Inter-Services Organisations, under the Department of Defence, are responsible for carrying out tasks related to common needs of the three Services like medical care, public relations and personnel management of civilians in the Defence Headquarters.

Information regarding the Ministers in the Ministry of Defence, the Chiefs of Staff, the Secretaries in the three Departments of the Ministry and the Financial Advisers who held positions from April 01, 1998 is given in Appendix II.

Planning for defence

The defence policy accommodates continuing changes in the strategic setting whilst ensuring that the armed forces deployed are well-equipped, properly manned and supported to allow them to undertake operations effectively. It is equally necessary to ensure that they are capable of responding to future challenges. The force structure is designed to provide a robust response to the new strategic environment whilst remaining sufficiently responsive to further development.

Systematic planning for effective implementation of the Defence Strategy and the security policy is the essence of planning for defence. The strategic and technological environment assessment based on the harmonised perception of experts, from all the concerned Ministries and Departments forms the basis for evolving the strategy. Planning for defence is a multi-disciplinary exercise involving, inter alia, an assessment and understanding of the trends in the international security environment, foreign policy, economic and international relations and the internal security environment.

The Directorate General of Defence Planning Staff (DPS), an Inter-Service organisation, provides inputs to the Chiefs of Staff committee in of Defence Planning. The DPS is designed to be a multi-disciplinary group with representation from the three Services Defence Finance, the Ministry of External Affairs and the DRDO. For sectoral planning, independent units function in the Services Headquarters which, in turn, are supported by the Departments of Defence, Defence Production and Supplies and Defence Research and Development.

Defence expenditure

Given India's size and security concerns, the outlay on Defence, assessed either as a percentage of the total Central Government expenditure or of the Gross Domestic-Product, continues to be one of the lowest amongst neighbouring countries. The two charts in this chapter represent Service /Department-wise break up of Defence expenditure for the years 1996-97,1997-98, 1998-99(RE) and 1999-2000(BE) and Service/Department-wise expenditure as a percentage of total Defence expenditure.

Army

The basic responsibility of the Army is to safeguard the territorial integrity of the nation against external aggression. Due to the country's long borders encompassing different geographical and climatic conditions such as desert terrain on the west, snow-covered mountains in the north and thick rainfed mountainous jungles in the east, the Army has to constantly prepare itself for diverse challenges. In addition, the Army is often required to assist the civil administration during internal security disturbances and in the maintenance of law and order, in organising relief operations during natural calamities like - floods, earthquakes and cyclones and in the maintenance of essential services. Demands on the Army have increased manifold due to continuous deployment of its forces in intense counter insurgency operations in Jammu & Kashmir and the North East parts of the country. To achieve these objectives, the Army has to be constantly modernised, suitably structured, equipped and trained.

Information Technology (IT) activities

Major IT Projects under implementation, Planning and Initiation are as under:-

(a) *Replacement of Mainframe Computer*: The obsolete mainframe computer of 1983 vintage at Army Headquarters Computer Centre has been replaced with a high-end server RS-6000 of IBM.

(b) *Army Intranet*: Local Area Networks (LANs) at Army Headquarters (HQs) have been established. The Wide Area Network (WAN) connectivity is under implementation to connect all HQs. With this connectivity, the flow of data and information with these HQs and within the HQs will improve manifold.

(c) *Automation of Research & Referral (R&R) Hospital*: The project for automation of the prestigious R&R Hospital, Delhi Cantt. is under consideration.

(d) Automation of Record Offices (Phase V) Automation of the remaining 17 Record Offices had been taken up during the year.

(e) *Automation of Indian Military Academy (IMA)*: The case for full automation of IMA, Dehradun has been initiated.

(f) *Pilot Project for Automation of a Corps*: A pilot project to evaluate the total automation requirements of a Corps, including Headquarters in the chain (Corps, Divisions and Brigades) and the units has been initiated. This Pilot Project will form the basis for automation of all the Corps of the Army.

(g) *Enhancement of LAN at Command Headquarters*: The project will enhance the present limited capacity at Command Headquarters for meeting their full-networked Management Information System (MIS) requirements. The case has been initiated during the current year.

Mechanised forces

With a view to enhancing combat efficiency of the Army, the following measures have been taken:

(a) The Defence Research Development Organisation (DRDO) has developed an indigenous Main Battle Tank (MBT) Arjun, which will be the mainstay of Indian Army during the 21st Century. Clearance has been accorded for production of tanks.

(b) Import of T 90 S tanks from Russia has been approved.

(c) Contract for Armoured Fighting Vehicle (AFV) Radio sets is likely to be concluded.

(d) FLAME anti-tank guided missile launchers are under the process of being delivered.

(e) The scheme for modernisation of T-72 tanks is under active consideration.

Artillery

For meeting the urgent requirement of Artillery, import of 155 mm smoke ammunition has been cleared and same is likely to be delivered shortly. Battle Field Surveillance Radar (Medium Range) [BFSR (MR)] and Thermal Integrated Observation Equipment (IOE) have been contracted for and would be available to troops in near future. Action has been initiated for procuring Weapon Locating Radar (WLR) in limited quantity ex-import.

Infantry

In order to provide mobility and protection to own troops against improvised explosive devices, Mine Protected Vehicle is being acquired. A contract has been signed and the first consignment of few vehicles is expected to be despatched shortly.

Snow mobiles have been procured and moved for use in Siachen Area. These will considerably ease out acute logistic problems of troops in Siachen Area.

The supply order for 5.56 mm Light machine Gun (LMG) & Passive Night Sight (PNS) for 5.56 mm Rifles/ LMG has been placed with various vendors.

Signals

During the year, significant development work has been done on some of the most critical equipment/ subsystem of Plan AREN.

(a) *Automatic Electronic Switch (AES MK II):* This has been developed as a product improvement of AES MK- I already in service. All evaluations of AES Mk 11 have been completed. Bulk Production Clearance (BPC) is likely to be granted shortly.

(b) *Radio Local System (RLS):* This system comprises of one Radio Local Centre (RLC) and upto ten Radio Local Extensions (RLE). The equipment is used in fluid and mobile operations when paucity of time does not permit laying of field cables. The system integrates RLE subscribers into the Army Radio Engineering Network (AREN) grid. RLSs have also been inducted.

(c) *Radio Frequency 'F' (RRF) type:* This Electronic counter measure (ECCM) fortified Frequency Hopping Radio Relay Set was introduced in June 3.11 1998. The RRF will be subsequently upgraded.

Trial and Evaluation: Trials and evaluation have been completed in respect of the following equipment:

(a) Fibre Optic Cable System (FOCS).

(b) Army Radio Engineering Network—Army Static Communication Network (AREN-ASCON) Pipeline Interface Unit (AAPIU).

(c) Radio Set HX

Army aviation

Limited series production of Advanced Light Helicopter (ALH) is progressing and likely to be delivered during 1999. Emergency Locator Transmitter, Personnel Locator Beacon and homers have been contracted for.

Engineers

Logistic upgradation in siachen: Due to extremely low temperatures obtaining in the Siachen glacier area, disposal of night soil poses a great problem and leads to organic pollution. In order to preserve the delicate ecological balance of the Himalayas, bio-digesters were tried out for disposal of human waste through biodegradation. After successful trials at the Base Camp, the bio-digester has been recently installed at the Glacier.

Pipeline project in siachen: Kerosene oil is the basic necessity for troops deployed on the glacier. It is the primary fuel used for warming and cooking purposes. A major portion of the stores being air dropped is kerosene. A pilot project to pump kerosene oil using pipelines was executed to ascertain its feasibility and efficacy. The pilot project has performed well and the pipeline network is being extended to other locations on the Glacier.

New mine field breaching systems: New minefield breaching system in the form of Engineer Mine Plough have been imported.

Army capital works: The management of Army Capital

Works has been streamlined over the years. Close monitoring and careful cost control has resulted in most of the high value projects being completed on schedule and within the estimated cost. Completion of on going works continued to get priority to achieve an optimum use of the available resources and minimise cost overruns. Modern construction techniques and materials are being instituted gradually. The allocation of funds for Capital Works for the Army during the Financial Year 1998-99 is Rs. 438.80 crore which includes Rs. 40-00 crore for special married accommodation under Quick Shelter Project initiated to achieve enhanced satisfaction levels of married accommodation. The emphasis continues on the construction of married accommodation expeditiously in a time bound manner. Towards achieving this end, all married accommodation projects are being treated as Fast Track Projects and works amounting to Rs. 16.32 crore have been sanctioned during 199899. During 1997-98, married accommodation comprising 729 units for officers, 571 units for JCOs and 3301 units for OR have been completed.

Revenue works: The allocation of funds for Revenue Works and Maintenance Services is Rs. 1145-81 crore during 1998-99. To optimise the use of the available funds and to achieve higher users satisfaction, innovative schemes like door-to-door Maintenance, Welcome maintenance and single window system for attending to maintenance problems introduced earlier have been given a major thrust.

Completed works: A few important time bound projects completed during 1997-98 and 1998-99 are given below:-

(a) Provision of Other Than Married (OTM) accommodation for a medium regiment at Jodhpur.

(b) Project Quick Shelter (Phase-I) in 39 out of 42 high pressure stations.

(c) Single officers accommodation for 164 Officers at Mhow.

(d) Provision of accommodation for two Air Observation Post Flights and Base facilities for Army Aviation BMC at jodhpur.

(e) Introduction of pre-fabricated construction of married accommodation at Gurgaon.

(f) Infrastructural work for international Aero-Space Exhibition 98 at Yelahanka, Bangalore.

(g) Construction of building for Controller of Defence Accounts (CDA) (Navy) in Mumbai.

(h) Augmentation of accommodation for Naval Hospital, Powai.

Electrical and Mechanical Engineers (EME)

The Corps of EME has dynamically moulded itself to keep pace with technological advancement in war like equipment in providing engineering support to the equipment deployed across all the frontiers.

Simulators: EME has actively associated itself in the design, development and manufacture of simulators for imparting cost effective and realistic training to the field Army. The following simulators have been developed:-

(a) 'B' Veh Driving Simulators.

(b) Hand Grenade Simulators

(c) Anti Tank Guided Missile (ATGM) Simulators.

Total Quality Management (TQM): Development and training of EME Officers and personnel were given a fresh impetus at the Military College of Electrical & Mechanical Engineering (MCEME), Secunderabad which led to the institution being awarded ISO - 9001 and Golden Peacock National Training Award for excellence in training. Achieving yet another milestone in the field of 'TQM, 510 and 512 Army Base Workshops have been awarded ISO - 9002 for excellence in technical output.

Overhaul/reoptimisation: In order to meet the challenges posed by changes in the international situation since 1991 and the recent United States (US) sanctions, the Corps of EME has resorted to medium repair/ overhaul/ reoptimisation of critical equipment such as T-72 tanks, BMP, Air Defence Weapon Systems, missiles, radars and communication equipment. Base workshops have also been geared up with modern CNC machinery for manufacture of selected spares of foreign origin.

Environmental protection: The Corps of EME has contributed towards environmental protection and pollution control. EME has been entrusted with the implementation of pollution norms for military vehicles and equipment. It has been instrumental in establishing pollution check centres in major cities and identifying old vintage vehicles for transfer from metros to other cities.

Product improvement: The following product improvements are in an advanced stage of implementation:-

(a) Modification of Power Supply of Radar Cymbeline.

(b) Modification of Audio Amplifier with Radio Sets ANPRC/VC.

(c) Modification of Alternator Circuit of Position and Azimutch Determining system (PADS) Mk - II.

(d) Modification Fuel Injection Pump (FIP) Solenoid of Tank Vijayanta.

(e) Fitting UTD - 20 engines in BAZ 5937 (CV) and 5939 (TLV) of OSA AK weapon system.

(f) Modification of the emergency gear controller of Vijayanta tank.

Territorial Army (TA)

The year was eventful due to heavy commitments of the units on embodiment of TA infantry units for 'Operation Rakshak' (Jammu&Kashmir) and security, guard/escort duties.

Ecological task forces: The Ecological Task Force (ETF) remained embodied for eight months. The ETFs have performed commendably in greening the limestone quarries scarred hills around Mussoorie in Dehradun District, carry out plantation and greening in Garhwal District, foothills of Samba in Jammu, greening around the desert in Jaisalmer District in Rajasthan, soil conservation and plantation in Chambal Ravines in Morena District of Madhya Pradesh.

Non-departmental units: These are infantry units which are financed entirely by the Ministry of Defence. During the year, some of these infantry battalions remained embodied for internal security duties in 'Operation Rakshak' in J&K for tasks, such as guarding of vulnerable areas and points, manning permanent vehicle check posts, road opening, convoy protection, cordon and search operations and detection of improvised explosive devices (IEDs). Few battalions were employed for guarding ASCON installations, Ordnance Depots, and Border Roads Organisation (in Doda J&K, Tripura, and Manipur areas). In addition some battalions were deployed for election duties in North East during February to April, 1998.

Reamount veterinary corps (RVC)

Raising of dog unit: Trained army dogs of the Indian Army have acted as force multipliers when deployed with the security forces in combating insurgency in Northern and Eastern sectors. Their successful deployment has yielded commendable results which have been highly appreciated. Accordingly, Govt has accorded approval for raising of more dog units which has already commenced.

Gifting of dogs to Bangladesh and training of their personnel: Government of India has gifted 8 trained dogs to Government of Bangladesh, which have been procured and trained by the Remount and Veterinary Corps of the

Indian Army. Bangladesh army personnel were also trained in handling and deploying the trained dogs.

Sale of horses/ dogs: Army is selling surplus animals to para military forces, state police, state governments and friendly foreign countries. This has led to generation of revenue worth Rs. 71,52,950.00 for the year 1997-98.

Veterinary camps and civic aid programme: Under the Civic Aid Programme, RVC is regularly conducting Veterinary Aid Camps and Area Breeding programmes by providing free services of horse stallions, especially in Northern and Eastern Commands. The Veterinary Aid Camps provide free consultancy and treatment facilities to sick animals of civilians living in remote and far flung areas. The local population is also advised about the latest animal husbandry practices, prevention and control of animal diseases and know-how to start poultry, sheep, goat and cattle breeding projects. Veterinary Aid Camps have become a very useful tool in the hands of formation commanders for effective fraternisation of border population.

Army dogs were deployed to fortify security arrangements along the route traversed by the pilgrims for Amarnath Yatra. Timely detection of IEDs by the Army dogs have not only saved the lives of many pilgrims but also thwarted an attempt of the saboteurs, thus enhancing the image of the Army in the minds of the people of the country.

UN peacekeeping operations

Indian Army is actively involved in the peacekeeping operation in Angola, Sierra Leone, Lebanon, Kuwait and Bosnia Herzegovina. Our troops with their professional approach and respect for human rights have earned respect from various non-government organisations and other UN agencies. One battalion group has taken over responsibilities as United Nations Interim Force in

Lebanon (UNIFIL) from a Norwegian Battalion in Lebanon as of November 27,1998.

Rashtriya rifles

The Rashtriya Rifles, under the operational control of the Army, remained fully committed in counter insurgency operations and have acquitted themselves creditably in the assigned role. A number of civic action programmes were conducted in the deployment areas in an attempt to mitigate the hardship faced by the people due to ongoing insurgency. Because of their valour and devotion to duty, 156 Rashtriya Rifles personnel have been awarded honours and awards during the period. A total of 96 Rashtriya Rifles personnel (7 Officers, 3 JCOs and 86 other ranks) laid down their lives during the year in the service of the nation.

Recruitment of personnel in the armed forces

New recruitment system: The New Recruitment System has been introduced from April 01, 1998 in order to make recruitment more transparent, accessible to the public and to eradicate exploitation of candidates by touts and agents. The recruitment is carried out through rallies in order to reach out to the prospective candidates in the districts and far flung/remote areas.

Relaxation in recruitment: Relaxation has been given to wards of servicemen/exservicemen/war widows in physical measurements and they are also awarded 20% bonus marks on passing the written examination. Provision of instant enrolment has also been made for sons of battle casualties.

Improvement in intake: The intake of cadets in the National Defence Academy, Indian Military Academy and Officers Training Academy has shown a marked improvement. This trend, if continued, will arrest the deficiency in the officers category of the Army in the next ten years and bring it within manageable proportions.

Introduction of new entries: With a view to providing opportunities to aspirants from within the ranks of the Army and outside, a number of new entries like the Special Commissioned Officers Entry (for service entries), 10+2 Entry, University Entry Scheme (Technical Graduates) and NCC Special Entry Scheme have been introduced.

Women Special Entry Scheme (WSES): The Women Special Entry Scheme has attracted a number of applications from potential women candidates for the Non Technical and judicial streams. The scheme has also been extended to widows of service officers killed in action. So far four widows have been commissioned into the Army during 1998. Vacancy capacity per course is 50 with an annual intake of 100.

Publicity campaign: An Image Projection Campaign on mass media through TV, Print and Radio was conducted by the Army with the assistance of a professional advertising agency. This campaign has been received very well by the target audience. The positive effect of the campaign is apparent in way of improved intake in the training academics.

Navy

India is a maritime nation strategically straddling the Indian Ocean, with a substantive sea borne trade. The country's economic well being is thus very closely linked to our ability to keep our sea-lanes free and open at all times. Besides, India has other maritime interests as well. Our island territories situated on our Western and Eastern seaboards are at considerable distances away from the mainland. To ensure their sustained development, umbilical linkages with the mainland and maritime security protection are essential prerequisites of our maritime security. Our offshore assets within the Exclusive Economic Zone (EEZ) of 2.02 million sq. kms, fisheries and deep sea interests, major and minor harbours and the overall seaward security of long coastline and island territories are other vital aspects of our maritime dimension and Navy's responsibilities.

Indian Navy has consciously taken the difficult route of indigenisation in consonance with the national endeavour towards self-reliance. The Navy embarked upon a programme for indigenous construction of ships and development of major sub systems, sensors and weapon systems with the help of Defence Research and Development Organisation (DRDO) and Defence Public Sector Understandings (PSUs). Commissioning of the indigenously built destroyer, INS Delhi on November 15, 1997, with two more of the class in the pipeline along with other frontline ships under construction at the Government Shipyards have enabled the Navy to become a builder's Navy and not just be a buyer's Navy. Self-reliance through indigenisation has been the Navy's guiding philosophy over the last half century.

Operations and Activities In its quest to maintain the highest level of vigil across the country's maritime boundary, the Navy conducted various activities during the year.

Fleet exercises: Naval ships conducted regular tactical exercises, including amphibious landings, involving the three services and the Coast Guard. Both the current and new doctrines were rehearsed.

Surveillance patrol: Naval ships, submarines and aircraft maintained continuous surveillance off the coasts of Maharashtra, Saurashtra and Orissa, as also in the Palk Bay, to prevent smuggling of arms, drug trafficking and illegal movement of personnel. Naval forces successfully undertook major operations in the Andaman sea against gunrunners and narcotic dealers and apprehended a number of militants alongwith large catches of arms and ammunition. Some of the major operations were:-

(a) "Leech" Feb 09-11, 1998 Vindhyagiri, Saryu, Two LCUs, CGS Vivek, Lakshmibai, Islanders, CG Dornier Elements from 3 Madras, 5 X MI-8 Helicopters

(b) "Poorab" May 29 to June 02, 1998 Saryu, Kuthar, LCU Islander, Dornier Kirpan, 34, 35 CG

(c) "Hibiscus" Aug 09-17, 1998 Khanjar, Himgiri, Saryu Kuthar,

Joint Exercises with Foreign Navies : The Indian Navy carried out joint exercises with naval units from Oman, Saudi Arabia, Kuwait, Iran, Mauritius, Seychelles, Maldives, Singapore, Vietnam, Philippines and United Kingdom. The units conducted Search and Rescue (SAR) exercises and other basic level exercises. Such interactions serve as good Confidence Building Measures (CBMs) and help foster friendly relations with these countries. These opportunities also provide a forum for disseminating the Navy's, as also the country's, perceptions and policies on issues of interest to other countries.

New acquisitions

Ships commissioned: INS Kora, the first of the four missile corvettes being constructed indigenously at M/s Garden Reach Shipbuilders and Engineers Ltd. (GRSE), Calcutta, was commissioned on August 10, 1998. Amongst the other acquisitions, an Extra Fast Attack Craft, INFACT-80, was commissioned on June 24, 1998. The second ship of the class is also expected to join the Indian Navy by early 1999. The first indigenous Fleet Tanker, 'Aditya' is in its final stages of construction at M/s GRSE, Calcutta, and is likely to be handed over to the Indian Navy (IN) by mid 1999 alongwith a Fast Attack Craft (under construction at M/s Goa Shipyard Ltd.).

New projects: The Government has approved indigenous construction of two submarines and three frigates as also the acquisition of three frigates and two submarines from Russia. Of the two, one submarine was delivered to the Indian Navy in December 1997. The Government has also approved modernisation of the aircraft carrier INS Viraat which is scheduled to commence by May 1999.

Ships proposed for decommissioning during the year

After rendering yeoman service, the following ships would be decommissioned during 1999:-

(a) INS Androth and Amala

(b) INS Mesh and IN LCU L-31

(c) INS Kesari

Cooperation with foreign countries

With the end of the Cold War, international relations have undergone radical changes affecting the world order. This has necessitated most countries to forego their traditional confrontationist approach and seek new strategic alliances with the dual aim of promoting regional stability as also to progress towards the economic wellbeing of the nation state. Various international maritime cooperation initiatives by the Indian Navy over the last few years have helped in building bridges with foreign navies which would go a long way in establishing a strategic relationship, based on mutual trust and confidence.

Goodwill visits: During the year, Indian Navy (IN) ships visited ports in Oman, Saudi Arabia, Iran, Mauritius, Seychelles, Maldives, Vietnam, Singapore, Malaysia, Philippines, South Korea, UAE and Bahrain. In addition, warships of most neighbouring countries in the Indian Ocean Region, as also ships from Italy, France and England visited Indian ports.

High level visits: Exchange visits by high ranking defence official help in strengthening the existing defence ties with other countries. Following Senior Naval dignitaries visited India during the year:-

(a) C-in-C Russian Navy - January 98

(b) Chief of Staff, Japanese MSDF - February 98

(c) Chief of Staff, French Armed Forces - February 98

(d) CNS Bangladesh Navy - March 98

(e) Chief of General Staff, Polish Armed Forces March 98

(f) C-in-C Royal Thai Navy - April 98

(g) Chief of General Staff, PLA of China

(h) CNS Singapore Navy - April 98 - July 98

(i) CNS South African Navy - October 98

(j) CNS Nigerian Navy - October 98

Training of foreigners in India: To meet the varied and multidimensional training requirements of foreign naval personnel, the Indian Navy has well established institutions/academies imparting both basic and specialist training. These institutions are adequately geared up to meet the training requirements of friendly countries. Training to foreign nationals is imparted under various schemes namely, International Technical and Economic Cooperation (ITEC) Programme, the Special Aid Scheme and the Self Financing Schemes (SFS). During the year 1997-98, 94 officers and 131 sailors from foreign navies were trained in India. 345 vacancies have been provided for training foreign nationals during the period 1998-99.

Hosting of meetings with foreign navies: The Indian Navy hosts a regional congregation of the Navies (MILAN) of the littoral countries on a regular basis. These meetings are aimed to foster close ties between countries for developing Confidence Building in the region. Following MILANs are planned to be held in early 1999:-

(a) MILAN 99: A meeting of the Bay of Bengal littoral

countries (MILAN 99) is scheduled to be hosted by the Indian Navy at Port Blair in April 1999. MILAN 99 is planned as a sequel to 'MILAN 95' and 'MILAN 97' with a wider scope for interaction. Highlights of 'MILAN 99' include hosting of discussions on maritime subjects of mutual interests like Laws of the Sea, Pollution Control, Regional SAR etc. and presentation of papers on professional issues to promote regional security dialogues and Confidence Building Measures, joint Exercises as also various sports/cultural activities.

(b) Naval Symposium. A naval symposium on 'Role of Navies in Littoral Warfare in the 2151 Century' was conducted by the Indian Navy from February 03-07, 1999, at Kochi. Delegates from Sri Lanka, Maldives, UAE, Oman and Mauritius also participated in the symposium.

Indigenous programme

Significant strides have been made towards indigenisation of various equipment required by the Navy. R&D efforts by DRDO's chain of laboratories and the Weapons and Electronic Systems Engineering Establishment (WESEE) of the Navy have been the mainstay in our efforts towards indigenisation of various equipment.

Weapon systems/spares: The acquisition, maintenance and product support of naval weapons and equipment used to be heavily dependent on foreign suppliers. In order to achieve better product support and move towards self reliance, the Indian Navy has been promoting indigenisation of spares, sub systems and systems used on board naval ships, through domestic industry in the 420 private and public sectors. Some of the major projects under progress are:-

(a) Triple Tube Torpedo Launcher.
(b) Super Rapid Gun Mount
(c) Anti Missile System Trishul.
(d) APARNA Radar
(e) Electro Optical Fire Control System—EQN 51.
(f) Sonar HUMSA.
(g) Submarine Sonar Panchendriya.

Underwater ranges: The project for setting up of an underwater range at Goa for measurement of magnetic and noise signatures of naval platforms is in the advance stage of execution. On completion, the facility would enhance the operational effectiveness of naval ships and submarines particularly for shallow water operations. Modernisation of Viraat: The modernisation of the aircraft carrier is scheduled to commence in India in May 1999. A major part of the onboard equipment is slated for replacement by indigenous equipment being supplied by Indian industries.

RF test range: The Government has approved the setting up of a scale model RF test range at INS Valsura (Jamnagar). The range would provide facilities for undertaking scale model studies of ships in a simulated RF environment with a view to optimise ship design in achieving electromagnetic compatibility.

Maintenance

Marine gas turbine overhaul centre: The IN is operating gas turbines for propulsion and power generation on board naval ships. These engines are in the range of 12-14 MW for propulsion and 900 KW for power generation. The centre would cater for overhauling and testing of the M15E and M36 gas turbines, which would be a major step towards self reliance.

Refit of floating dock: The only Floating Dock, FDN-1,

with the Navy is being refitted for the first time at M/S Hindustan Shipyard Ltd, Visakhapatnam.

Overhauling large capacity alternator: Naval Dockyard (Mumbai) has successfully undertaken rewinding and overhauling of a 1MW alternator in May 1998. Until now the dockyard had undertaken repairs of alternators upto 750 KW capacity.

Delegation of financial powers

Delegation of financial powers in the Navy, with the institutationalisation of 'New Management Strategy' (NMS) has resulted in greater efficiency in all field formations. The areas where the Navy has benefited the most on account of delegation of revenue powers are refit of ships, procurement of stores and training. The net gain has been in greater operational availability of ships, submarines and aircraft

In its quest to build upon the advantages, which have accrued through NMS, the Navy has automated its entire procurement process through creation of a WAN -Integrated Logistics Management Systems (ILMS). The Navy has also achieved computerisation of its financial management requirement which is proposed to be linked with the Management Information System.

The greatest fallout of the delegation of Financial Powers is that, the Navy today is more budget aware and expenditure is being prioritised to achieve the "best value for money".

Hydrography

India, with its hydrographic traditions dating back to the seventeenth century, is the foremost hydrographic nation in the Indian Ocean Region. The National Hydrographic Department (NHD) compares favourably with all the major hydrographic countries in terms of resources and expertise. The National Hydrographic Department (NHD) is recognised as a regional leader for undertaking training as well as hydrographic surveys.

The NHD has six indigenously designed and constructed survey ships fitted with the latest hydrographic instrumentation and equipment. The ships are capable of 4-31 undertaking all types of survey assignments. Two more ships of the same class are under construction in an Indian Shipyard and are likely to be delivered by 2000-2001 AD.

The NHD earned revenue for the Navy during 1997-98 by undertaking contract surveys including Coastal Zone Management Surveys.

The department is undertaking trials of the Electronic Navigational Charts prepared by it as part of the programme to produce such charts for the entire area covering the Indian coast/waters. The department is also involved in surveys related to the Continental Shelf and baselines as per requirements of the UN Convention on Laws of the Sea.

Commercial diving

The Navy will conduct the following 'Commercial Diving Courses', on a payment basis :-

(a) Indian Diving Standards (IDS) I to IV courses

(b) Conversion Courses from one level to another within IDS.

(c) Training of divers from commercial diving companies for undertaking specific diving tasks.

(d) Specially tailored diving courses for personnel of Police, Port Trusts, Hydel Projects, Fire brigades etc.

Personnel: The importance of creating the software and human resource base, which will anticipate as well as respond simultaneously to the changing technology, needs no further emphasis. Naval warfare, by nature, remains at the front end of high technology and therefore, requires continuous upgradation of the technological and innovative skills of its personnel. Towards this quest, the induction pattern, training facilities and methodologies at the Training Schools/ establishments and repair yards, as well as the on job training on board ships and submarines has been constantly reviewed to adopt modern practices and enable seamless integration.

Women in all branches of the Indian navy: Induction of Women as Short Service Commission (SSC) officers in the support branches /cadres of the Indian Navy commenced in 1992. 99 women officers have been inducted during the last six years in the Education Branch and Law, Logistic & Air Traffic Controller cadres of the Executive Branch. The Government has now approved induction of women, as SSC officers, in all branches of the Indian Navy. Women technical graduates will also be able to join the operational cadres in the field of highly sophisticated propulsion machinery, weapons systems and sensors with a network of information technology. The Indian Navy will be one of the very few Navies in the world wherein women officers have been actively employed on board ships.

Sports and adventure activities

Sports and adventure activities continued to play an important part in naval life. The Navy Adventure Cell 'at Naval Headquarters organises various activities in the Navy. During the year, hot air ballooning, rafting, trekking, powered hang gliding, para sailing, skydiving, wind surfing, kayaking, mountaineering and skiing were undertaken for naval personnel and their families.

Sky to ocean expedition: A multi disciplinary expedition from Indira Col (Saichen) to Indira Point (Andaman & Nicobar Islands) named "Sky to Ocean" was conducted by the Army from August to November 1998. The expedition, encompassing 14 disciplines of adventure activities, was flagged off by Hon'ble Raksha Mantri on September 03,1998 in New Delhi. The naval participation in this expedition was in the following disciplines:-

(a) Trekking, mountaineering and skiing

(b) Rowing/rafting

(c) Skydiving and hot air ballooning

(d) Motor cycle expedition

(e) Wind surfing

(f) Scuba diving

International achievement of naval sportsmen/coaches: Naval sportsmen participated in various international fixtures and brought laurels to the country by winning medals in the various events. Participation by NC Dingko, Petty Officer (Steward) and D Wilson, Petty Officer (Steward) in boxing and weightlifting respectively at the Commonwealth Games -1998, in Malaysia are cases in point.

Welfare

Various activities to improve community development in the IN as also its quality of life were initiated. Prevention of AIDS and family planning were accorded high priority. Other welfare measures instituted in the IN included the rehabilitation of widows, computer coaching classes, yoga training, protection of environment etc.

Education: The Indian Navy established a 'Naval Maritime Academy' (NAMAC) at Mumbai to conduct courses for retiring naval personnel/ children of service personnel interested in seeking employment in the Merchant Navy. In addition, the KV Sangathan has granted additional concessions, at the insistance of the Navy, to ease problems faced by serving and retired defence personnel seeking admission of their wards to Kendriya Vidyalaya schools.

Air force

The Indian Air Force (IAF) today, having completed more then six decades of dedicated service to the nation, is a modern, technology-intensive force distinguished by its commitment to excellence and professionalism. Keeping apace with the demands of contemporary advancements, the IAF continues to modernise in a phased manner and today it stands as a credible air power as the nation marches into the next millennium.

With the ever escalating costs of operations, great emphasis is being placed on cost effective training, reducing expenditure, optimising output and minimising wastage. The Air Force has implemented a number of measures to enhance the quality of life of its personnel in key welfare areas of housing, education and hostel facilities.

In addition to the traditional wartime roles of the IAF of counter air, counter surface, strategic and combat support operations, the Air Force has provided significant aid to civil authorities during natural calamities like the Gujarat cyclone and the Malpa tragedy. The Siachen glacier lifeline continues to be monitored by the Indian Air Force, fully supporting the Indian Army in fighting on the world's highest battlefield. The IAF has also provided aid to civil authorities for the large scale movement of military and para military personnel to maintain law and order as well as to cater for the needs of a large number of airmen and jawans in remote and inaccessible outposts.

Modernisation

Air superiority today is a mandatory prerequisite to land and sea battle. Keeping in mind the acquisitions and capabilities of our potential adversaries, a continuous review of the state and performance of existing assets is indispensible. Where cost factors do not permit replacements, indigenisation and mid life updates have been selected as alternatives, extending the life and effectiveness of valuable and expensive aircraft over a larger span of time. In some cases, the Air Force has upgraded the avionics and associated systems, while in others, it has inducted multi- role capability at minimal cost to the exchequer.

Upgrade of combat aircraft

The upgrade of the MiG 21 Bis has commenced in earnest and those for the MiG 27 and Jaguar aircraft are on the anvil. This would provide a fresh lease of life to these fighters, maintaining them as a potent force till well into the next century. The mid life update on the MiG 21 Bis is going on as per schedule. Currently, two aircraft are in Russia for upgrade. The subsequent plan is to overhaul and upgrade the remaining aircraft at the Hindustan Aeronautics Ltd. (HAL).

Advanced Jet Trainer (AJT)

In the absence of an optimally designed advanced jet trainer, the IAF has inducted a large number of MiG 21 trainers to ensure continuity to the fighter pilot training programme on the MiG 21.

Electronic welfare support systems

Electronic Warfare Systems enhance survivability in a dense and lethal air defence environment. The IAF today has placed great emphasis on such systems and most aircraft are now equipped with state-of-the-art electronic systems for Radar Warning and Counter Measure Dispensing Systems to upgrade their survivability and enhance their operational effectiveness.

Operations

Air defence: The air defence of the nation is the foremost task of the IAF. To further strengthen its air defence shield, the IAF is continuously improving upon the performance of ground radars, their integration, automation of data transfer and displays. Combined with dedicated interceptors and guided missiles, the layered structure presents an effective and efficient air defence system.

Offensive strike capability: The IAF has a variety of multi-role and dedicated strike aircraft to present a formidable combat capability acting both as an effective deterrence against adventurism by our adversaries and to effect a crippling strike should the necessity arise. The SU-30 -multi-role air superiority fighter was formally inducted into the IAF last year. The aircraft and the aircrew are now operationally well prepared. With this acquisition, the IAF's strike as well as air defence capability have taken on a new dimension.

Operational training: The Indian Air Force has continued to carry out extensive operational training in the form of major air exercises both within own elements as well as extensive interaction in joint exercises with the Army and the Navy New concepts, philosophies and tactics have been evolved to conform with the changing threat scenario. These elaborately planned, single as well as joint exercises have helped in improving our capabilities and fostering inter-service cooperation and jointmanship. Such joint exercises have been held in all the various terrain and climatic conditions obtaining in our environment both on land and over the sea. The exercises have constituted high points of the training activities for the year, ensure crew fitness and re-confirm our confidence in our capabilities.

Shifting of Headquarders South Western Air Command (SWAC)

The South Western Air Command shifted its headquarters. The move was conducted very fluently, without any break in the effective functioning of the headquarters during the change. The Government of

Gujarat extended all cooperation and support in facilitating the establishment of the headquarters at its new location.

Displays

The flying displays saw participation by front line fighters including the highly agile SU-30 attired in the national tricolour performing most impressively. The original IAF aerobatic team called the 'Thunderbolts' equipped with the redoubtable Hunter aircraft were rested due training requirements of the Air Force. The IAF has revived its formation aerobatic team reinstated as the "Surya Kiran". Along with the sky diving team 'Akash Ganga' they have performed most professionally across the country. The National Golden Jubilee celebrations were enjoined befittingly by the Air Force by organising numerous static displays and flypasts at several cities throughout the country including Mumbai, Chennai, Cochin, Srinagar, Jodhpur, Lucknow and Visakhapatnam.

Information Technology (IT) projects in the IAF

As an ongoing development of a comprehensive IT base, the IAF has initiated Project "Inventory Material Management On-Line System (IMMOLS)" to computerise its inventory. The project is well under progress. Operational and maintenance management activities are also being completed under project "Computerised Operations & Maintenance Management Package (COMMPACK)". On completion, the project would computerise the entire operations/maintenance/miscellaneous activities of flying bases and ground weapon systems and thus would lead to a total computerisation in the IAF.

Administration

The Indian Air Force has made significant progress in improving the quality of life of its personnel. Improving the quality and the numbers of dwelling units of residential accommodation has been a priority area for the Air Force. During the current financial year, the construction of an additional 2600 dwelling units is planned.

Family welfare

Prevention of AIDS and family planning continued to be high priority areas. The Air Force has implemented the family welfare programme through seven Class I and 29 Class II welfare centres. Amongst a myriad of other welfare thrusts of the Air Force are the setting up of dental Chairs, rehabilitation of widows of personnel losing their lives while still in harness, subsidy for dwelling units for widows, establishment of numerous computer awareness programmes and setting up of a marriage bureau.

Adventure sports

The momentum generated by IAF adventure activities during the Golden jubilee celebrations last year continued into this year also. A highly successful and popular sequence of air shows continued with the Air Devils carrying out sky diving demonstrations at Port Blair, Lucknow, Mumbai, Chandigarh and Calcutta. In addition, existing adventure activities such as mountaineering, water sports, horse riding, trekking, hang gliding were undertaken. The para sailing camp drew active participation by over 3000 Air Force personnel. An adventure camp for Air Force school children at Mount Abu and Dalhousie drew enthusiastic response during the summer holidays.

Super speciality veterans' hospital

Currently there are certain serious diseases whose treatment is not authorised in service hospitals. In order to alleviate the suffering of retired Air Force personnel against such life threatening situations, a Super Speciality Veterans' Hospital has been established in Delhi with facilities available for Radiotherapy, Haemodialysis. Bronchoscopy and Physiotherapy.

Senior citizens institute

An old age home for lonely retired Air Force personnel is under construction at Tughlakhabad, New Delhi. This care centre would have facilities like messing, canteen, clinic, dispensary, library and a physiotherapy centre located within the complex.

Educational programmes

Ab-initio trainees are being given inputs in computer education throughout the Indian Air Force. Advanced PCs have been procured and supplied to all training institutes of the IAF for widespread training in computer education.

Flight safety

The entire flight safety organisation in the IAF remained geared during the year to reducing flying accidents and conserving precious resources required to maintain high standards of operational preparedness at all times. During the last two years, accidents due to human error and bird strike have shown a marked downward trend. The IAF, during 1996-97, recorded its lowest ever accident rate. This was repeated in 1997-98 and efforts are underway to reduce these figures even further. Some of the measures in this regard are :-

(a) *Accident Investigation*:. Each accident or incident is thoroughly investigated. Specialists from the Ministry of Defence and manufacturers are involved in Courts of Inquiry, as and when required. The recommendations made by these courts are implemented to avoid a recurrence.

(b) *COFAA*: Committee on Fighter Aircraft Accidents

(COFAA) is a high powered committee, which was initially set up to monitor accidents on fighter aircraft. The scope of the committee was subsequently enlarged to cover accidents on other aircraft also. The recommendations of this committee are expected to go a long way in further enhancing flight safety in the IAF.

(c) *Bio-acoustic devices*: Bio-Acoustic devices have been procured and installed for bird strike prevention on vulnerable airfields. These have been found to be effective. Regular monitoring of bird strike incidents is being carried out to check the efficacy of these aids. Zon guns are noise devices intended to scare birds. The Liquefied Petroleum Gas (LPG) fired zon guns have been procure and installed at some of the vulnerable airfields.

Institute of flight safety

The Institute of Flight Safety, the only one of its kind in South Asia, trains officers and other personnel in accident investigation and prevention. It has been conducting regular courses for the IAF, Army, Navy, HAL and the Directorate General of Civil Aviation (DGCA). It is also engaged in research and analysis and publicity to build up flight safety awareness. During the beginning of the year, the Institute of Flight Safety conducted an International Flight Safety Seminar on Human Error Accidents. Delegates from over 40 countries attended and valuable lessons were drawn from the experiences of Air Forces the world over on human error accidents.

Prevention of bird strikes

Sanitisation of airfields: In order to reduce the probability of bird strikes to aircraft, it is proposed to sanitise 10 priority airfields within a radius of 10 km. A project report is being prepared on the subject by Housing & Urban Development Corporation (HUDCO). The

Ministries of Agriculture, Urban Affairs and Dairying will install modern abattoirs, carcass utilisation plants and ensure general cleanliness in the sanctioned areas, which would go a long way in further enhancing the anti-bird programme of the Air Force. In addition, an environmental inspection of all airfields is being carried out to monitor the flight safety environment at each base. This obviously pays dividends in the accident/ incident prevention programmes at the airbases.

Flight safety zones: Flight Safety zones have been created at all airfields as a bird strike prevention measure.

Induction and Training (IAF)

Induction in officer cadre of IAF

Induction into the officers cadre of the Indian Air Force is done through:-

(a) Union Public Service Commission (UPSC).

(i)National Defence Academy (NDA) Examination

(ii)Combined Defence Services (CDS) Examination

(b) Direct recruitment

(c) In-service recruitment.

A common entrance examination is held by the UPSC for NDA and CDS examinations, the syllabi for which is widely publicised and made known to all aspirants. All successful candidates based on the results of the written examination are sent to Air Force Selection Boards for further interviews and Officer Like Qualities (OLQ) tests. The results of the Air Force Selection Board tests are announced openly immediately after the completion of the test at the Service Selection Boards. Thereafter, recommended candidates are detailed for medical examinations. Whilst calling the candidates for Selection Board tests, complete details pertaining to the medical requirements are also intimated to them in writing so that they are aware of the medical fitness levels that would be required from them. The Selection Board marks are forwarded to the UPSC who finally release the merit list through newspapers.

In so far as direct recruitment is concerned, the advertisements giving complete details of the qualification requirements and other details are published in the Employment News, Rozgar Bulletin and leading national dailies at least one year in advance. On receipt of applications, in response to the advertisements, the same are thoroughly, checked for eligibility and eligible candidates are subsequently called for Service Selection Board (SSB) interview. The selection process at Service Selection Boards involves well publicised information which has been disseminated through books, magazines, brochures and even television programmes The results of the SSB tests are openly announced

In-service induction into the officers cadre is done through a widely publicised written examination. Those who qualify in the same are sent for Service Selection Board tests.

Recruitment of airmen to the air force

Recruitment of airmen is done through the Central Airmen Selection Board, New Delhi. There are thirteen selection centres spread all over India and they make necessary arrangements for the conduct of selection tests and final enrolment.

After seeking applications through advertisements in National and Regional Dailies and through the Mass Media, a written test on an All India basis is held and an All India Merit List drawn up for purpose of recruitment. Enrolment is done in order of merit. Allocation of trades is done on the basis of Trade Allocation Tests. The number of personnel recruited varies as per requirement.

5

Defence Policy

India's defence policy aims at promoting and sustaining durable peace in the subcontinent and equipping the defence forces adequately to safeguard aggression.

The Supreme Command of the armed forces is vested in the President of India. The responsibility for national defence, however, rests with the Cabinet. The Defence Minister is responsible to Parliament for all matters concerning defence. Administrative and operational control of the armed forces is exercised by the Ministry of Defence and the three services headquarters.

At the Army Headquarters in New Delhi, the Chief of the Army Staff is assisted by the Vice-Chief of the Army Staff and seven other Principal Staff Officers, namely, the two Deputy Chiefs of the Army Staff, Adjutant General, Quarter-Master General, *Master General* of Ordnance, Military Secretary and Engineer-in-Chief.

The Army is organised into five operational Commands, *viz.*, Southern, Eastern, Western, Central and Northern Command and one Training Command. Each Command is under a General Officer Commanding-in-Chief who holds the rank of Lieutenant General. General Officer Commanding-in-Chief commanding an operative command is the commander of demarcated geographical area and has both field and static formations under the command. The major field formations are Corps, Division and Brigade commanded by a General Officer Commanding of the rank of Lieutenant General, a General Officer Commanding of the rank of Major General and Brigadier, respectively. The major static formations are Area, Independent Sub-Area and Sub-Areas. An Area is commanded by a General Officer Commanding of the rank of Major General and an independent Sub-Area and Sub-Area by a Brigadier.

The Army consists of a number of arms and services. These are Armoured Corps, Regiment of Artillery, Corps of Air Defence Artillery, Army Aviation Corps, Corps of Engineers, Corps of Signals, Mechanised Infantry, Infantry, Army Service Corps, Military Nursing Service, Army Medical Corps, Army Dental Corps, Army Ordnance Corps, Corps of Electrical and Mechanical Engineers, Remount and Veterinary Corps, Military Farms Service, Army Education Corps, Intelligence Corps, Corps of Military Police, Judge Advocate General Department, Army Physical Training Corps, Pioneer Corps, Army Postal Service, Territorial Army, Defence Security Corps. In addition, the Army has its own Recruiting Organisation, Record Offices, Depots, Boys Establishments and Selection Centres and Training institutions.

Navy

The Navy is responsible for defence and security of India's maritime interests and assets, both in times of war and peace. The Chief of the Naval Staff at the Naval Headquarters, New Delhi, is assisted by four Principal Staff Officers, namely, the Vice-Chief of Naval Staff, Deputy Chief of Naval Staff, Chief of Personnel and Chief of Material.

The Navy has three commands, *i.e.,* Western, Eastern and Southern, with their headquarters located at Mumbai, Vishakhapatnam and Kochi respectively. Each command is headed by a Flag Officer Commanding-in-Chief in the rank of Vice-Admiral. Western Command and Eastern Command have under them operational fleets, *i.e.*, Western and Eastern Fleets comprising warships, submarines, aircraft and other support ships. Southern Naval Command is responsible for all training activities of the Indian Navy.

The Indian Navy is a well-balanced three-dimensional force consisting of sophisticated missile-capable warships, aircraft carriers, minesweepers, advanced submarines and the latest aircraft in its inventory. Many of the warships are of indigenous design and have been constructed in Indian shipyards, These ships compare well with the ships of similar capability constructed by the advanced countries. The Naval forces are maintained and supported by modern dockyard facilities encompassing state-of-the-art technology. At present, it has two major Naval bases at Mumbai and Vishakhapatnam.

Coast guard

The Coast Guard came into being on 1 February 1977 and was constituted as an independent Armed Force of the Union of India with the enactment of CG Act 1978 on 18 August 1978. The Coast Guard's broad Charter of Duties includes : (a) Safety and protection of offshore installations and artificial islands: (b) Providing protection to fishermen in distress; (c) Protection of maritime environment; (d) Assisting Customs in anti-smuggling operations; (e) Enforcement of MZI Act; and (f) Safety of life and property at sea.

The general superintendence, direction and control of the Coast Guard is exercised by the Director General Coast Guard under Ministry of Defence.

The entire coastline of India and the national maritime zones have been divided into three Coast Guard Regions, namely, Western, Eastern and Andaman and

Nicobar Islands, under the respective Commanders of the regions. The Regional Headquarters are located at Mumbai Chennai and Port Blair.

The Coast Guard Regions are divided into eleven Coast Guard Districts based in our maritime states. There are five District Headquarters on the West Coast, namely Porbandar, Mumbai, Goa, New Mangalore and Kochi. Four on the East Coast, namely Chennai, Vishakhapatnam, Paradip and Haldia and two District headquarters in Andaman and Nicobar Islands, namely, Diglipur and Campbell Bay. In addition, there are Coast Guard stations and Air Enclaves at various locations.

Beginning with two frigates and five Seaward Defence Boats (SDBs), the Coast Guard service has made rapid progress in the last 20 years. The service has now developed into a full-fledged maritime organisation with nine Offshore Patrol Vessels (OPVs), two Advanced Offshore Patrol Vessels (AOPVs), 24 Fast Patrol Vessels (FPVs), 15 Interceptor Boats (IBs) and ICs, 17 *Dornier* Aircrafts and 15 *Chetak* Helicopters. The third Advanced Offshore Vessel is expected to be commissioned shortly.

Air force

The Air Force is organised both on functional and geographical basis. There are five operational commands. These are: Western Air Command, South-Western Air Command, Central Air Command, Eastern Air Command and Southern Air Command. In addition, Maintenance Command and Training Command are two functional commands.

At the Air headquarters in New Delhi, the Chief of the Air Staff is assisted by the Vice-Chief of Air Staff, Deputy Chief of the Air Staff, Air Officer In-charge Personnel, Air Officer In-charge Administration, Air Officer In-charge Maintenance and Inspector General (Flight Safety and Inspection). Each of these Principal

Staff Officers is assisted by Assistant Chiefs of the Air Staff.

Today, the Air Force has an array of modern aircraft on its inventory besides other high-tech electronic and support equipment. The aircraft fleet consists of fighter bombers, air superiority fighters, interceptors, transport and logistic aircraft and helicopters. The fighter force comprises MiG-21 variants, MiG-23s, MiG-25s, MiG-27s and *Jaguars* which represent the modern generation strike aircrafts. Older generation aircrafts like the Hunters and *Canberras* are presently used in training and ancillary roles. MiG-29s and Mirage-2000 are air defence aircraft of the present generation. The transport fleet consists of *IL-76s,* AN-32s, the indigenously produced HS-748, Dornier-228 which are manufactured under licence by HAL and *Boeing*-737 are used for VIP duties. While the *IL*-76s provides the Air Force with heavy-lift capabilities, AN-32s and HS-748s are also used in training role besides performing air maintenance and communication duties. The helicopter fleet consists of *Chetak, Cheetah,* MI-8s, MI-17s and the heavy lift MI-26. All these aircraft are used for high-altitude operations and provide logistics support to our ground forces. *Chetak/Cheetah helicopters* manufactured by HAL for the Air Force, are also used in Anti-Tank Guided Missile (ATGM) carriers, airborne Forward Air Controller (FAC) and for search and rescue operations. *MI-8* Helicopters are specially modified to undertake tasks in Antarctica. In addition, the force has been supplemented with *MI*-25 and *MI*-35 attack helicopters. *HPT*-32 and *HJT*-16 (K*iran*) aircraft, both manufactured by HAL, are used as basic and applied-stage trainers respectively, with the Kiran being supplemented by Polish Iskara aircraft. The first batch of women pilots were commissioned on 17 December 1994. Since then women pilots have been serving in frontline Air Force transport and helicopter squadrons. Women officers are also serving in Technical, Administrative, Logistics, Education and Medical branches. The first batch of women Air Traffic Controller and Fighter Controller/DATS was commissioned in May 1996. Thus all branches of the IAF now have women serving.

Commissioned Ranks

The following are the commissioned ranks in the three services; each rank is shown opposite its equivalent in the other service:

Army	Navy	Air Force
General	Admiral	Air Chief Marshal
Lieutenant General	Vice Admiral	Air Marshal
Major General	Rear Admiral	Air Vice Marshal
Brigadier	Commodore	Air Commodore
Colonel	Captain	Group Captain
Lieutenant Colonel	Commander	Wing Commander
Major	Lieutenant Commander	Squadron Leader
Captain	Lieutenant	Flight Lieutenant
Lieutenant	Sub-Lieutenant	Flying Officer

Recruitment

The Armed Forces symbolise the unity of the country and the ideals of national integration. Recruitment to the Armed Forces is open to all Indian nationals, irrespective of caste, creed, community, religion and region. The endeavour has been to provide free and equal opportunities to all sections of the population to join the Armed Forces and render service in accordance with the ideals of secularism, democracy and social justice. India's Armed Forces offer challenging openings to our youth.

A remarkable feature of recruitment to the Armed Forces is that it is entirely voluntary. The competition for entry into the service is intense, reflective of the increasing numbers of educated youth in the country, coupled with the attractive terms and conditions of service, and the high level of respect commanded by the Armed Forces. Recruitment is made from different states/ Union Territories on the basis of their recruitable male population. Conscious efforts are made to take care of the special needs of the border areas and hilly and other remote areas, by lowering educational and certain other criteria to suit their requirements.

Induction of women into the armed forces

While provision has all along existed for women to join the Armed Forces Medical Services, the Armed Forces Dental Services and the Military Nursing Service, Section 12 of the Army Act provided that women would not normally be eligible for enrolment in the Army. Similar provisions also existed in the cases of the Air Force and the Navy. However, in acknowledgement of the changing times, the Government has approved the induction of women into selected noncombatant branches in the three Forces. The entry of women has, however, been restricted to the officer cadres, and they are on Short Service Commission basis. Further continuance of schemes would be decided on the basis of the experience gained. In pursuance of this decision, several women officers have since joined the Service, in the EME, Signals, Engineers, Army Education Corps, Army Ordnance Corps, Army Service Corps and in the Judge Advocate General Department.

The response to this entry was encouraging and the courses were almost fully subscribed. Therefore, the existing planned intake of 50 officers per annum has been increased to 100 per annum. In addition, the Government has also approved grant of antedate seniority to those women officers who possess a technical qualification. Till date, 219 women officers have been commissioned in various Arms/Services.

Recruitment of commissioned officers

Entry into the officer cadres in the Armed. Forces is primarily through the Union Public Service Commission (UPSC). Graduates are eligible to join the Armed Forces through an examination known as the Combined Defence Services Examination (CDSE) conducted by the UPSC twice a year. Candidates who qualify in the examination join the Indian Military Academy (IMA), the Air Force Academy, and the Naval Academy for pre-commission training. Individuals selected for Short Service Commission are trained at the Officers Training Academy.

The candidates seeking a career in the Armed Forces after completion of 10+2 general education join the National Defence Academy (NDA). UPSC holds an entrance examination twice a year for entry in the NDA. Candidates who qualify in this examination join the respective Service Academies, *viz.*, the Indian Military Academy (IMA) for the Army, the Air Force Academy for the Air Force and the Naval Academy for the Navy, for their pre-commission training.

There is also direct entry of officers through the Service Selection Boards (SSBs) for the Army and Navy, and through the Air Force Selection Board for the Air Force, without any written examination by the UPSC. Candidates in the age-group of 20 to 27 years with Engineering Degree and Post-Graduates in specified subjects in the age-group of 23 to 27 years are eligible for interview by the respective Selection Boards of branches of the Armed Forces.

In July 1992, the Government approved a University Entry Scheme, initially for a period of three years, for induction of engineering students in their final year/pre-final year into the Army. This scheme is already operating in the Air Force and the Navy. Engineering students of various disciplines studying in the final/ pre-final years in recognised universities/ institutions are eligible for induction into the technical branches/services of the Army as short-service commissioned officers with the rank of 2nd Lieutenants (now Lieutenants) under this scheme. Their salary, however, is paid in one lump-sum on their joining the IMA for training, on the successful completion of which they will be granted permanent commission in the Army. An intake of 100 officers per year has been planned under this scheme.

In order to mitigate the shortage of Technical Officers (Engineering) in the Army, the Government also approved a Short Service Commission (Tech) Entry scheme. This envisages recruitment of qualified technical graduates through the SSBs and their enrolment in the Officers Training Academy (OTA), Chennai after medical tests for a ten-month course. At the end of the course, the successful candidates will receive Short Service Commission. Thereafter, they will be governed by the Rules applicable to the other short-service commissioned officers.

Recruitment of medical officers in the Armed Forces is done through two sources. All MBBS graduates passing from the Armed Forces Medical College, Pune, are granted Permanent Commission. Apart from this, post graduates/MBBS degree-holders passing from civilian medical colleges are selected through competitive examinations, on an all-India basis, conducted by the Directorate General of Armed Forces Medical College, Pune, partly for grant of Regular Commission and partly for grant of Short Service Commission.

The Government has already approved a scheme of induction of NCC 'C' certificate holders to SSC (NT) stream only, through SSB interview without passing UPSC (CDS) examination. This scheme will help in improving the intake in this entry.

A special Commissioned Officers, entry scheme has been introduced in the Army. Under this entry serving JCOs/NCOs/ORs in the age-group of 30-35 years, with an Army Senior School Certificate Pass (Class XI CBSE pattern) qualification, will be eligible for commission after screening/selection through SSB and a Medical Board. The officers so commissioned will earn promotion up to the rank of Colonel. The officers will be employed in unit as platoon commanders/sub-unit commanders or equivalent/QM job/ERE appointments, etc., up to the rank of Major. They will retire at the age of 55 years, after serving for about 20-25 years as officers, The scheme will not only improve the career prospects of existing JCOs/NCOs/ORs but also help in making up for the deficiency of officers in the Army.

Recruitment of other ranks in Army and in Navy

There are 12 Zonal Recruiting Offices (ZROs) and 58 Branch Recruiting Offices (BROs) spread throughout the country. In addition, there is an Independent Recruiting Office (IRO) at Delhi. In order to inform the potential candidates of the commencement of recruitment well in advance, extensive recruitment publicity is undertaken throughout the country, including in remote areas.

Recruitment rules provide for relaxation in respect of educational and physical standards to the candidates from certain specified backward, remote and tribal regions to give them due representation in the Army. Special physical standards for certain classes/regiments/tribes and categories have been laid down. Besides, relaxation in physical qualifications is being provided to certain categories of candidates like those between 16 to 18 years of age-group, national/state-level sportsmen and one son in the case of every serving soldier, ex-serviceman and war widow.

Airmen

Recruitment of Airmen to the Indian Air Force is done through the Central Airmen Selection Board located at the Air Force Station, New Delhi. There are 13 Selection Centres under this Board and they make the necessary arrangements for the conduct of selection tests and the final enrolment. A Pilot Project has been undertaken for the direct recruitment of trained manpower from, the civil stream in the trades, such as clerks, drivers, and Surveyor Automated Cartography. Besides direct recruitment of technically qualified civilian personnel as JCO (catering) has been introduced.

Territorial army

The Territorial Army is a voluntary part-time civilian force which plays a useful role in the defence of the country. It was raised in 1949 and since its inception, has rendered valuable service to the nation. The territorial army consists of departmental and non-departmental TA units, The departmental TA units are raised from amongst the employees of Government departments and public-sector undertakings. There are at present 27 departmental and 25 non-departmental TA units. The five ecological battalions are also part of the departmental TA units.

As a result of internal disturbances and terrorist activities in Punjab, Jammu and Kashmir and other states and the prevailing conditions along our northern, eastern and western borders, the TA has of late been called upon to play an active role in assisting the local Army formations in these areas. As a result of these demands, all the 25 infantry battalions (TA) have been embodied since 1990-91, for varying periods.

The five ecological battalions of TA (called Eco Task Forces) have continued their excellent work of environmental upgradation of the degraded areas in

Rajasthan, Madhya Pradesh, Uttar Pradesh and Jammu and Kashmir. In consultation with the Ministry of Environment and Forests several steps aimed at reducing the cost of these Eco Task Forces, without actually lowering their output or efficiency, have been taken up. A proposal to reorganise 16 infantry battalions (TA) initiated by the TA Directorate, has been approved by the Ministry of Defence.

National cadet corps

The National Cadet Corps (NCC) established on 15 July 1948 has emerged as the single largest structured youth movement in India. It has 11.6 lakh boys and girls in the Senior and junior Divisions in the Army, Navy and Air Force Wings. This strength covers four per cent of the eligible student population in the country. Director General, NCC located at New Delhi controls and oversees various activities of the NCC through 16 NCC Directorates spread across the country. There is a Central Advisory Committee for the NCC to provide overall policy guidelines. NCC is manned by the service personnel, whole time NCC officers, teachers /professors and civilians. One lecturer/teacher in each educational institution is appointed Associate NCC officer.

The NCC whose motto is 'Unity and Discipline' has the following aims: (a) To develop qualities of character, courage, comradeship, leadership, secular outlook, spirit of adventure and sportsmanship and the ideal of selfless service among the youth to make them useful citizens; (b) To create a human resource of organised, trained and motivated youth to provide leadership in all walks of life including the Armed Forces and to be always available for the service of the nation.

During 1997-98, 17 Centrally organised camps were held. Forty National Integration Camps were conducted across the country in which nearly 49,885 cadets participated. A total of 4,99,677 cadets attended Annual Training Camps during 1997. The NCC has an ongoing youth exchange programme with Canada, Singapore, U.K., Bangladesh and Sri Lanka. A team of three officers and 24 cadets (12 boys and 12 girls) went to Canada; eight NCC cadets (four boys and four girls) visited United Kingdom; one officer and four NCC cadets (two girls and two boys) to Air Wing attended the NCC Air Wing Programme at Singapore; one officer and two cadets (one boy and one girl) visited Australia for the first time to attend the youth exchange programme and one officer and four NCC cadets (two boys and two girls) participated in the Naval programme of Singapore and a team of two NCC cadets (one boy and one girl) went to Sri Lanka.

Training Institutions

Sainik schools

The scheme to establish Sainik Schools was started in 1961 to broadbase the recruitment to the officers cadre of the Defence Forces. Sainik Schools are joint venture of the Central and state governments. At present 18 Sainik Schools, one each in all major states are managed by the Sainik Schools Society. Boys from a state which does not have a Sainik School of its own are admitted to schools located in adjoining states. Sainik Schools are fully residential and admit students in classes VI and IX strictly in order of merit obtained in the All India Sainik School Entrance Examination held in February each year. These schools are affiliated to the Central Board of Secondary Education and follow the 10+2 pattern, in science stream.

The pass percentage of Sainik School students in the class X and XII CBSE examinations during the academic session 1996-97 was 98.6 per cent and 86.7 per cent respectively. Students from 110 Sainik Schools joined the

NDA in 1997. So far 4,901 students from the Sainik Schools have joined the NDA. The tuition fee has been raised to Rs. 14,000 per annum from academic session 1997-98.

National defence academy

The National Defence Academy (NDA), Khadakwasla, is a joint services institution for training young cadets as future officers of the Defence Services. The motto of the Academy is *Sewa Paramo Dharma* (Service Before Self). As part of their training, cadets are provided academic inputs. The syllabus of the Academy has been approved by the Jawaharlal Nehru University for the grant of BA/ B.Sc. degree at the time of passing from the Academy, As on date, the strength of cadets is 1,870. This includes 71 cadets from Bhutan.

Indian military academy

The Indian Military Academy (IMA), Dehradun, established in 1932 caters to the training of cadets for commission into the Army. The training enables the Gentlemen Cadets to develop intellectual, moral and physical qualities through basic military training and broad academic education; qualities of dynamism, initiative and understanding which form the very basis of leadership, in war as well as in peace. The motto of the Academy is *Veerta Aur Vivek* (Valour and Wisdom). The present strength of the IMA is 1,207 Gentlemen Cadets which includes 23 Gentlemen Cadets from friendly countries. Army Cadet College is a wing of IMA which caters to training of service cadets selected for commission. The academic format is similar to the NDA on the lines of 10+2+3 and the syllabus is common. On completion of the course these cadets also qualify for a BA/B.Sc degree, recognised by the Jawaharlal Nehru University.

Officer's training academy

The Officers' Training Academy, (OTA) Chennai, imparts pre-commission training for the following courses: (a) Short Service Commission Course of 44-weeks for university graduates who qualify in the Union Public Service Commission; (b) course of six months for lady cadets (Women Special Entry Scheme); and (c) Permanent Commission on Special List (PCSL) to selected service candidates, who qualify after a training of four weeks. Authorised training strength of the Academy is 500. So far 297 lady cadets have been granted Short Service Commission.

Rashtriya Indian military college

Education on public-school lines is imparted at the Rashtriya Indian Military College, Dehradun, principally for the boys who subsequently desire to join the NDA with a view to obtaining a commission in the Armed Forces. The College admits students in class VIII through a written examination-cum-*viva voce* test conducted under the aegis of the state governments throughout India twice every year in February and August. The college has the distinction of having had on its rolls three Chiefs of Army Staff and a Chief of Air Staff.

National defence college

The National Defence College (NDC) was founded in 1960 to prepare senior Defence and Civil Service officers for a comprehensive understanding of major problems of national security and strategy. The aim of the NDC course is to equip future planning of national strategy in the context of world polity. Commandant NDC and Senior Directing Staff (Foreign Services) participated in the Asia Regional Forum (ARF) Meeting of the heads of National Defence Colleges /Institutions held in Manila in September 1997. The Prime Minister addressed the participants of 37th NDC Course on 'India's Role in a Changing World'.

Army cadet college

Army Cadet College is a wing of IMA which caters to the training of service cadets selected for commission. The academic format is similar to the NDA on the lines of 10+2+3, and the syllabus is common. On completion of the course these cadets also qualify for a BA/B.Sc. degree recognised by the Jawaharlal Nehru University.

Army school of physical training

Army School of Physical Training (ASPT), Pune, established in 1947 is the cradle of physical and recreational training in the Army. It has training infrastructure to impart systematic and comprehensive instructions on physical training. Selected candidates from all ranks of the Army, students from the police, paramilitary forces and friendly foreign countries attend various courses on physical training and allied subjects at ASPT.

Other training centres and schools

The College of Combat, Mhow, conducts the higher command, senior command and junior command courses for Army Officers. It also conducts a Combined Operational Review and Evaluation (CORE) programme for selected senior officers of the rank of Major General and equivalent of the three Services once every year. College of Military Engineering, Kirkee (Pune), imparts training to the officers and other ranks in all aspects of military engineering. Long courses of over two years, duration are also conducted to train officers up to degree standards. The Military College of Telecommunication Engineering, Mhow imparts basic and advanced technical training in telecommunications and signal tactics. The Armoured Corps Centre and School, Ahmednagar, conducts training in tactical handling of armoured fighting vehicles, driving and maintenance. The School of Artillery, Deolali, provides training in field branch artillery. The Air Defence Guided Missiles School at Gopalpur-on-sea trains personnel of the Air Defence Artillery. The High Altitude Warfare School located at Gulmarg and Sonmarg trains personnel in the art of mountain warfare including rock, snow and ice-craft. The Counter Insurgency and General Warfare School, Vairengate, trains officers and men in the art of combating insurgency.

The Mechanised Infantry Regimental Centre conducts basic and technical training for recruits of mechanised infantry. In addition, it runs basic and instructor courses on anti-tank guided missiles for officers, JCOs and other ranks of mechanised infantry. It also carries out conversion training of units when they are converted to mechanised infantry or when change in equipment is involved. The College of Materials Management, Jabalpur, imparts specialised training in materials management including ammunition and explosives and also in contemporary materials management techniques. Some of the other Army training centres and schools are Army Service Corps School, Bareilly; EME School, Vadodara; Military College of Electronics and Mechanical Engineering, Secunderabad; College of Defence Management, Secunderabad; Remount and Veterinary Corps Centre and School, Meerut; Army Education Corps Training College and Centre, Pachmari; Army School of Physical Training, Pune; Army/Air Transport School, Agra; Military Intelligence Training School and Depot, Pune; Army School of Mechanical Transport, Bangalore; Corps of Military Police Centre and School, Bangalore; Institute of Military Law, Kamptee; Armed Forces Medical College, Pune; Institute of National Integration, Pune and Army Medical Corps Centre and School, Lucknow.

Production and Supplies

Department of Defence Production and Department of Defence Supplies were merged in December 1984 to constitute the present Department of Defence Production and Supplies. The primary role of the Department is to equip the armed forces of the country with the latest equipment and weaponry systems and to contribute to modernisation of armed forces. This task is being undertaken through 39 ordnance factories and 8 defence public-sector undertakings.

Ordnance factories

The Ordnance Factory Organisation is the largest departmental undertaking engaged primarily in the production of defence hardware for the armed forces and paramilitary/police. At present 39 ordnance factories with a manpower of 1.48 lakh ' spread all over India operate a wide range of discipline and technologies and supply critical lethal as well as non-lethal stores to defence forces. Some of the important products are field guns, anti-aircraft guns, mortars, various small arms and ammunition for weapons and guns, rockets, projectiles, pyro-technics, bombs, grenades, mines, demolition charges, depth charges, infantry combat vehicles, battle tanks, transport trucks and patrol vehicles, high-altitude and combat clothing, optical and fire control instruments, engineering equipment, supply dropping equipment including parachutes, rubberised items, various knitted and woollen items like blankets, web equipment and a wide range of general stores. The OFB's bulk production today is 54.56 mm Indian small armed system.

Besides meeting the requirement of the army, OFB produces a range of products for the Air Force and Navy including Air-dropped bombs for Air Force. Liquid Fuel required for successful flight trials of *Prithvi* and *Agni* missiles, igniters and copper liners for the warheads are also supplied during development/production of Prithvi missile.

The production of Ajeya tank (T-72) and Sarath (BMP-II), Infantry combat vehicles are carried out at Heavy Vehicle Factory, Avadi and Ordnance Factory, Medak, respectively. A sophisticated opto-electronic production unit has been set up at Dehradun to produce the opto-electronic fire control and night vision devices required for Ajeya tank (T-72-MI) and Sarath vehicle (BMP-II).

Productionisation of Main Battle Tank (MBT) *Arjun*, which has now been accepted by the Army is also being taken up. To meet the Army's requirement of high calibre ammunition, a new Ordnance Factory is being set up in Bolangir District of Orissa. The state-of-the-art plants are expected to be commissioned in the current year.

As part of diversification efforts, Vehicles Factory, Jabalpur (VFJ), has taken up modification and upgradation of the *Jonga* to cater to the civilian market, besides introduction of new generation transport vehicles for armed forces under technology collaboration.

Defence undertakings

The Defence Public Sector Undertakings (DPSUs) were structured with a flexible form of operation, decentralised management and adequate operational autonomy so as to utilise the defence technological base to a wide and diversified range of applications, in addition to the basic task of catering to the needs of the armed forces.

Eight public-sector undertakings (PSUs) currently function under the Department of Defence Production and Supplies. These are Hindustan Aeronautics Limited (HAL), Bharat Electronics Limited (BEL), Bharat Earth Movers Limited (BEML), Mazgaon Dock Limited (MDL), Garden Reach Ship-builders and Engineers Limited (GRSE), Goa Shipyard Limited (GSL), Bharat Dynamics

Limited (BDL) and Mishra Dhatu Nigam Limited (MIDHANI). The value of production of the Defence PSUs during 1997-98 has been of the order of Rs 6,327 crore as against Rs 5,599 crore in 1996-97. The average value of sales by these PSUs during the last 5 years is Rs 5,017.8 crore.

Hindustan Aeronautics Limited (HAL) was set up in 1964 with its corporate office at Bangalore. The company has 13 divisions located in six states. The principal functions of the company are to design, manufacture, repair and overhaul various types of aircraft helicopters and related aero-engines, avionics, instruments and accessories. HAL is currently manufacturing *Jaguar, Dornier*-228 and MiG-27M aircraft, *Cheetah* and *Chetak helicopters* and various types of aero-engines. HAL is also engaged in the design and development of an Advanced Light Helicopter (ALH). All divisions of HAL have obtained the ISO 9001/9000 certificate by the International Accreditation and Quality Agencies.

The Bharat Electronics Limited (BEL) was established in 1954. It is the country's premier electronics organisation, having nine manufacturing units located at Bangalore, Chennai, Hyderabad, Machilipatnam, Pune, Taloja, Panchkula, Ghaziabad and Kotdwara. Its corporate office is at Bangalore. BEL is engaged in the design, development and manufacture of sophisticated state-of-the-art electronic equipments for the use of defence services and paramilitary organisations. Other users are All India Radio, Doordarshan, Department of Telecommunications, Police, Meteorological Department, etc. It has a very wide range of over 350 products, comprising communication equipment, radars for military and civil use, optical and opto-electronic equipments, sound and vision broadcasting equipment and electronic components. All the manufacturing divisions of BEL are equipped with the most advanced test and measurement and quality-control facilities for NIL grade /International civilian standards. ISO 9002 accreditation has been achieved by almost all the manufacturing units of BEL.

Bharat Earth Movers Limited (BEML) was incorporated as a DPSU in May 1964 and commenced its operations in January 1965. It has three modern production units at Bangalore, Kolar Gold Fields and Mysore. Besides, a subsidiary unit, Vigyan Industries Limited (VIL) in Tarikere (Karnataka), has been established by taking over an existing venture of the state government. Its corporate office is at Bangalore. The company is presently engaged in the design, development and manufacture of a wide range of sophisticated equipments and systems, particularly earth-moving machines, rail coaches, track-laying equipments, heavy-duty trucks, trailers, diesel engines, etc. BEML is a leader in the earth-moving industry with over 70 per cent market share. Its equipments and systems are productively deployed in India and over 30 other countries across the globe. The company has acquired ISO 9000 certificate.

Mazagon Dock. Limited (MDL) is the country's leading shipbuilding yard and can build warships up to 6,000 DWT displacement and merchant ships up to 27,000 DWT. It has units at Bombay, Nhava and Mangalore and headquarters at Bombay. Its major activities include construction of submarines, missile-boats and destroyers, etc., for the Indian Navy and off-shore-supply vessels and well-head platforms, etc., for the Oil and Natural Gas Commission (ONGC). The company also provides diving services as well as services for coating/laying sub-sea pipes.

Garden Reach Shipbuilders and Engineers Limited (GRSE) was established in 1884 as a small ship-repair workshop. It was taken over by the Government of India in the early 1960. It is a multi-unit shipyard-cum-general engineering company. It has six units in and around Calcutta and a Diesel Engine Plant at Ranchi (Bihar). Its corporate office is at Calcutta. It has three distinct divisions, namely, ship, engineering and engine divisions. It is presently engaged in the construction of warships and auxiliary vessels of various types for the Navy and Coast Guard to undertake repair of vessels of these two organisations.

The activities of Goa Shipyards Limited (GSL) located at Vasco da Gama, primarily comprise construction and repair/refit of ships/vessels. It has undertaken construction/refit of variety of vessels for the Indian Navy and the Coast Guard as well as for the non-defence sector. It is currently building advanced off-shore patrol vessels of in-house design.

Bharat Dynamics Limited (BDL), Hyderabad, was established in 1970 to manufacture guided missiles. It has two units at Kanchanbagh and Bhanoor. It is also the prime production agency for missile weaponry systems. The company utilising the spare capacity available has diversified into small arms production to meet the requirement of paramilitary forces of the country.

Mishra Datu Nigam Limited (MIDHANI) located at Hyderabad was incorporated in 1973. MIDHANI's product range includes super alloys, maraging steels, heat-resistance alloys, controlled expansion alloys, tungsten, molybdenum, etc., in a variety of all mill forms to serve the strategic needs of the country including, defence, atomic energy, spare aeronautics with a view to attaining self-reliance in this sophisticated field. The company has obtained ISO 9002 certificate for the entire plant.

Research and Development

The Defence Research and Development Organisation (DRDO) was established in 1958 by amalgamating Defence Science Organisation and some of the Technical Development Establishments. A separate Department of Defence Research and Development was formed in 1980 which operates through a network of 50 laboratories/ establishments. The department is engaged in the pursuit of self-reliance in critical technologies of relevance to national security. It formulates and executes programmes of scientific research, design and development leading to induction of state-of-the-art weapons, platforms and other equipments required by the Armed Forces. It functions under the control of Scientific Adviser to Defence Minister who is also Secretary, Defence Research and Development.

The major achievements towards indigenous development of defence weapons and systems are: (a) development leading to production of surface-to-surface missile, Prithvi; (b) state-of-the-art main battle tank, *Arjun;* (c) flight simulators for aircraft; (d) pilotless target aircraft, *Lakshya;* (e) parallel super-computer pace plus; and (f) small arms and ammunition.

The DRDO has acquired world class core competence in the area of Guided Missiles, Super Computer, UAV, armaments and ammunition including illuminating ammunition, night vision devices, secured communication, military bridging systems and fire detection and suppression systems. India is now self-reliant in armours, armaments, super computers and missile systems. The DRDO has launched a 10-year national mission for enhancing self-reliance in Defence Systems with the goal of increasing the indigenous content in the annual defence acquisition from the level of 30 per cent in the year 1995 to 70 per cent by the year

2005. It has also accorded high priority for development of systems in critical areas of technologies which have been denied by advance countries or which are likely to be denied in the future. The weapons and ammunition developed by the Organisation and produced by production agencies include Indian field gun, INSAS rifle, LMG 5.56 mm, charge line mine-clearing for safe passage of vehicles in the battlefield, illuminating ammunition for enhancing night field-fighting capability, cluster weapon system for fighter aircraft, new generation bombs for high-speed aircraft, naval mines and 105 mm FSAPDS, 105 mm and 125 mm. FSAPDS ammunition. Multibarrel rocket system *Pinaka* is undergoing user trial. In the area of Electronics and Instrumentation, the significant developments are low-level tracking radar *Indra* I, Indra II for Army and Air Force, light-weight field artillery radar, battlefield surveillance radar, secondary surveillance radar, avalanche victim detector, tidex, EW systems, night vision devices and secured telephone SECTEL. Installation and commissioning of facilities and equipment for fabrication of Galleum Arsenide Wafers at GAETEC and artillery combat command and control systems. Some of the development successes in the area of engineering systems are bridge layer tank *Kartik*, military bridging systems, various types of shelters, crash fire-tenders, rapid intervention vehicle and state-of-the-art fire-detection and suppression system for tanks, naval ships, missile launchers and barbette areas.

In the area of naval systems and materials the organisation has developed an advanced ship sonar system, the marine accoustic research ship *Sagardhwani*, underwater anti-fouling paints, torpedoes, naval simulators and jackal steels. The submarine sonar and weapon control system *Panchendriya is* getting ready for harbour/sea trials. The indigenous light combat aircraft (LCA) is getting ready for maiden flight trials by 1998.

The advanced technology aero engine *Kaveri* of LCA is undergoing multi test-bed trials. The Kaveri engine has been successfully tested for about 500 hours on multiple test beds. The remotely-piloted vehicle Falcon has successfully undergone 25 developmental flight trials and is getting ready for user trials. The Integrated Guided Missile Development Programme (IGMDP) comprises four missile systems, Prithvi, surface-to-surface tactical battle field missile; *Akash,* medium-range surface-to-air missile; *Trishul,* short-range surface-to-air missile; and Nag, third-generation anti-tank-missile. *Trishul is* getting ready for user trials. *Akash and* Nag are in advanced stages of development. The programme also included successful development of re-entry technology demonstrator under project Agni.

The Department has developed preserved and convenience foods for the Armed Forces. State-of-the-art technologies developed for missile programme LCA and other high technology systems are being channelised to make available to the common man bio-medical equipment at a fraction of the prevailing price of imported systems. A society of bio-medical technology has been formed for this purpose. Extra light-weight floor reaction orthosis (FROs) for polio-handicapped persons, cardiac stress analyser, cardiac pacemaker and cytoscan for early detection of cancer cells have been developed and the technology has been transferred to industry.

In addition to the above, the Department has been rendering many services to the Armed Forces.

Resettlement and Welfare of Ex-Servicemen

In order to maintain the youthful profile of the Armed Forces, over 55,000 service personnel are retired /released every year at a comparatively young age. As per statistics a total of 13.55 lakh ex-servicemen and 2.43 lakh widows have been registered with them and were reported to be surviving as on 31 December 1996. The Directorate General of Resettlement (DGR) under the Ministry of Defence (MOD) has been set up to look after all matters connected with resettlement and welfare of ex-servicemen and their dependents. A Kendriya Sainik Board under the Chairmanship of Defence Minister has been established for laying down the general policy for the welfare of ex-servicemen and their dependents for the administration of Welfare Funds, and also for coordinating the work of the Sainik Boards in the country. At the state level, the Rajya Sainik Boards, and at the District level the Zila Sainik Boards, have been established. The Government of India bears 50 per cent of the expenditure incurred on the organisations of Rajya and Zila Sainik Boards, the remaining expenditure being borne by the respective state governments.

Resettlement

Resettlement activities for the retired /retiring service personnel consist of the following: (a) Training programmes to reorient retiring Defence personnel towards civil employment; (b) Providing re-employment opportunities in Government/ semi-Government/public sector organisations; and (c) Schemes for self-employment.

Training

For retiring service officers the following training programmes were introduced during the year 1996-97: (a) Diploma in Industrial Security and Labour Laws; (b) Coaching for Airline Transport Pilot Licence/Senior Commercial Pilot Licence/ Commercial Helicopter Pilot Licence; (c) Consultant in ISO-9000; (d) Quality Assurance Manager ISO-9000; (e) Deputy Quality Assurance Manager ISO-9000; (0 Consultancy as a career; (g) Equity and Portfolio Management; (h) LAN Engineering; and (j) POXPRO Oracle. During the training year 1996-97, 1,145 officers were trained. The vocational training, ITI training and on-the-job training are presently being conducted for retiring Service personnel other than officers.

Re-employment

Re-employment constitutes a major means of rehabilitation or resettlement of ex-servicemen. To achieve this goal both the Central and state governments have provided various concessions/ facilities. These include reservation of posts, relaxations in age/ educational standards, priority in employment, etc. The Central Government has reserved 10 per cent of Group 'C' and 20 per cent of Group 'D' posts for ex-servicemen in Central ministries and departments. The percentage of reservation in public-sector undertakings and nationalised banks in these categories are 14.5 and 24.5 per cent respectively. Besides, there is 10 per cent reservation for the post of Assistant Commandant in paramilitary Forces. Reservations under the state governments vary from two per cent to 20 per cent. There is no reservation for ex-servicemen in Bihar, Kerala and Meghalaya.

DGR has been nominating ex-servicemen security agencies to various PSUs and private-sector organisations. These security agencies provide employment opportunities for officers and other ranks. There are over 300 ex-servicemen security agencies which are registered with DRG, of which 130 have been sponsored for work. This alone has generated employment opportunities for over 7,000 ex-servicemen and over 400 officers. There is considerable scope for absorption of ex-servicemen in paramilitary forces like CRPF, BSF, ITBP, CISF.

The concept of Ecological Task Force was mooted in 1992 for the purpose of restoring the forest cover in regions where significant deforestation had taken place. These units were initially raised in three states, namely,

Uttar Pradesh, Rajasthan and Jammu and Kashmir. The task forces are manned by ex-servicemen who are paid salaries as per Territorial Army scales. Every individual, irrespective of his rank prior to retirement, is re-employed as a sepoy. The Ministry of Defence provides officers to command these units.

Schemes for Self-employment

Important schemes for self-employment for ex-servicemen are SEMFEX-I, SEMFEX-II and SEMFEX-III. These schemes have been launched in collaboration with the Small Industries Development Bank of India, NABARD and the Khadi and Village Industries Commission for providing extensive self-employment opportunities for ex-servicemen and their dependents.

Under SEMFEX-I Scheme launched in April 1987 financial assistance is provided to ex-servicemen to set up small industrial projects for self-employment. Loans under this Scheme are provided by the respective State Financial Corporation. As on 31 December 1996 there were 6,697 beneficiaries and the amount sanctioned was to the tune of Rs 179.48 crore since inception.

The SEMFEX-II Scheme was launched in January 1988 by the DGR in collaboration with the National Bank for Agricultural and Rural Development (NABARD) to provide assistance for agricultural and allied activities. Under the Scheme, financial assistance up to Rs 10 lakh for setting up of industrial units/service establishments is given. The ceiling of Rs 10 lakh is, however, not applicable for setting up of units relating to agro-industries and non-agro industries and they can be supported up to SSI limit under non-farm sector activities. However, all agro and food processing units including processing of forest produce will be assisted without any ceiling on the project cost. Eligible borrowers may also be financed for acquisition of a maximum of two transport vehicles. Interest-free soft loan assistance for all schemes under non-farm sector as also the innovative hi-tech projects, export-oriented units and agro-processing projects are covered under the farm sector. Since inception and up to December 1996 loans amounting to Rs 2,057.82 crone have been sanctioned to 3,550 beneficiaries.

The SEMFEX-III Scheme was launched in October 1991 in collaboration with the Khadi and Village Industries Commission (KVIC) but was implemented from 1992-93. It provides self-employment opportunities for setting up village industries in the purview of KVIC. Under this Scheme, ex-servicemen and their widows are eligible to take up self-employment ventures. Financial assistance for such ventures is provided under a liberalised pattern of assistance by the KVIC. Margin money requirement is only five per cent of the project cost. The project proposals up to Rs. 25 lakh will be financed under the scheme. Grant up to 30 per cent will be provided for the project cost up to Rs 10 lakh and 10 per cent for the remaining cost of the project. The KVIC has earmarked 10 per cent of the states allocated budget under the Scheme. The loan granted to village industries under this Scheme carries an annual rate of interest of 17 per cent and 4 per cent on loan for Khadi units. The Scheme is picking up. Up to December 1996, a loan of Rs 295.33 lakh was sanctioned to 467 beneficiaries.

Welfare

Kendriya Sainik Board (KSB) is responsible for progress in the various welfare benefits and concessions provided, by Central and state governments to ex-servicemen, war widows, disabled ex-servicemen and dependents. The undermentioned concessions and facilities are available to eligible personnel: (i) Re-possession of land/house owned by ex-Servicemen which they had rented out during their service career; (ii) Children of Defence personnel killed or disabled in action or disabled, who are studying in educational institutions under the Department of Education of both Central and state governments, are entitled to total exemption from tuition fee and other fees levied by the institutions. Grants are provided to meet hostel charges towards cost of books, stationery and uniform where it is compulsory; (iii) 25 seats in the MBBS, one seat in BDS and two seats in Engineering are available through KSB for wives/widows and wards of those servicemen killed in action, disabled in action and boarded out from service, died while in service with death attributable to Military service, died while in service and boarded out with disability, attributable to service and Gallantry Award winners; (iv) 25 per cent seats are reserved for the wards of serving and ex-service personnel in Sainik Schools; (v) States/UTs have made reservation of seats in professional colleges /ITI / Polytechnics for wards of serving and retired Defence personnel; (vi) A grant of Rs 600 p.m. per student is provided to wards of war-bereaved, disabled and attributable peacetime casualties housed in 35 War Memorial Hostels, to enable them to pursue their studies; (vii) Ex-servicemen, their families and families of deceased service personnel drawing pension of any kind are entitled to free out-patient treatment in Military hospitals subject to certain conditions. In addition to the existing Military Hospitals, 24 MI Rooms and 12 Dental Centres have been specially created from the funds provided by the Services and KSB for providing medical facilities to ex-servicemen pensioners and their dependents. Ex-servicemen suffering form serious diseases are provided 60 per cent reimbursement of the total expenditure for treatment in Civil Hospitals in case they have not been provided assistance from other sources. Assistance for Dialysis is restricted to Rs 75,000 only; (viii) 75 per cent concession in rail fare for travel in 11 Class is available to war-widows including those of IPKF casualties, on production of I Card issued by KSB. In addition, Government of India has announced free travel for recipients of Gallantry Award *(Chakra* Series only) in First Class/II AC throughout the country. The passes are issued by the office of the divisional Railway Manager. 50 per cent concession in fare for air travel in domestic Rights of the Indian Airlines, is available to the recipients of *Param Vir Chakra, Maha Vir Chakra, Ashok Chakra and Kirti Chakra* and permanently disabled officers who have been invalidated out of service, and dependent members of their families; (ix) Financial assistance form *Raksha Mantri's* Discretionary Fund (RMDF) is provided to ex-servicemen and widows of ex-servicemen in penury, for marriage of daughters, education of children, repair of house and medical assistance; (x) The majority of States have made reservations for serving/retired Armed forces personnel in allotment of house sites/ houses; (xi) Financial assistance is provided to war-widows/war-disabled for repair of houses on 50 per cent cost sharing basis with state governments up to a maximum of Rs 10,000; (xii) Over 252 Sainik Rest-Houses have been created in the country which provide transit facilities to ex-servicemen and dependents at nominal rates; and (xiii) The states/UTs provide Cash Award / Annuity/Cash in lieu of land for Gallantry/Non-Gallantry Award Winners.

Armed forces flag day fund

Before April 1993 there were four separate funds, namely, Amalgamated Special Fund for War-Bereaved, War-Disabled and other ex-Servicemen /serving personnel; (ii) Flag Day Fund; (iii) St. Dunstan's (India) and KSB Fund; and (iv) Indian Gorkha Ex-servicemen's Welfare Fund. These separate funds have been merged into an Armed Forces Flag Day Fund.

A number of welfare schemes are funded from the Armed Forces Flag Day Fund administered by the Kendriya Sainik Board. The fund has a corpus of Rs 54.73 crore as on 31 March 1997, and the interest earned on the investment of the corpus is utilised for various welfare activities/schemes approved by the Managing Committee of the Fund. Financial assistance is also provided to institutions such as Military Hospitals, Paraplegic Homes at Kirkee and Mohali, Red Cross Society, Cheshire Homes, St. Dunstans After Care Organisation (for the blind).

Concessions to ex-servicemen

The concessions provided to the ex-servicemen *inter alia* include: (a) Free education for children of Armed Forces personnel killed or disabled in action; (b) Reservation of 25 seats in MBBS and one seat in BDS to the wards of ex-servicemen killed in action, disabled and boarded out, died in service, where death is attributable to military service etc.; (d) Reservation of seats in professional colleges by various states/Uts for wards of serving and retired Armed Forces personnel; (e) Grant of Rs 400 pm to wards of war-bereaved, housed in 35 War Memorial Hostels; and (f) Financial assistance from RM's discretionary funds to old and infirm ex-servicemen and their widows in indigent circumstances. In addition, the ex-servicemen have also been extended the following facilities : (i) Ministry of Railways has issued instructions to the GMs of all Indian Railways for allowing the benefit of two complimentary passes in 2nd AC/1st Class to the Service Personnel/ex-Servicemen who have won gallantry awards like *Param Vir Chakra, Maha Vir Chakra* and *Vir Chakra; (ii)* Ex-servicemen are entitled for free medical treatment from the Military Hospitals. If not treated from the Military hospitals they are granted financial assistance equal to 60 per cent of total expenditure for treatment of serious diseases. Funds have also been provided for procurement of the Intraocular lenses for ex-Servicemen; (iii) The ex-servicemen and their families are entitled to the CSD (1) canteen facilities available in Units/ Establishments; (iv) *Saini Bhawans*/ Rest-Houses have been provided in selected centres for the stay of the ex-servicemen who visit these places in connection with settlement of their problems; and (v) The Indira Awaas Yojana has been extended to the families of servicemen and paramilitary forces killed in action irrespective of the income criteria subject to the condition that; (a) they reside in rural areas, (b) they have not been covered under any other shelter rehabilitation scheme; and (c) they are houseless or in need of shelter or shelter upgradation. Other ex-servicemen are also given priority provided they fulfil the normal eligibility conditions of the Indira Awaas Yojana and have not been covered under any other shelter rehabilitation scheme.

Ex-Servicemen need to be rehabilitated in civil life after their release from the Services on account of their truncated career in the Armed Forces. About 60,000 service personnel are retired/ released each year Majority of ex-Servicemen prefer to settle down near their home towns after their release from the Services. Accordingly, resettlement and welfare of ex-Servicemen has been accepted as a joint responsibility of the Central as well as State Governments. Both the Central and State Governments have introduced a number of schemes for welfare of ex-Servicemen, and to provide them rehabilitation through re-employment in the organised sector or through self-employment. The benefits extended to Ex-Servicemen and their dependants vary from state to state.

At the Centre, the Ex-Servicemen Welfare Wing of the Ministry of Defence is responsible for the formulation of the policy guidelines and schemes for resettlement of ex-Servicemen. The Director General of Resettlement (DGR), under the Ministry of Defence (MOD) is the nodal agency for overseeing execution and proper implementation of the central schemes for ex-Servicemen. DGR is also responsible for liaison with the State/UT Governments. In the States and Union Territories, the Departments of Sainik Welfare at the state level and Zila Sainik Welfare offices at the district level are functioning to attend to the problems of ex-Servicemen and to execute the rehabilitation and welfare schemes at the state and district levels respectively.

Ex-Servicemen Population

A total of 14,53,013 ex-Servicemen and 2,74,632 widows of the Service personnel were registered with various Zila Sainik Boards in the country as on June 30, 1998. The ex-Servicemen population is mainly concentrated in the states of Uttar Pradesh (2,53,644), Punjab (1,80,539), Haryana (1,46,155), Maharashtra (1,30,397), Kerala (1,21,965), Tamil Nadu (99,746), Rajasthan (94,460) and Himachal Pradesh (73,981).

Resettlement

The efforts are constantly on to explore various avenues for employment of Ex-Servicemen. The Central Government is providing the following avenues for resettlement/ re-employment of Ex-Servicemen:-

(a) Training programmes to re-orient retiring defence personnel towards civil employment;

(b) Reservation of posts for providing re-employment opportunities in Government/Semi-Government/ Public Sector organisations;

(c) Schemes for self-employment.

Training Programmes

Training for preparing both ex-Servicemen and retiring Service personnel for their resettlement in civil life is one of the major functions of the Directorate General of Resettlement. Emphasis has been on employment/ self-employment oriented training programmes so that new resettlement avenues, both for officers and other ranks, are opened. A number of new courses and job-oriented training programmes have been included in the training schedule. Training includes inputs on managerial science as well as technology and know-how required in the civil field. Constant endeavour is made to improve the quality of training to enhance the post-employment opportunities of defence personnel and to equip them with necessary qualifications and expertise commensurate with the skill and aptitude of each individual in the desired field of settlement in civil life.

Officers Training

During the training year 1998-99, (until October 1998) 393 officers have been trained in various disciplines. The resettlement training programmes range from vocational courses of 3 months duration to degree/diploma courses in Business Administration, Personnel Management, Hotel Management and Tourism, Human Resource Training and Development etc. of one to three years duration.

JCOs/OR and Requirements Training

Training programmes were also undertaken for the retiring as well as retired JCOs/OR and their equivalent from the three Services. These programmes included vocational courses like Security Management, Export/ Import Management, Marketing/Sales Management and Tourism & Travel Agency Management. In an endeavour to further increase their employment potential, courses like Computer Hardware Maintenance, Diploma in Medical Laboratory and X-Ray/ECG Technology, Ceramic Handicrafts, Electroplating, Machinist and Lens Making, Computer Science & Applications, Office Automation,

Computer-Aided Designing (CAD), Printing Technology and Desk Top Publishing (DTP), Bee-keeping, Poultry Farming, Crop Production, Dairy and Animal Husbandry, Assistant Security Officer, Industrial Security and Fire Fighting courses etc. are being conducted. The Directorate General Resettlement (DGR) has been conducting more than 400 courses for vocational training, besides courses at more than 200 ITIs for pre-and-post release training and On-the-Job-Training (OJT) courses at 85 PSUs / Departmental Undertakings as well as ex-Servicemen resettlement training schemes.

Re-Employment

The Central and State Governments provide a number of concessions to ex-Servicemen for their re-employment in Central/State Government posts. These include reservation of posts/ relaxation in age and educational qualifications, exemption from payment of application/ examination fees, priority employment to disabled Ex-Servicemen and dependants of deceased service personnel on compassionate grounds.

Reservation for Ex-Servicemen in Government Jobs

The Central Government has reserved 10% of Group 'C' posts and 20% of Group 'D' posts for ex-Servicemen. Central Public Sector Undertakings and Nationalised Banks provide 14.5% reservation in Group 'C' and 24.5% in Group 'D' posts to ex-Servicemen. 10% posts of Assistant Commandants in Para-Military Forces are also reserved for Ex-Servicemen. In addition, most of the State Governments, except the states of UP, Bihar, J&K, Kerala and Meghalaya, are providing reservations to ex-Servicemen in the State Government jobs. It has, however, not been possible to have statutory backing to the reservations being provided to Ex-Servicemen because of the overall ceiling of 50% imposed by the Supreme Court and as 49.5% reservation has already been provided in Government jobs for SC/ST/OBC. Therefore, the reservation being provided to ex-Servicemen is not of vertical nature as is the case of reservation for SC/ST/OBC but it is of horizontal nature, which implies that ex-Servicemen selected against the vacancies reserved for them are subsequently adjusted against the relevant category i.e. SC, ST, OBC or general to which they belong. There is also no carry forward of unfilled reserved vacancies under horizontal vacancies. Besides, with the shrinking of job opportunities in civil employment, large scale unemployment in the country and ever increasing competition, difficulties are faced in providing re-employment to Ex-Servicemen.

Relaxation in Age

Ex-Servicemen have been provided age relaxation to the extent of military service plus three years- against reserved/ unreserved vacancies in Group 'C' and 'D' posts and also in Group 'A' & 'B' posts, which are filled otherwise than by way of competitive examinations. The age relaxation is restricted to 5 years in Group 'A' & 'B' posts which are filled by competitive examinations.

Relaxation in Educational Qualification

Ex-Servicemen are being granted relaxation in prescribed educational qualification. Army class I, II and III certificates have been equated to 8th, 6th and 4th class respectively in civil. For reserved vacancies for which the minimum educational qualification is matriculation, an Ex-Servicemen who has put in at least 15 years of service and has passed Army class I certificate or equivalent is considered eligible. For the reserved jobs for which the minimum educational qualification is graduation, an Ex-Servicemen who has put in at least 15 years of service in the Army and has passed matriculation or equivalent examination is considered eligible.

Security Agencies

The Directorate General of Resettlement registers/ sponsors Security Agencies for providing Security Guards to various Public Sector Undertakings and industries in private sector. The scheme offers self-employment opportunities to retired Defence Officers and employment opportunities to retired Defence Officers and employment opportunity to ex-PBOR. The Department of Public Enterprises (DPE) had issued instructions toll the PSUs to get security personnel through DGR sponsored Security Agencies. The scheme had shown good results. However, in December 1997, the said instructions were unilaterally withdrawn by the DPE. The matter was taken up with Ministry of Industry, who have revived the scheme with effect from February 1, 1999. Instructions have been issued to all the Departments of Government of India to implement the scheme for PSUs under them.

Officers Employment

During the year 1998 (until October 1998), a total number of 319 officers are registered with the DGR. Officers' names were sponsored for employment for 307 posts during the same period. There has been a significant drop in fresh registration cases due to enhancement of the retirement age since May, 1998.

Schemes for Self-Employment

As it is not feasible to provide Government jobs to all ex-Servicemen after their retirement from the Armed Forces, Government have formulated several schemes for encouraging and giving financial support by way of loans to ex-Servicemen entrepreneurs intending to set up small and medium industries. Important Self Employment Schemes are SEMFEX-I, SEMFEX-II and SEMFEX-III. Applications for sanction of loans are submitted by Ex-Servicemen directly to concerned Zila Sainik Boards in the states. The applications are scrutinized and those who satisfy eligibility criteria and other terms and conditions are recommended for sanction of loan through State Financial Corporations aided by Small Industries Development Bank of India (SIDBI), Scheduled Commercial Banks, District Central Cooperative Banks, State Land Development Banks and Regional Rural Banks aided by National Bank for Agriculture and Rural Development (NABARD).

Ex-Servicemen Coal Transport Companies

Special provision exists for sponsoring Ex-Servicemen coal transport companies for the execution of work in the coal subsidiaries of Coal India Limited. The unemployed retired officers and JCOs registered with DGR are selected to form ex-Servicemen coal transport companies and are sponsored to respective coal subsidiaries for five years, extendable by another two years. 114 companies of ex-Servicemen employing over 6000 personnel are operating in six different coal subsidiaries of Coal India Limited.

Allotment of Oil Product Agencies to the Ex-Servicemen/ Widows/Dependants Under Defence Quota

Ministry of Petroleum and Natural Gas have reserved 8% of the Oil Product Agencies i.e. LPG, Petrol Pumps, Kerosene etc. for disabled soldiers with disability of 50% and above attributable to military service and widows and dependants of those who died in war/ peace due to causes attributable to military service. DGR sponsors eligible candidates for selection by the Oil Selection Board constituted by the Ministry of Petroleum & Natural Gas. Final allotment is made by their concerned oil company. Approximately 70-80 certificates are issued every year.

Allotment of Army Surplus Class VB Vehicles

Ex-Servicemen and serving personnel due to retire within six months, can apply for Army Surplus Class V-B vehicles. The allotment is made by the Army Headquarters through nine vehicles depots. On an average, 2000 applications are registered every year under this scheme.

Reservation of CSD & LOW Technology Items Manufactured by the Ex-Servicemen Entrepreneurs

The Canteen Stores Department of India (CSDI) has reserved 15% of the 30 selected CSD items and the Ministry of Defence have reserved 10% of the 262 selected items, manufactured by Ex-Servicemen entrepreneurs under the Defence Purchase Programme. Only the ex-Servicemen's manufacturing units are eligible.

Grant of Price Subsidy to the Ex-Servicemen's Small Scale Industrial Units

The ex-Servicemen manufacturing units supplying stores to Defence Establishments under Defence Purchase Programme are eligible for 10% price subsidy of the total value of stores supplied or Rs. 50,000/ whichever is less, in a financial year for five consecutive years. 39 ex-Servicemen units have been granted over Rs. 60 lakhs under the scheme so far.

Allotment of Parking Sites in New Delhi

New Delhi Municipal Committee is currently has 105 parking lots in the area under their jurisdiction. 50% of these parking lots are reserved for ex-Servicemen which are allotted to them on the basis of open limited tenders.

Allotment of Typewriters/Duplicators

Ex-Servicemen are eligible to apply for a maximum of 5 repairable typewriters and one duplicator through DGR. These typewriters and duplicators are allotted by Directorate of Military Records & Forms through Regional Stationery Depots on nominal payment. An average of 60 applicants are allotted these machines every year which includes officers and JCOs. As per feedback, these are used for setting up typewriting institutions in rural areas.

Allotment of Mother Diary/DMS Milk Booths and Fruit & Vegetable Outlets

This scheme was launched in consultation with National Dairy Development Board (NDDB) to provide ready made booths with deep freezers, electronic weighing machines and other accessories costing approximately Rs. 8 lakh borne by NDDB. Ex-Servicemen up to the rank of JCO or its equivalent, below the age 55 years are eligible for allotment of Mother Dairy milk booths and fruit & vegetable outlets till such a time they attain 60 years of age. More than 4500 ex-Servicemen have benefited under the scheme since 1987 on a rotational basis. Based on the success of this scheme, other States have also been approached to provide similar facilities to ex-Servicemen. Tamil Nadu and Karnataka have already responded with 50% and 100% reservation for allotment of automatic milk vending booths in their States. Rajasthan Government is also considering giving preferential treatment to ex-Servicemen for allotment of milk vending booths.

Welfare

The Kendriya Sainik Board (KSB) under the Chairmanship of Raksha Mantri has been established for laying down the general policy of the welfare of ex-Servicemen and their dependants; for the administration of Welfare funds and also for coordinating the work of the Rajya Sainik Boards (RSBs) and Zila Sainik Boards (ZSBs). The expenditure on the resettlement work in the states is shared by the Central and the State Governments in the ratio of 50:50. The KSB also administers the Armed Forces Flag Day Fund collected on Flag Day through sale of car flags and token flags. Various welfare activities are financed from the interest earning of the Fund. Financial assistance is provided to institutions such as Paraplegic

Homes at Kirkee and Mohali, the Red Cross Society, Cheshire Homes, Military Hospitals, St. Dustan's After Care Organisation and the Homes for taking care of old and physically handicapped Ex-Servicemen and their dependants. Financial assistance is also provided to individual Ex- Servicemen and their families who are in a state of penury to meet specific needs.

Financial Assistance from Raksha Mantri's Discretionary Fund (RMDF)

A portion of the earnings of Armed Forces Flag Day Fund is set apart as Raksha Mantri's Discretionary Fund and is used to provide financial assistance to poor and needy ex-Servicemen who are in penury. This is given for various purposes viz., medical treatment, marriage of daughters, repair of houses, education of children. Monthly financial assistance up to a period of two years is also provided to old and infirm ex-Servicemen/ widow of Ex-Servicemen living in penury.

Concessions and Facilities

Undermentioned concessions and facilities are available to eligible personnel :-

(a) Free educational facilities to children of defence personnel killed or disabled in action.

(b) 25 seats in the MBBS, one seat in BDS and two seats in engineering stream are available through KSB to dependants/ wards of certain categories of defence personnel.

(c) 25% seats are reserved for the wards of serving and Ex-Servicemen personnel in Sainik Schools.

(d) States/UTs have made reservation of seats in professional colleges/ITIs/ polytechnics for wards of serving and retired defence personnel.

(e) Two educational grants of Rs. 600/- and Rs. 300/- p.m. per student is provided to wards of war bereaved, disabled, attributable and non-attributable peace time casualties respectively, housed in 35 War Memorial Hostels to enable them to pursue their studies.

(f) Medical facilities

(i) Ex-Servicemen, their families and families of deceased service personnel drawing pension of any kind are entitled to free outpatient treatment at Military Hospitals. These personnel can also be provided inpatient treatment in Military Hospitals subject to certain conditions. In addition to the existing military hospitals, 24 MI Rooms and 12 dental centres have been specially created from the funds provided by the Services and KSB for providing medical facilities to ex-Servicemen pensioners and their dependants.

(ii) Ex-Servicemen suffering from serious diseases are given financial assistance of up to 60% of the total expenditure for treatment in civil hospitals in case they cannot raise funds from other sources. These are bypass surgery, open heart surgery/valve replacement, pacemaker implant, angiography/angioplast, kidney/renal transplantation, dialysis, cancer and spastic paraplegics. Assistance for dialysis is restricted to Rs* 75,000/- only.

(iii) The leading hospitals throughout the country have been empanelled from where the ex-Servicemen can get treatment for serious diseases on payment of 40% of the total expenditure. The remaining 60 % is paid directly to the hospitals by the KSB. For this purpose, the Ex-Servicemen is required to submit a letter issued by KSB, to the hospital.

(iv) Ex-servicemen not availing medical facilities from military hospitals can choose to draw Rs. 100/- every month for medical purposes.

(g) Travel concessions : Following concessions are available to war widows/ gallantry award winners, which can be availed on production of identity card issued by KSB:-

(i) Rail travel concession: 75% concessions in rail fare for travel in II Class is available to war widows, including those of IPKF casualties. Besides, recipients and widows of posthumous recipients of Chakra series of gallantry awards are entitled or free rail pass for travelling in Class I/II AC Sleeper.

(ii) Travel Concession: Certain categories of personnel are eligible to 50% concession in fare for air travel in domestic flights of the Indian Airlines.

(h) Reservation of house-sites/houses: Majority of States have made reservations for serving/ retired Armed Forces personnel in allotment of house sites/ houses.

(i) Grant for repair of houses: Financial assistance is provided especially to war widows/war disabled for repair of houses on 50% cost sharing basis with State Governments up to an extent of Rs. 10,000/-.

(j) Sainik rest house facilities: Over 252 Sainik Rest Houses have been created in the country which provide transit facilities to Ex-Servicemen and their dependants at nominal rates.

(k) Cash award/annuity/cash in lieu of land for gallantry/non-gallantry award winners: The States/ UTs provide Cash Award/ Annuity/Cash in lieu of Land for Gallantry/Non Gallantry Award Winners.

Achievements 1998-99

The major welfare measures/ achievements made by the KSB during 1998-99 are mentioned below :-

(a) Based on the recommendations of the Ministry of Defence during the recent past, a few States i.e. Goa. Kerala, Mizoram, NCT of Delhi and UT of Chandigarh have enhanced the rates of monthly financial assistance to Rs. 300/ - or more for their World War-II veterans /widows.

(b) Assam Government has decided to provide Rs. 2 lakh to next of kin (NOK) of defence personnel belonging to Assam, killed in counter-insurgency operations in the State. The Government of Tripura has also enhanced rates of ex-gratia payment from Rs. 25,000/ - to Rs. 50,000/- for the defence personnel who are killed in extremist violence while on duty in the State.

(c) During the year (till November 16, 1998), a record amount of Rs. 22.56 lakhs has been sanctioned as financial assistance to 248 ex-Servicemen/ dependants in penury, from Raksha Mantri's Discretionary Fund.

(d) During this period (till November 16, 1998), 202 ex-Servicemen/ dependants have been provided financial assistance of Rs. 85 lakhs for treatment of serious diseases from Armed Forces Flag Day Fund.

(e) The Government orders on the recommendations of the Fifth Pay Commission on pensionary benefits to Ex-Servicemen, have been forwarded to all the Rajya Sainik Boards for further dissemination to the Zila Sainik Boards under their jurisdiction for information.

Pension to Armed Forces Personnel

The Armed Forces are required to maintain a youthful profile at all times for the maintenance and upkeep of the highest degree of combat efficiency. Service personnel are retired/ released at a younger as compared to civilian employees. Approximately 50,000 Service personnel retire every year. In recognition of their difficult service conditions, early retirement and the supreme sacrifice of life in the interest of the nation, Armed Forces personnel are granted pensionary benefits at somewhat liberal scale as compared to their civilian counterparts. The nature of retirement/release from service determines the admissibility of the type of pension in the cases of Armed Forces personnel. The rates, eligibility conditions etc., for grant of these pensions are enunciated in the succeeding paragraphs.

Retiring/Service Pension

The Commissioned Officers of the Army, Navy and Air Force after rendering the prescribed 20 years of minimum qualifying service (without weightage - 15 years in the case of late entrants) and the Personnel Below Officer Rank (PBORs) after completion of 15 years of service (20 years in the case NCsE), become eligible to retiring/ service pension. Retiring/ service pension is calculated at 50% of the average reckonable emoluments as in the case of civil pensioners. In view of their early retirement ' the benefit of added years of service is given to the Armed Forces personnel while calculating their qualifying service for pension. This benefit ranges from 9 years for Captains and below to 3 years for Generals and 5 years in the case personnel below officers rank. While in the case of officers, pension is calculated on the basis of the average pay drawn during the last ten months of service, in the case of PBORs, it is calculated with reference to the maximum pay of the rank held for 10 months preceding retirement. For calculating gratuity, a uniform weightage of 5 years added service is given to all ranks. Armed Forces personnel are also permitted higher commutation of their pension as compared to civilians.

Disability Pension

Disability pension is granted to an Armed Forces personnel who is disabled during service and is boarded out on account of a disease/injury/wound attributable to or aggravated by military service provided that the disability assessed by the Medical Board is 20% or more. Disability pension is granted in addition to service pension and/or gratuity as admissible depending on the length of service. Disability pension consists of service element and disability element. The amount of service element is equal to the normal retiring/ service pension. The service element subject to a minimum of Rs.1275/- is also payable when the length of service rendered is less than the minimum pensionable service. Personnel with 100% disability are also paid a Constant Attendance Allowance on the recommendations of the Medical Board. In all other cases, where the personnel are invalidated out of service with a disability neither attributable to nor aggravated by military service, invalid pension is granted, if the service rendered is 10 years or more. If the service is less than 10 years, invalidating gratuity depending upon the length of service is paid.

The 5th Central Pay Commission has made recommendations inter alia for enhancement of the minimum disability element of disability pension from Rs. 375/- per month to Rs. 1350/- per month. Final decisions with regard to the various recommendations relating to disability pension are yet to be taken by the Government and the same will be suitably notified in due course.

War Injury Pension

In case of 100% disability in war or war like operations, the pay last drawn at the time of invalidment is paid to the Service personnel as war injury pension on monthly basis. The amount of war injury pension in case of invalidment is proportionately reduced where the degree of disability is less, subject to a minimum of 60% of the last pay drawn in the case of Commissioned Officers and 80% of the last pay drawn in the PBORs. War injury pension at this rate is also paid in cases where the disability is less than 20% on invalidment. Armed Forces personnel who are retained in service despite war injury and retired subsequently are given an option either to draw lump sum compensation in lieu of war injury element or to draw war injury pension at the time of subsequent retirement foregoing lump sum compensation. The 5th Central Pay Commission's recommendations relating to grant of war injury pension are at present under consideration of the Government. Appropriate orders would be issued by the Ministry of Defence as soon as decisions on these recommendations of the Commission become available.

Family Pension

Ordinary family pension: Families of Armed Forces personnel who die during service or after retirement with pension, are granted ordinary family pension at uniform rate of 30% of the reckonable emoluments. The amount of minimum family pension which earlier was Rs. 375/- per month has been raised to Rs.1275/- per month with effect from January 01, 1996 on the basis of the recommendations of the 5th Central Pay Commission. If the deceased personnel had rendered 7 years or more service, then the family is given family pension at double the rate of the first 7 years or up to the time when deceased would have reached the age of 65 years, whichever is earlier. The amount of enhanced family pension will, however, not be more than 50% of the emoluments, or the retiring pension if the death takes place after retirement but before 65 years of age.

Special family pension: If a Service personnel dies on account of causes attributable to or aggravated by military service, the widow with children is granted special family pension at the rate of 60% of the reckonable emoluments drawn by the deceased, subject to a minimum of Rs. 750/ and a maximum of Rs. 2500/ (pre-revised). The 5th Central Pay Commission's recommendations for grant of Special Family Pension in such cases at the rate of 60% of reckonable emoluments without ceiling, are under consideration of the Government and appropriate orders would be issued as soon as the decisions in this regard are taken.

Liberalised special family pension: In recognition of sacrifice of life in war or war like operations/ counter-insurgency operations/ action against terrorists/ extremists etc., the families of the deceased Armed Forces personnel are granted Liberalised Special Family Pension equal to the pay last drawn by the deceased. Dearness relief as revised from time to time is also paid along with the pension.

In addition to the grant of Special Family Pension/ Liberalised Special Family Pension, orders have also been issued by the Ministry of Defence, effective from August 01, 1997, in pursuance of the recommendations of the 5th Central Pay Commission for payment of ex-gratia amount to the family of a Service personnel in the event of his death during the course of performance of bonafide official duty as given below :-

(a) Death occurring due to accidents in the course of performance Rs. 5.00 lakh of duties

(b) Death occurring in the course of performance of duties Rs. 5.00 lakh attributable to acts of violence by terrorists, antisocial elements, etc.

(c) Death occurring during (i) enemy action in international war or Rs. 7.50 lakh border skirmishes and (ii) action against militants, terrorists, extremists, etc.

Implementation of 5th Central Pay Commission's Recommendations

Decisions on other recommendations of the 5th Central Pay Commission relating to enhancement/ revision of the rates of disability pension/special family pension/ war injury pension etc. are yet to be taken by the nodal Department of the Central Government i.e. the Department of Pensions & Pensioners' Welfare. Necessary orders in this regard would be issued when the same become available.

In pursuance of the decisions taken by the Government on the recommendations of the 5th Central Pay Commission, orders have been issued by the Ministry of Defence for revision of pension with effect from January 01, 1996 of pre-January 01, 1986/ pre and post January 01, 1996 defence pensioners/ family pensioners. The important features of these orders, inter alia, include grant of minimum retiring pension/family pension at Rs.1275/- per month, enhancement of the maximum limit of service/death gratuity from Rs. 2.5 lakh to Rs. 3.5 lakh and payment of a medical allowance at the rate of Rs. 100/- per month to all Armed Forces pensioners who are not provided medical facilities as outdoor patients in Armed Forces hospitals/MI Rooms. These orders have been published in April-June 1998 issue of Sainik Punarvas, a quarterly magazine issued by the Directorate General of Resettlement.

Armed forces and civil authorities

Apart from their main responsibility of defending the borders of the country, the Armed Forces render assistance to civil authorities, when called upon to do so, for the maintenance of law and order, essential services, and for organising relief and rescue operations during natural calamities. To ensure a timely response, the Armed Forces maintain regular liaison with the civil authorities and meetings are held at different levels with civilians officials to coordinate various facets of aid. The assistance provided by the Armed Forces during the year is outlined in the succeeding paragraphs.

Maintenance of LOW & Order and Anti-Militant Operations

The Army's active assistance to the state governments of the North East in counter insurgency/anti militancy operations has helped them to contain the insurgency. In Assam, sustained military operations under the aegis of revitalised Unified Headquarters, resulted in effective neutralisation of militants besides keeping them holed up in 'trans-border safe sanctuaries'. Consequently, during the period under review, insurgency in the State remained at low ebb. However, in a bid to show to the masses that their writ still runs in the state, militant outfits specially United Liberation front of Assam (ULFA), continued to engage soft targets/indulge in sabotage activity. Bodos on the other hand focused their attention on Bodo Autonomous Council issue and to draw attention of the Centre/State Governments towards their demands, resorted to sabotage and other depredatory activities including ethnic cleansing in areas of Bodo Autonomous Council. However, timely Army deployment in affected areas helped to stabilise the situation.

In Nagaland the ceasefire with the National Socialist Council of Nagaland (ISAK -Muvah) [NSCN(IM)] and other groups has been monitored/ enforced virtually single handed by the Army since August 1997. While the ceasefire has been holding out with NSCN(IM) and other groups, the National Socialist Council of Nagaland (Khaplang) [NSCN (K)] remained recalcitrant. The Army, therefore, was compelled to recommence operations against the outfit. However, in view of overtures by tribal organisations, the operations against the Group were suspended for a period of two months w.e.f. November 15, 1998. Involvement of all groups in the peace initiative will facilitate finding a lasting solution to the Nagaland problem.

In Jammu & Kashmir local support for militancy declined progressively as the local population had seen through the designs of the sponsors of terrorism. A desperate effort is being made by the external sponsors to sustain the proxy war by infiltrating more foreign mercenaries specially trained in assembling and planting sophisticated improvised explosive devices (IEDs) for standoff attacks against soft targets/VIPs. An estimated 700-800 foreign mercenaries are operating in the state. Measures such as synergisation of operations of all security forces, improved intelligence and redeployment of forces resulted in the elimination of 793, apprehension of 468 and surrender of 104 militants, while recovering a total of over 1606 weapons during the year. Relentless operations continue throughout the winter to eliminate the mercenaries who had infiltrated into the State.

The Army's assistance was requisitioned by the Government of Tamil Nadu following a series of bomb blasts that had rocked Coimbatore town on the eve of a proposed political rally. The spontaneous response by the Army contributed to restoring normalcy besides recovering a huge cache of pipe bombs, explosives and lethal weapons.

Assistance During Natural Calamities

During the period under review, the Army's assistance was sought by various State Governments, for relief and rescue operations at a number of flood affected areas in the country. Army personnel evacuated thousands of marooned people besides assisting the civil administration in medical and material relief. Of significance, were the relief/rescue operations in the following States/Areas :

(a) Floods in Uttar Pradesh and Bihar: Eastern Uttar Pradesh (UP) and Champaran districts of Bihar were virtually cut off from the rest of the country owing to heavy floods, causing serious losses to both life and property. A total of 28 columns, along with medical teams, were provided by the Army from July to September 1998, to restore normalcy. The Army's assistance was rendered in terms of evacuation of marooned civilians, provision of medical aid and large scale distribution of food packets/relief material, both by land and air.

(b) Malpa tragedy (Kumaon Hills, UP): Braving tough and inclement weather, approximately one thousand Army men provided immediate assistance in rescue and safe transportation of survivors, besides retrieval of dead bodies from the debris. Other facets of the aid rendered by the Army included provisioning of communications, track construction, distribution of rations/ essential supplies, medical aid and air effort by the Army Aviation helicopters.

(c) Cyclone in Gujarat: Apropos cyclonic storms that engulfed coastal Gujarat and the Rann of Kutch during June 1998, the Army had provided five relief columns along with specialist equipment and medical teams.

(d) The Army also provided similar assistance to the Governments of West Bengal, Assam and Delhi during 1998.

Maintenance of Essential Services Army

The Army assisted the civil administration in maintenance of essential services in the following disciplines:

(a) Provision of Army Nursing Staff to various Government hospitals in the Union Territory of Delhi during May 1998, following a strike by nurses in the capital.

(b) Provision Of five technical columns to the Uttar Pradesh Government in July 1998, following a strike by the Uttar Pradesh State Electricity Board (UPSEB) Staff.

Other Types of Assistance

Antarctica expedition: The Army logistic support contingent comprising two officers, two JCOs and nine other ranks was provided to the Department of Ocean Development, the Government of India for the 17th and 18th Antarctic Expeditions. Tasks undertaken by the contingent are construction, repair and maintenance of permanent stations; running of life support systems and overland transportation of men and material on the continent. Army teams have also been undertaking other humanitarian tasks, over and above their laid down charter. On June 01, 1998, Army personnel, despite difficult weather/terrain conditions, rescued four survivors from a Russian helicopter that had crashed on the continent.

Restoring national highway-22 in Himachal Pradesh: Consequent to the flash floods resulting in the severe disruption of NH-22 during September 1997, the Army assistance in the form of seven bridges were provided to the State Government of Himachal Pradesh to restore vital communication link.

Restoration of water supply in North West Delhi: To ensure continuous water supply to the residents of North West Delhi, the Army launched a bridge at Hyderpur during July/ August 1998 to provide support to the water pipes that had sagged due to a breach in the embankment of the canal.

Navy

Cyclone relief operations - Port Kandla and Jamnagar :The severe cyclonic storm, which hit the coast of Gujarat just north of Porbandar on June 9, 1998 left a trail of havoc with a large number of lives lost both at sea and ashore. The severity of the storm was the most at Kandla port. The Indian Navy responded quickly by pressing in all available resources into undertaking relief operation in a swift and efficient manner to provide succour to the affected. The Navy also undertook efforts to restore communication links and essential services as also the port operations in a record time thus saving vital earnings to the exchequer.

Flood relief operations: Heavy rains in the northern Gangetic plains resulted in unprecedented floods in vast areas of Bihar and West Bengal. The magnitude of the calamity was of alarming proportion. The Navy mobilised immediate relief operations by providing medical and diving relief operations through 29 naval doctors, 50 medical personnel, 25 divers and 19 personnel from different trades. Relief operations spanned from September 15 to October 09,1998 and spread over Malda district in West Bengal and Samastipur in Bihar Covering the village of Hasanpur, Kaliachak, Mahananda Tola, Bhilaimar Delta and Panchanandpura and areas in and around Malda itself. In addition, a total of 36 tons of rations contributed by the Navy was distributed in the affected areas.

Similar relief operations were undertaken in many districts along the Godavari river following heavy rains in Andhra Pradesh. Naval relief teams were despatched to areas near Vijaywada to provide relief in villages which were cut off and had no means of communications.

Other relief operations: During the year, naval divers provided assistance to various State Governments and

District Administrations for rescue of personnel and recovering of bodies in various accidents viz., operations in Wardha river to rescue coal miners at Ambernath, to rescue passengers of Konark Express in October 1998, etc. Responding to a call for medical assistance from a merchant vessel Pearl of Abu Dhabi on October 21/22, 1998, a mother and her prematurely born baby were airlifted by Naval units and safely brought ashore. Assistance rendered by the Navy highlights its commitment towards nation building in addition to its primary role in war.

Indian Air Force (IAF)

Flood relief: The Indian Air Force has rendered yeoman service in aid to civil power. Extensive flood and cyclone relief operations were carried out by the Indian Air Force during the year. Numerous sorties were carried out airdropping tons of relief load as well as rescuing stranded people in the affected areas of Gujarat, Bihar, Rajasthan, Uttar Pradesh, Arunachal Pradesh, Assam and West Bengal. Indian Air Force helicopters were also pressed into service towards emergency requests by the Governments of Jammu and Kashmir and Uttar Pradesh to assist in dealing with massive landslides and floods.

Malpa tragedy: There was a massive landslide at Malpa village in the Uttar Pradesh hills during August 1998. The 12th batch of Kailash Mansarovar Yatris camping at Malpa village were swept away and buried under the landslides caused by the torrential rains. This resulted in the loss of approximately 120 lives. The Indian Air Force swung into action to provide immediate relief to stranded pilgrims conveying the survivors to safety and carrying the bodies of the deceased to Dharchula and Pithoragarh.

Disaster relief : The IAF has been extensively involved in disaster relief particularly during the latter half of 1998.

For flood relief and natural calamities, over 900 sorties were launched in 1998, representing an eighteen fold increase over 1996. The figures for casualty evacuation and aid to civil power have shown dramatic increases over previous years as the Air Force strives to meet all tasks required of it.